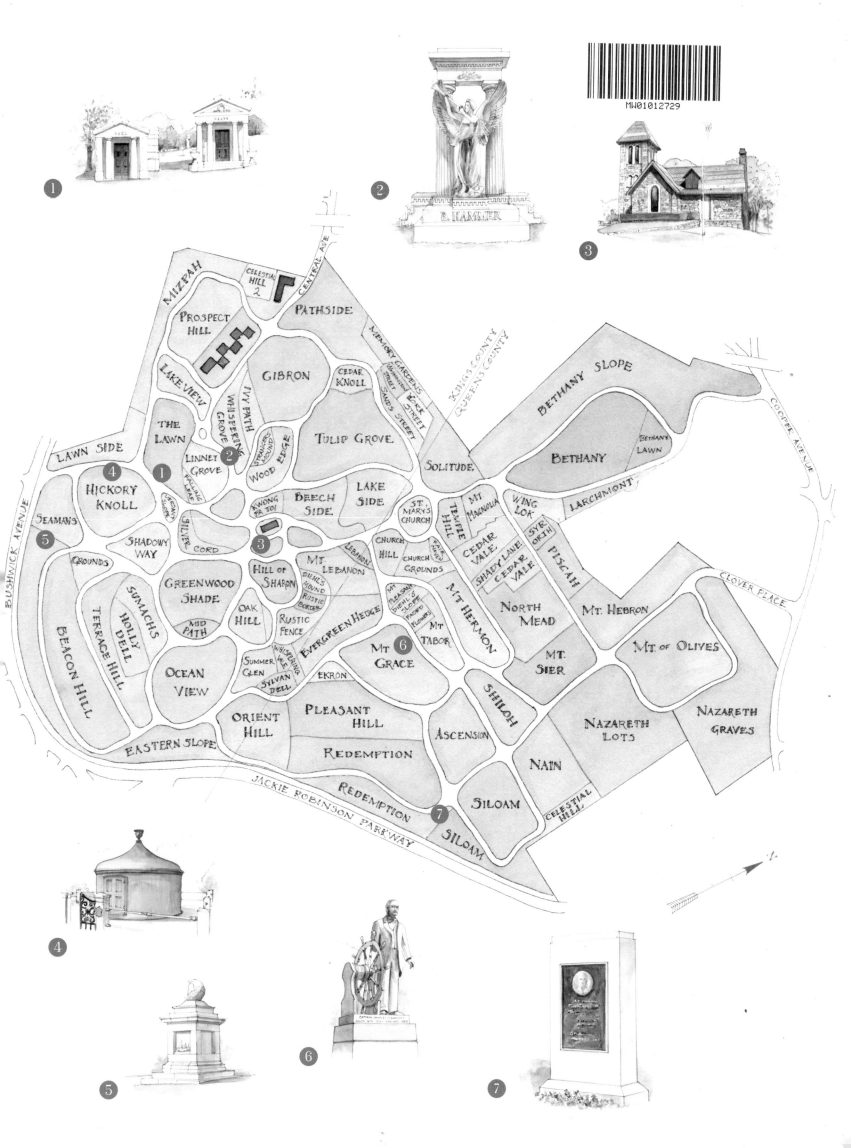

1

2

B. HAMMER

3

CELESTIAL HILL 2

MIZPAH

PROSPECT HILL

PATHSIDE

LAKE VIEW

WHISPERING GROVE

IVY PATH

GIBRON

CEDAR KNOLL

MEMORY GARDENS

MONUMENT STREET

YORK STREET

SANDS STREET

KINGS COUNTY
QUEENS COUNTY

BETHANY SLOPE

THE LAWN

LAWN SIDE

LINNET GROVE

2

STRANGERS MOUND

WOOD EDGE

TULIP GROVE

SOLITUDE

BETHANY

BETHANY LAWN

COOPER AVENUE

BUSHWICK AVENUE

HICKORY KNOLL

4

1

VERONA SLOPE

KWONG FA TOI

BEECH SIDE

LAKE SIDE

ST. MARYS CHURCH

TEMPLE HILL

MT MAGNOLIA

WING LOK

LARCHMONT

SEAMANS

5

SILVER CORD

3

CHURCH HILL

CEDAR VALE

SYR ORTH

PISCAH

SHADOWY WAY

GROUNDS

HILL OF SHARON

MT LEBANON

LEBANON

DIEHLS MOUND

RUSTIC BORDER

CHURCH GROUNDS

SHADY LANE

CEDAR VALE

SUMACHS

GREENWOOD SHADE

OAK HILL

RUSTIC FENCE

EVERGREEN HEDGE

MT PLEASANT

DIEHLS SLOPE

FAIRD

FLOWERS

MT TABOR

MT HERMON

NORTH MEAD

MT HEBRON

CLOVER PLACE

TERRACE HILL

HOLLY DELL

MID PATH

SUMMER GLEN

WHISPERING VALE

SYLVAN DELL

MT GRACE

6

MT SIER

MT OF OLIVES

BEACON HILL

OCEAN VIEW

EKRON

SHILOH

NAZARETH LOTS

NAZARETH GRAVES

EASTERN SLOPE

ORIENT HILL

PLEASANT HILL

REDEMPTION

ASCENSION

NAIN

CENTRAL AVE

JACKIE ROBINSON PARKWAY

REDEMPTION

SILOAM

7

SILOAM

CELESTIAL HILL

4

5

6

7

GREEN OASIS
in BROOKLYN

THE EVERGREENS CEMETERY
1849–2008

GREEN OASIS
in BROOKLYN

THE EVERGREENS CEMETERY
1849–2008

JOHN ROUSMANIERE

Photography by Ken Druse

Seapoint Books

An imprint of Smith/Kerr Associates LLC

Kittery Point, Maine

www.SmithKerr.com

Distributed to the trade by National Book Network
Generous quantity discounts are available through
Smith/Kerr Associates LLC, 43 Seapoint Road,
Kittery Point, ME 03905 (207) 439-2921 or
www.SmithKerr.com

The Evergreens Cemetery
1629 Bushwick Avenue
Brooklyn, New York 11207-1849
718-455-5300

Cataloging-in-publication data is on file at the Library
of Congress.

ISBN-13 978-0-9786899-4-0

ISBN-10 0-9786899-4-1

Cover and book design by Claire MacMaster,
 Barefoot Art Graphic Design
 Printed in China through Printworks Int. Ltd.

contents

OPPOSITE TITLE PAGE, MT. GRACE

LEFT, OCEAN VIEW

foreword

I FEEL PRIVILEGED to have been invited to write the history of a magnificent plot of land and its people. A little-known gem of Brooklyn and New York, The Evergreens Cemetery is a place of stories, beauty, and traditions stretching back nearly one hundred sixty years. It is a fine example of what the cemetery historians Blanche Linden-Ward and David C. Sloane were saying when they described the typical American rural cemetery as "a museum, arboretum, bird sanctuary, park, historical archive, and landmark"—as well, of course, as a sacred place of burial. On the bucolic Green Hills of Brooklyn, with its vistas of Manhattan and the Atlantic Ocean, a great many families, races, ethnic groups, and professions are brought together in both mourning and hope. There is an abiding connection among the people of the Evergreens—those who have worked to create and maintain it, and those who are buried there. When the cemetery's president, Paul Grassi, told me, "We're a cemetery and a *community*," he was referring to the generations of men and women who have watched over and cared for this place, and to the more than 526,000 men, women, and children who have been buried there since 1849, and their families, friends, and admirers.

It is ironic but true that no place provides a more accurate picture of the life of a community than the city of its dead, its cemetery. If the picture shown by the Evergreens sometimes appears chaotic and paradoxical, such are New York and Brooklyn. Among the permanent residents are many great successes: the Son of Liberty John Berrien, the Hudson River School painter Martin J. Heade, the vaudeville impresario Tony Pastor, the pioneering cartoonist Winsor McCay, the first world champion of chess William Steinitz, and a long line of entertainers that includes Bill "Bojangles" Robinson and the saxophone genius Lester "Pres" Young. Some here were more infamous than famous, including one of baseball's most notorious cheats, Tammany Hall crooks, and a large number of men and women connected to the conspiracy to assassinate Abraham Lincoln.

Many who have been laid to rest here would have had trouble finding decent graves elsewhere because of their races or trades. At the heart of the story of any great institution is the story of *its* heart. The Evergreens was still young when it began opening its grounds to people whom most Americans regarded as pariahs— Chinese, African Americans, suicides, executed criminals, merchant seamen, and actors. Their stories wind through this narrative, along with accounts of New York's and Brooklyn's worst calamities, including the loss of the steamship *Slocum*, the Triangle Shirtwaist fire, the 1918–19 influenza pandemic, and the race incidents of the 1980s, all of which are memorialized at the Evergreens.

A proper account of a proper cemetery has four threads: the people who are there (of whom I have said only a little), the people who created and maintained it, its place, and its rituals. Created out of a desperate need by New Yorkers during its prolonged burial crisis, the Evergreens was organized and led by some remarkable men. One was William R. Grace, the self-made shipping tycoon who became New York's first Irish and Roman Catholic mayor, who helped bail the cemetery out of a scandalous bankruptcy, and who influenced the Evergreens for over a century.

The third thread is the story of the place itself and its surrounding community. The "high rustic enclosure" (as the grounds were called at the time of its founding in 1849) was shaped originally by a great glacier, then by Dutch farmers, and finally by some of the best architects of their time, including Alexander Jackson Davis and Calvert Vaux. This is the only cemetery to which Andrew Jackson Downing, the pioneering landscape architect, set his hand. The Evergreens is an example of what Downing called "a green oasis for the refreshment of the city's soul and body"—in other words, a bucolic park. Its roles as both park and burial ground are summarized in the phrase that has historically been used to describe the Evergreens and similar cemeteries, "rural cemetery." Often the two words and goals complement each other, but sometimes there is a tension and even a conflict that can make the history of a cemetery surprisingly lively, as we will see in the last chapter.

"Brooklyn, of ample hills, was mine," proclaimed Walt Whitman, who buried his father and mother at the Evergreens. Diverse and always changing, Brooklyn has provided a toehold for people as different as the social worker and refugee from Nazi Germany Alice Salomon, the science fiction writer Isaac Asimov (who found refuge in the Evergreens' hills and forests and called it his "lonely Eden"), and the black Civil War soldiers who were sent off to fight in glory but were later ignored, including by history.

The fourth thread in the story of a cemetery is that of its rituals. It is a place where ceremony is taken seriously, and we have three chapters about it. One concerns the celebration of Decoration Day, the great American "festival of our dead," when cemeteries served as national monuments and thousands of people scattered flowers on soldiers' and sailors' graves. Another chapter is about the rituals of mourning that families traditionally observed when burying their dead from their homes. The third is about Chinese-Americans at the Evergreens, and their days of ancestor worship. The sense of ritual does not end there, of course. When Whitman defined a good, independent life as one in which there is a guarantee of a decent burial, he represented the universal longing to avoid a pauper's grave.

As I regretfully come to the end of this fascinating project, I recognize that the Evergreens and its place and history have become very dear to me. There is the satisfaction of knowing that I have become a member of its community.

—JOHN ROUSMANIERE
New York
October 22, 2007
Year's mind of my father's death

CHAPTER ONE

A PROPER PLACE IN THE AMERICAN REVOLUTION

I N THE YEAR 1849, one of the cemetery's founders, Samuel E. Johnson, would recall, "the attention of certain persons was directed to the ground now occupied by the Evergreens, as a proper place, from its central position and natural beauties, for a rural cemetery." Several deep concerns propelled the initiative to create the burial ground and park that came to be called the Cemetery of the Evergreens. The first was the innate human yearning for a respectful burial in a respectable grave. Another was the new romantic understanding of the role of pastoral nature as a mediator between life and death. The third was the crowding of old downtown churchyards, which damaged public health and restricted development. And then there was the blend of philanthropic spirit and private financial self-interest on the part of the civic leaders who founded the cemetery, including the man quoted above, a friend and publisher of America's poet-democrat, Walt Whitman, whose path repeatedly crosses the Evergreens' early history.

As important as they were as building blocks for the Evergreens, these four factors would have been mere pebbles without that "proper place" on a ridge sprawling over the border of Kings and Queens counties. Because location is crucial to a cemetery, and because this particular location is historic—for its land and setting, for the people buried there, and for the men and women who have cared for it—this story of a Brooklyn cemetery begins with this place and the part it took in the American Revolution.

First, however, we should introduce the then-unusual purposes of the Evergreens' founders. This was not to be a burying field of the type too well known to Americans—a gloomy museum of mossy gravestones and doom-laden, chiding epitaphs. The Cemetery of the Evergreens was intended to be two things: a lovely place of rest for the dead, and a place of spiritual renewal and a park of true re-creation for the living. That double goal was summarized in the formula that the founders chose to describe it: "rural cemetery." In those two words are bundled several paradoxes. Though remote from the city, the Evergreens served urban needs. Though a burial ground, it was not located (as most American cemeteries were) within walking distance of a church or neighborhood. Though dedicated to death, the site was a place of natural beauty for the living. And finally, despite its constantly self-renewing landscape, the cemetery was shaped by human hands.

The land itself is a character in our story, and so is the subtle conflict implicit in that formula, "rural cemetery." A tension between the holy role as a burial ground and the secular role as a recreational center and park runs as a thread throughout the history of the Evergreens.

A Piece of Forest Land

On a fine, fair day in late October 1849, a number of people of social concern, charitable spirit, and inquisitive mind boarded ferry boats in Manhattan and crossed the East River to Brooklyn. There they were met by other men and women guided by similar lights. The

EAST NEW YORK.

Long associated with the owners of the famed Halfway House, Howard Point was renamed Beacon Hill when the Seaman's Monument was built and became a landmark for living navigators.

company climbed into carriages, and the horses turned their noses eastward on a wood-planked turnpike, keeping a long ridgeline to their right as they trotted toward a green highland standing proud on the horizon at the eastern border of Kings County. They passed through the town of Williamsburg, already becoming crowded with German immigrants, and crossed through far less populated Bushwick, its fields punctuated by curved-roof Dutch farmhouses. In time the turnpike veered right through a natural cut in the ridge, called Jamaica Pass. There the horses turned off the main road and climbed a dusty wagon trail up a steady grade, first bordering farms and then diving under thickets of the brown autumn leaves of old-growth trees. A newspaper reporter who came along remembered a "splendid piece of forest land" where "the oak, the maple, the beach and the hickory, indeed every tree of the American forest, are mingled." High above them all towered a few examples of "the lordly tulip tree," rising, it seemed, to the sky.

Once clear of this dense forest, the horses and carriages clip-clopped onto old, somewhat unkempt, stone-walled, marshy pastures that one passenger described as "a wilderness of thorns and tangled brushwood" with "a dreary aspect." Here was property that had been farmed for at least a century by several of Kings County's oldest families—Schencks, Remsens, Meseroles, Lotts, Suydams, and Howards (all of whose names are on gravestones at the Evergreens today). Passing by seven ponds, the carriages finally climbed one more hill to reach a dead end at a high south-facing promontory that locals called Howard Point in honor of an important local family, but that later was known as Beacon Hill for the shaft that stood there as a memorial to the thousands of merchant seamen buried nearby.

There on Howard Point the passengers took in the full, grand circle of a panoramic view of land and sea. To the west stood Manhattan, where the tallest structures were church spires spiking above the low, jagged line of commercial and residential buildings that ended abruptly at Forty-Second Street, the city's northern limit. When the spectators faced south, squinting into the sun, the vista was very different. Near the foot of the hill stood an old tavern, and behind it the scraggly but grandly named settlement of East New York, its few houses haphazardly scattered among the straight and near-empty streets that had been laid out by ever-optimistic land developers. Beyond the village to the south lay more farms, and beyond them the blue vastness of the Atlantic Ocean, thickly dotted with sails.

One of the Evergreens' links to the American Revolution, the Rockaway Footpath played a crucial role in the Battle of Brooklyn. Its probable route has been marked.

To the newspaperman, the seascape further confirmed the impression of diversity that he had formed while conducting his survey of the trees. "The sails of all nations were slowly approaching each other as they came from the far east and far west, the north and the south, to the metropolis of the Western World." Like any good New Yorker, he understood the city's magnetism and variety. So it seemed right to him that these rolling acres of former farmland were about to be dedicated to a whole new purpose. "Anywhere on that chain of hills a man may rest well," he decided. "It is the proper place for the repose of a citizen." This place on the hill was not intended to serve as the site of another real estate development, or a rich man's mansion. Rather, some of Brooklyn's and New York City's leading clergymen and political figures, aided by two of the day's most influential architects, hoped to convert these hills, kettles, forests, and meadows into something much less familiar—a carefully landscaped burial ground to receive all people.

Among the visitors that day were several Protestant clergymen whose congregations were wrestling with a serious problem. American churches were by far the leading source of good works, including burial of the dead in nearby churchyards, but their near-monopoly on interments was breaking up in the 1840s. Urban crowding and epidemics of yellow fever and cholera were causing governments to shut down local church and private burial grounds and order the removal of remains to distant rural places. Caught in this bind were several of Manhattan's and Brooklyn's most prestigious churches, including St. Ann's in Brooklyn Heights, St. Mark's in the Bowery, and another Manhattan institution, Brick Presbyterian Church. The Brick Church's rector of sixty-seven years was The Reverend Dr. Gardiner Spring, and he was appointed one of the new cemetery's chaplains. When the congregation decided to sell its almost eighty-year-old brick-walled church and surrounding burial ground and move farther uptown, Dr. Spring arranged with the Evergreens to reserve a part of a round-topped knoll called Church Hill for remains transferred from his church.

The son of a Continental army chaplain, Gardiner Spring was trained as a lawyer but was teaching school in Bermuda when a sermon on the text "To the poor the Gospel is preached" inspired him to follow his father into the clergy. Raised a rigid Calvinist, Spring gradually softened. He wrote in his book on mourning, *The Mission of Sorrow*, "It must be a hard heart that is not touched with the sorrows of the bereaved." It was said that his concern about merchant seamen, whom most people treated as pariahs, dated to the night a fire broke out in a nearby building and a sailor climbed high on the Brick Church's steeple and tossed burning brands to the ground. From that moment on, Spring included sailors in his special concerns, and the first large plot at the Evergreens was dedicated to them.

John Berrien's Triumph

Among the sailors attracted to the Brick Church was John Berrien, a leading figure of the Revolutionary era. He was buried in the Brick Church's churchyard in lower Manhattan and later transferred to what Dr. Spring called "a beautiful location in the Cemetery of the Evergreens." Dr. Spring himself was subsequently interred a few feet away on Church Hill, near a spire engraved with the statement, "In memory of those whose mortal remains were removed with pious care." The epitaph on John Berrien's sandstone tablet-style grave marker reads:

John Berrien Esq.
Who Having Practiced Every Virtue of Private Life
& given the Highest Evidence of Faithfulness & Ability
In Legislative & Other Offices
during the Memorable Revolution of America
d. Sept. 25, 1784, in 49th year of his age.

DEFENCE OF THE LIBERTY POLE IN NEW YORK.

The road to revolution was laid by John Berrien and other Sons of Liberty when they knocked redcoat heads in New York's Liberty Pole riots.

"Firm for his Country, Zealous in her Cause,
Foe to her foes, and Friendly to her Laws,
A Glowing Bosom, a Liberal Mind
True to his Friends, & just to all Mankind
Inclined to Please, yet shun'd the noisy crowd,
For praise too meek, for Flattery too proud
Friendship may weep, Humanity may sigh,
But Berrien triumphs in the Fields on High."

This charming epitaph only hints at the accomplishments of this faithful shunner of the noisy crowd. John Berrien was a man to be reckoned with—a successful ship captain, an active member of the revolutionary Sons of Liberty, and an official during the Revolution. It is ironic that though he was originally buried within sight of the place where he became well-known for resisting the British, he ended up at the Evergreens, just a few minutes' walk from the path that 10,000 redcoats took on their way to defeat George Washington's army in the Battle of Brooklyn.

Berrien was descended from a French family that settled in the Netherlands, moved to Flatbush in the middle of the seventeenth century, and then dispersed. (Another John Berrien was a judge in New Jersey, and a third, the judge's son John Macpherson Berrien, was a multiterm U. S. Senator from Georgia and attorney general under Andrew Jackson.) Our John Berrien started out under modest circumstances as a boatman working around New York. He rose to freeman—meaning he was a citizen and enjoyed the right to sell goods in the city— and then in his twenties attained the status of property owner (as the "Esquire" in the epitaph indicates) as the captain and owner of a small merchant ship. It is not inconceivable that Captain Berrien augmented his

CHURCH HILL, BRICK CHURCH GROUNDS, (BACK TO FRONT) DR. SPRING HEADSTONE, CHURCH MONUMENT, BERRIEN STONE

income with a little lucrative privateering during the French and Indian War. He did well enough to own a house, some slaves, and a wharf at Beekman Slip, on the East River.

It was risky work, both physically and economically. Bound from New York Bay for Philadelphia in a small schooner on a windy day in February 1768, Berrien (according to a newspaper's Shipping News column) was "obliged to return to the Bay, in Distress, having meet with a Gale of wind." Any number of good ships and skilled captains might be lost on such days, yet Captain John Berrien must have enjoyed a happy blend of good luck and good seamanship because he survived that storm and many more before he came ashore when he was in his mid-thirties, in about 1770, to be a merchant.

By then Berrien had a reputation as a protest leader. When the British government began to tax colonial trade with the Stamp Act and other laws, a coalition of merchants, ship captains, and sailors formed the Sons of Liberty in 1765. These "plain-spoken, self-taught, self-made men" (as Edwin G. Burroughs and Mike Wallace characterized them in their history of New York, *Gotham*) took to the streets and quickly helped bring about the Stamp Act's repeal. Not stopping there, they became a relentless thorn in the British hide. Gathering on the city's Commons (now City Hall's park), they raised poles and old ship's masts, and from them flew "Liberty" banners and dangled pots of burning tar representing "the fire of liberty." Once a Liberty Pole was put up, soldiers from the nearby British garrison came over and pulled it down, shredding the banner and stamping out the fire. The Liberty Boys then reassembled and raised a larger pole. As this street theater proceeded, noses were bloodied, and many bruises were given and received.

On August 11, 1766, John Berrien, his brother Cornelius, and another ship captain named Isaac Sears led a mob of Liberty Boys that was estimated at 2,000 in a defiant effort to reerect a Liberty Pole that the redcoats had torn down the previous day. As the rebels got to work, the British regiment's drum major appeared and issued a challenge. "Do you resent it?" he shouted, referring to the destruction of the old pole.

Berrien stepped forward and declared, "I do resent it."

The drummer drew his flintlock and was taking aim when a fast-thinking bystander hauled the angry soldier away. As other redcoats appeared, they raised the stakes dramatically by waving bayonets. A flintlock was dangerous, but a bayonet was lethal. "The terror weapon of the eighteenth century," according to the historian David Hackett Fischer, "British bayonets were a fearful sight, with their long blades gleaming in the light." They did more than gleam. According to a sworn deposition by another Liberty Boy, the soldiers were "cutting and slashing every one that fell in their Way." Among the Sons of Liberty left bleeding was John Berrien. Appearing in bandages at a hearing before the British governor, he heard the British officers blame the Sons of Liberty for everything. The governor, unpersuaded, demanded that the citizens and soldiers stop harassing each other, and the liberty pole went back up.

That was not Berrien's last skirmish with the law. He protested the quartering of British troops at colonists' expense, publicly refused to sell tea until the British revoked new import duties, and worked with a Committee on Vigilance to seize imports and sell them at public auction. In May 1774 he was one of sixty rebels who created a new provisional revolutionary government of New York. A year later, Berrien was appointed as financial officer for a commission fortifying the Hudson highlands, near West Point. He later served on a committee that inspected ships for contraband and weapons, and assisted a Conspiracy Committee (part-FBI, part–Department of Homeland Security) that imposed loyalty oaths, made arrests, identified Loyalists, and collected arms.

Then the redcoats came. In July 1776, as the Declaration of Independence was being read across the colonies, New York Harbor filled with the largest expeditionary force in British history, comprised of 40 percent of the Royal Navy and more than 30,000 troops who were put ashore on Staten Island. As Manhattan

RUSTIC FENCE, LOOKING
TOWARD SYLVAN DELL

Island barricaded itself against an expected invasion, General George Washington appointed Berrien as chairman of the General Committee of the City of New York with several responsibilities. One was to control the spread of smallpox, another was to stop soldiers from deserting and fleeing to the mainland, and a third—on the eve of the expected invasion in mid-August—was to prepare for a mass evacuation of civilians, with a special assignment to look out for the infirm and helpless. So many houses were shut down and so many people fled that "it seemed as if the Plague had been in it," said a clergyman.

When a direct assault on Manhattan seemed imminent, on August 12 Berrien's committee issued a public order calling for the immediate evacuation of "Women, Children, and infirm Persons," as well as "poor Persons in this city," with the expenses of their removal and resettlement in the city to be covered by the government. "Every Tide," they wrote, "we expect an Attack will be made on this City from the piratical Fleet at Staten Island."

William Howard and the Rockaway Footpath

Here we leave John Berrien. The British did not attack until August 27, and when they did it was in Kings County, today's Brooklyn, with a decisive maneuver through the land that is now the grounds of the Evergreens Cemetery. An eyewitness to this action, though not an entirely reliable one, lies buried at the Evergreens about a quarter mile south of John Berrien's grave, on the promontory from which those visitors in 1849 marveled at the crowd of sail entering New York Bay.

William Howard Jr. would live long enough to sell his property on Howard Hill to the founders of the Evergreens, who in 1853 would bury him on that hill. But in 1776 he was the sixteen-year-old son and namesake of the keeper of a tavern that was alternatively called Howard's, the Rising Sun, or (most often) the Halfway House, because it was about five miles along the ten-mile road from downtown Brooklyn to Jamaica, the most important market town in Queens. Built by

William Howard's grandfather in 1715, the tavern stood for many years under an immense white oak tree near Jamaica Pass, on ground now occupied by the Metropolitan Transit Authority's maintenance yards.

Early in the unseasonably cool morning on August 27, as the last of the farmers with their carts of produce were making their daily way west toward the dawn ferry to Manhattan, the door to the Halfway House was flung open and in strode two splendidly uniformed British army generals, William Howe and Henry Clinton. They informed the landlord, William Howard Sr., that they and their troops required a guide to lead them through the hills to the other side of the ridge. Five days earlier, 21,000 British and Hessian soldiers had put ashore at Gravesend Bay, just north of Coney Island, and were split into three prongs for the attack on George Washington's disorganized little army of 7,000. The goal was to pierce the long ridgeline running through the future sites of the Evergreens, Prospect Park, and Green-Wood Cemetery, and then pin Washington against the East River. Two of the three assaults were direct from the south at passes in the western part of the county, at Gowanus and Flatbush. But the third and largest attack was the flanking maneuver that brought Generals Howe and Clinton to the Howards' front door at the head of a column of 10,000 soldiers, with twenty-eight pieces of field artillery. Expecting resistance in Jamaica Pass, Howe chose to go cross-country over the hills, and once on the northern side of the ridge, pivot left and race west toward Washington's troops, which would already be preoccupied with the two-pronged frontal assault.

Although the Woody Heights of Guana (as British mapmakers called the highlands of the glacial moraine) was familiar to his Loyalist scouts, Howe decided to requisition a local guide. "You are my prisoner and must lead me across these hills and out of the way of the enemy" were Howe's words to the senior Howard—at least according to his son's colorful but occasionally self-serving story of that night's events.

"We belong to the other side, General, and can't serve you against our duty," Howard replied (again, so

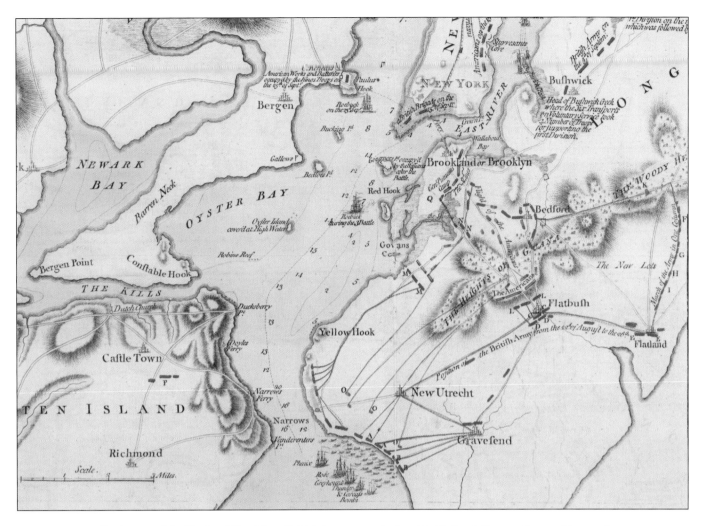

On the eve of the Battle of Brooklyn, British troops marched east to Flatland, then north over "the woody heights of Guana," the site of the Evergreens, before turning west to outflank George Washington.

his son recalled).

"That is all right, stick to your country or stick to your principles, but, Howard, you are my prisoner and must guide my men over the hill."

When Howard again demurred, Howe snapped, "You have no alternative. If you refuse, I shall have you shot through the head."

Late in his long life, decades later, William Howard, Jr., would say with a somber face that this threat was decisive. "My father, thus compelled to serve the cause of the enemy," he told all who listened, "was marched out under a guard, who had orders to shoot him."

As sentimentally patriotic as this story is, it sounds a little too pat, the stuff of a Mel Gibson military fantasy.

Howe hardly had to threaten execution in order to gain a guide in this part of the world, which was filled with Loyalists, some of whom had already got him this far and surely were prepared to lead him across the heights. As for the local farmers, most of whom were Dutch, at the very least they were apathetic about the revolution. Fighting was no good for business. The thought that the master of their local tavern was a secret rebel would have been ludicrous. Anyway, harsh threats were not Howe's style. A humane man who sympathized with the colonists' cause, he repeatedly stated that his purpose was pacification, not punishment. Another British general who was with him at the Halfway House, Lord Charles Cornwallis, shared Howe's sympathies, once

Now the cemetery's grounds, the rolling forested slopes of the Green Hills rise
onto the terminal moraine overlooking the Howards' Halfway House.

stating publicly that the Americans were nothing more or less than "free Englishmen, such as we, who are simply standing up for their rights." If Howe showed an excess, it was in lenience and a settled indecisiveness that, many historians believe, won the Revolution for George Washington.

Whatever the political convictions of the generals and the Howards, the father and son guided the British forces. Not wanting to risk exposure under a nearly full moon to American lookouts who were assumed to be posted down in Jamaica Pass, they worked their way along a footpath on the hill that had long been followed by the Rockaway Indians as they moved between their fishing grounds on Jamaica Bay and Long Island Sound. The terrain, now in the center of The Evergreens Cemetery, was not easy—rolling, heavily forested, and spotted by ponds and marshes. Pausing frequently to look for American troops and saw down trees to make way for

the cannon (axes were too loud), the large party needed well over three hours to travel less than two miles. A British officer later said that no march during his career had been so disagreeable and that "by daybreak my stock of patience had begun to run very low."

The precise location of the Rockaway Footpath is not known for certain. When the Evergreens Cemetery's Board of Trustees decided to locate and mark it, Assistant Superintendent Anthony Salamone, an Army veteran, applied a foot soldier's logic to the problem. "Where would I want to walk and pull artillery pieces?" he asked rhetorically. "The answer is not anywhere near Howard Point. I'd want to be as far away from a steep climb as I could get." He believed the British entered the cemetery grounds approximately on the Kings-Queens line, on a shallow slope near the present-day Orient Hill burial section, then pushed west across the hillock on which the Evergreens chapel-administration building is now located, before descending toward the present-day entrance at Central Avenue, coming out well clear of Jamaica Pass on the road to Brooklyn. (It turned out that much of the effort was unnecessary. Due to confusion in the Americans' command, Jamaica Pass was guarded by just five raw recruits.) Soon after dawn the British were moving fast toward the weakly defended left flank of the surprised Yankees, and the Howards were returning to the Halfway House, where the boy conveniently forgot whatever patriotic feelings he may have had, cheerfully whiling away the next few days by chatting with British soldiers and watching daredevils pole-vault over the tavern's mansard roof.

The rout of the Americans was total. In his poem "The Centenarian's Story," Walt Whitman described "The British advancing, rounding in from the east, fiercely playing their guns." Observing the slaughter, Washington wrung his hands and exclaimed, "Good God! What brave fellows I must this day lose." Within a few hours, more than 2,500 Americans were dead, wounded, or taken prisoner, and destined for starvation in the British prison ships in Wallabout Bay. The British suffered only three hundred sixty casualties. When General Howe inexplicably declined to extend his triumph with a sustained offensive, the American troops escaped across the East River in small boats and beat a tactical retreat toward eventual victory. Meanwhile a fire (likely caused by arson) destroyed more than one-half the houses of lower Manhattan. If William Howard Jr. had climbed up to the promontory that would eventually be his last resting place, and looked miles to the west, he would have seen the blaze clearly.

The Halfway House and its environs remained occupied for several years. It became the subject of numerous tales told by rebels, among them a claim that when the news of the victory in the Battle of Bennington reached New York, a spunky revolutionary who was being held prisoner by the British in New Lots—perhaps Ethan Allen, the hero of Ticonderoga—walked out of confinement, climbed up on the roof of the Halfway House, and gave three rousing cheers before he was subdued and tossed back into prison. Even if this tale were true, it would not be as striking as the one William Howard would tell about the night Lords Howe and Cornwallis came to call on the Green Hills of Brooklyn.

As William Howard Jr. lived out a long life in or near the Halfway House, he repeatedly told the story of the Battle of Brooklyn—a story so intriguing and important that he can be forgiven the embellishments he applied from time to time. In 1849, his son-in-law, a lawyer named Philip Reid, arranged for the sale of his land to the founders of the Evergreens Cemetery. After he died five years later at the age of ninety-four, Howard's family and friends carried him up to the promontory. William Howard and the Reids lie there today in a place where, when the leaves are down in winter, an imaginative eye can still view the sails of all nations slowly approaching from the far east and far west, the north and the south, to the metropolis of the Western World.

John Berrien's War

As for Captain John Berrien, who had helped start the war that William Howard told such a colorful story about, after the Battle of Brooklyn he very likely assisted in the hasty evacuation of the city. Following brief service as a lieutenant in a private company of foot soldiers known as the Corsicans, he spent the war as an elected member of New York's State Assembly, which met in Poughkeepsie, Albany, and other places upstate, and served as commissary for the hospital department of the Revolutionary Army, corresponding (and sometimes disputing policy) with Washington. Berrien incurred debts during his service that were only covered for his heirs a century later in a special act of Congress.

Following the war, he went back into his old trade as an international merchant. In December 1783, a month after the last of the Loyalists evacuated New York, John Berrien and his partner, Leake Hunt, advertised that they had a goodly selection of rum, sugar, tea, and Madeira wine available to sell. Less than a year later, Berrien died at the age of forty-nine and was buried in the Brick Presbyterian Church churchyard, under a stone proclaiming him as a bastion of the Revolution. In his will, as befits a man who flaunted his status as an Esquire, he left sufficient funds to provide an annual lifetime income for his wife and daughter, and also a small library of books of "history, Philosophy, poetry, and amusement."

Seventy-two years later, this mobile and versatile individual made one last move as his bones were carried to the Brick Church's new burial ground on Church Hill, a short stroll from the Rockaway Footpath.

A TYPICAL AUTUMN SCENE
ON THE GROUNDS

CHAPTER TWO

A PRETTY NATURAL SITUATION: FOUNDING A RURAL CEMETERY

J UST WHO RECOMMENDED this proper place for a burial ground is unclear, and in any case it is unimportant. The area was too well known to require a Columbus. Any of the Evergreens' founders—Luther Bradish, president of the New-York Historical Society, former Brooklyn Mayors Edward Copland and George Hall, or the others— might have visited on a sleighing or skating adventure with children or grandchildren, or stayed over at the Halfway House, where they would have heard William Howard's colorful if somewhat amazing stories of the Revolution. The area went by several names, each referring to one or both of its most obvious features—the forests and the rolling hills. The Dutch who farmed there, leaving behind flintlocks and muskets that are sometimes turned up by gravediggers, called the area *Oost-Wont* (East Woods). Native Americans used *Guan* (hills), the British compromised with Woody Heights of Guana, and there were names like Greenwood, Jamaica Hills

PAGE 26, THE LAWN, WITH VIEW OF MANHATTAN

LEFT, LINNET GROVE AND 116-FOOT TULIP TREE

(referring to the Jameco Indians), and a somewhat exaggerated Green Mountains. As an indication of how parochial parts of old Kings County were, sometimes the terminal moraine east of Jamaica Pass was called Bushwick Hills, and west of it, toward downtown Brooklyn, there was Bedford Hills.

But the name that seems have been used most often was Green Hills, and that is good enough for us. If this jumble of names means anything, it is that the site of the Evergreens Cemetery was extremely well known ever since the early Dutch settlers arrived there in the 1600s. In the 1840s the rector of a Presbyterian Church in Williamsburg, the Reverend John D. Wells, took his daily horseback ride out there on most mornings. He grew so fond of the place that, after it became a cemetery, he helped decorate it with evergreen trees and arranged to be buried there.

The Human Obligation

Whether or not they knew the place, the founders agreed on one thing: New York and Brooklyn needed a big cemetery. Ten thousand New Yorkers and Brooklynites were dying every year, but the two cities' hundreds of crowded burying grounds and churchyards were being shut down for health reasons and to make room for real estate development. Add to these practical concerns the inherent, natural desire of all civilized people to find a respectable last resting place. When a nineteenth-century religious magazine observed that "death in the city is for more reasons than one a terror for the poor," the author conjured up the universal shame of a passing without decent burial. One of the most frightening prophecies in the Bible has to be Jeremiah's promise that King Jehoiakim's corpse would be "cast out to the heat by day and the frost by night" (Jeremiah 36:30). More acceptable, but not by much, was interment in a charity burial ground, variously known as a pauper's field, a public burying ground, a sojourners' or strangers' plot, and a potter's field (named after the burial site of Judas Iscariot in Matthew 27:7).

As the population frontier of New York City moved north, so did potters' fields, from Washington Square near Eighth Street, to Madison Square at Twenty-Third, then to what is now Bryant Park at Forty-Second. After that, the bodies were dug up yet again and taken out to islands, first Ward's Island near One Hundred Sixth Street, and finally (in 1869) Hart Island, today the world's largest potter's field with more than 700,000 graves, most unmarked. The convicts and common laborers do burial duty under the prayerful inscription on a cross: "He Calleth His children by name." Meanwhile, by both law and custom, churchyards and community burial grounds were expected to reserve a portion of their property for the interment of destitute people politely referred to as strangers or sojourners.

Strangers they may have been, but they still were attended to. "Show me the manner in which a nation cares for its dead," British Prime Minister William Gladstone has been quoted as saying, "and I will measure with mathematical exactness the tender sympathies of its people, their respect for the law, their loyalty to higher ideals." Untended corpses violated what a philosopher of cemeteries, Robert Pogue Harrison, calls "the human obligation to the corpse." Another humiliation was the prospect of the absence of mourners. For medieval people, as for us, to die meant to enter a great silence," writes a historian of English religion, Eamon Duffy, "and the fear of being forgotten in that silence was as real to them as to any of the generations that followed." This sentiment goes a long way toward suggesting why so much energy and so many resources have been applied not just to creating and maintaining cemeteries, but to providing burial. The many group plots at the Evergreens and other cemeteries are a constant reminder that the oldest form of life insurance, dating back to the ancient Greeks and Romans, is burial insurance provided through membership in a club or fraternal society. Burial insurance is no less important in modern times. "Without that policy, I don't know what I would have done," said a Mississippi woman who had buried her granddaughter using an insurance policy for which she paid $2 weekly. "You just don't want to put

Winter Scene in Brooklyn captures the diversity (and accidents) of the rustic
riverside village and its people on Fulton Street in 1820. Under the thick chimney smoke in the
distance are churchyards whose remains were later transferred to the Evergreens,
including the body of the painter of this delightful streetscape, Francis Guy.

your loved one away any old kind of way."

All this was instinctive to Americans of the mid-nineteenth century. As a group and individually, the founders of the Cemetery of the Evergreens were motivated to go through the complicated steps of assembling a new graveyard that was not just many times the size of even the largest churchyards, but that would profoundly change some of the ways in which New Yorkers buried their dead. Each founder was old enough to remember

the days when a proposal for a cemetery in the remote rural outskirts would have been a laughing matter. Their youthful neighborly world in the village of old Brooklyn on the banks of the East River is shown in the painting *Winter Scene in Brooklyn*, produced by Francis Guy during the winter of 1819–1820, looking out the second-story window of his house near the Fulton Ferry dock. When Guy died later in 1820, he was buried in the churchyard of the Sands Street Methodist Church, which lies beyond the cloud of chimney smoke in the painting. In 1849, when the Evergreens was founded, this small world was a distant memory. Forty years later construction of the Brooklyn Bridge forced Sands Street and other churches to sell out and transfer the remains in their cemeteries— among them, those of Francis Guy—to the Evergreens.

Today this solution to the crowding problem seems obvious when the Brooklyn-Queens border is less than a half-hour's drive from where Guy painted his townscape. A century and a half ago, however, that same trip could entail a several hours' journey from downtown Brooklyn to the Green Hills. Besides demanding considerable funding and tremendous energy, to locate a cemetery there required a leap of faith by everybody involved, not the least of whom were the cemetery's founders and investors.

An aristocratic abolitionist, and a former Lieutenant Governor of New York, Luther Bradish was the cemetery's founding president.

Mayors, Philanthropists, and Radicals

The founding Board of Trustees of, and company of investors in, The Cemetery of the Evergreens included many well-known names. The aristocratically jut-jawed president, Luther Bradish, was a former Lieutenant Governor of New York State and now in 1849 the president of the well-established New-York Historical Society and a leading antislavery figure who once went so far as to state in public that skin color was no cause for distinction. "Aristocratic" also describes one of the two founding vice presidents, William Bedloe Crosby. One of New York's richest men, he was related to several old Dutch families and, according to the rector of his church, "had the stately figure and the air of an English duke; those of us who knew him best knew well that a more genial, humble, devout, and benevolent heart could not be found in a Sabbath day's journey." Another

founder with close connections to New York churches was Abijah P. Cumings, a newspaper publisher and manager of the American Bible Society, which published and distributed inexpensive bibles (Crosby and Bradish were Bible Society's trustees).

Also active in the Evergreens founding were two mayors of Brooklyn. Evergreens Vice President Edward Copland was a retail grocer who had served as a Brooklyn judge, city clerk, and member of the school board. His term as mayor in 1849 was marked by his frequent vetoes of pork-laden legislation, his approval of Brooklyn's first park, and his insistence on hiring professional street cleaners and stopping dependence on scavengers, dogs, and pigs to pick up the trash. The *Long Island Star* (a local paper) praised him for his "urbanity, dignity, decision, promptitude, energy, and the most minute and careful attention to business"—not a set of skills usually associated with an urban mayor in those corrupt days.

The other founder-mayor was George Hall, the Evergreens' first general agent, or sales manager, working out of a downtown Brooklyn office. The child of Irish immigrants, he had worked his way up the ladder of government to be elected mayor in 1834. His platform was simple: temperance and no pigs. He wanted to close down all unlicensed saloons and liquor shops, and he wanted to clear Brooklyn's roads and paths of free-running hogs. Those were brave opinions for a politician at a time when whisky was so cheap that men were knocking it down at breakfast, and when butchers lined Fulton Street down to the ferry wharf. Hall succeeded. According to the *Star*, under Hall a town that was "formerly full of uproar" became "peaceful and attractive." Two decades after helping found the Evergreens, Hall ran again on the prohibition ticket and was elected the first mayor of the newly consolidated city of Brooklyn.

A CHARACTERISTIC SETTING
OF STONES, NATURE, SHADES,
SHAPES, AND TERRAIN

Hall was one of several employees of the new cemetery. Another was Roswell Graves, a surveyor who had brokered the purchase of the cemetery's land, going door to door in the late 1840s to negotiate with owners of old farmland. They were the descendents of some of Kings County's oldest families, people with names like Schenck, Lefferts, Furman, Ditmas, Duryea, Remsen, Rapelya, and Meserole, not to mention an ancient retired pub keeper named William Howard, who loved to tell stories about British generals—names seen on Brooklyn street signs, in Brooklyn history books, and on Evergreens Cemetery tombstones. Graves bought more than two hundred acres of land and sold it by prior agreement and at a modest profit to the founders, who in turn exchanged it with the cemetery corporation.

The Walt Whitman Connections

The paperwork founding the Evergreens was signed on October 3, 1849, in the home of Samuel E. Johnson. A member of one of Brooklyn's leading families, he was a lawyer, a future judge, and a member of the committee under Mayor Copland that created Brooklyn's first public park, which was first called Washington Park and then was renamed Fort Greene Park. Johnson was an active and vehement Free Soiler, meaning that he opposed slavery's spread in the United States. In 1849 he founded an antislavery newspaper, *The Brooklyn Daily Freeman,* and hired the cheerful, sociable, and slightly scruffy former editor of the *Brooklyn Daily Eagle* to edit it. This was Walt Whitman, six years before the publication of his epic poem *Leaves of Grass.* Whitman had championed Johnson's and Copland's park idea, but his enthusiasm for the Free Soil agenda had got him fired by the *Eagle* thanks to the pressure of Brooklyn's and New York's large pro-Southern faction.

Walt Whitman (shown here around 1855, when he wrote *Leaves of Grass*) roamed the Green Hills and buried his parents at the Evergreens.

Whitman personified and adored Brooklyn and Kings County. "I too lived—Brooklyn, of ample hills, was mine; / I too walk'd the streets of Manhattan Island," he wrote in his poem "Crossing Brooklyn Ferry." Manhattanites had flat streets, and its people were either rich or poor—"there is no medium between a palatial mansion and a dilapidated hovel." But Brooklyn's "ample hills" welcomed the common man. Whitman appreciated that there was something important about Brooklyn cemeteries. "What a history is contained in them!" he once exclaimed. And he also admired the Green Hills. His travels took him out there to a village boasting the name of East New York. When a real estate developer named John Pitkin in the 1830s heard that a railroad was under construction from downtown Brooklyn out to Long Island, he bought up farmsteads along the route and laid out streets for a new town whose future seemed so grand that he named it for the big city itself. Pitkin's scheme collapsed during a financial crisis, but in 1847 someone from the *Eagle*—Whitman, judging by the writing style—took a slow train out to take a look. He was struck less by the town than by the neighboring hills. "The settlement is quite a flat," he wrote. Not so its surroundings. "To the north rises a spur of that range of hills which runs nearly through the island," and this ridge, he explained, "gives the settlement a relief from the character of monotony which most flat places possess." For the average man and woman, this varied landscape "did really offer a pretty natural situation."

A natural situation for what? Whitman would have found it hard not to think of cemeteries. In that same year, 1847, the state legislature, concerned that cities were filling up with graves, passed the Rural Cemeteries Act—"rural" meaning outside city limits, though it would soon come to mean a distinctive bucolic land-

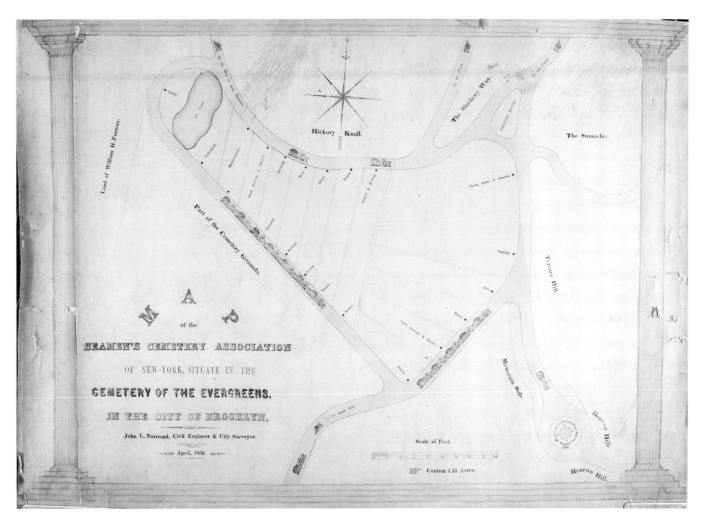

This early map shows the Seaman's Grounds, one nationality per section. The pond at the left was later filled in and the main entrance today is near its location. The Seaman's Monument (lower right) was moved without its column to its present location in the 1950s.

scape design. At the time of Whitman's visit to East New York, the Green Hills already had one rural cemetery, Cypress Hills, and another, the Evergreens, was in the early stages of planning by his friends.

Whitman was deeply sympathetic to such projects. He had no trouble understanding the human yearning for a decent grave and a dignified funeral. In the introduction to the first edition of *Leaves of Grass*, he briefly set aside his usual exuberance for a moment to lay down some rules about achieving true independence. To be independent, he said, required three things: One was ownership of a suitable house. Another was access to decent clothing and food. And the third was "a little sum

laid aside for burial-money." An anonymous charity grave in a potter's field was no sign of true independence. He did not write these words lightly. As he was preparing *Leaves of Grass* for the press, his father, Walter Whitman, died on July 11, 1855, in his house on Ryerson Street in Brooklyn. After the funeral, he was carried up and into the Green Hills and the new Cemetery of the Evergreens, where, just below the crest of a knoll with a sweeping easterly prospect, he was lowered into a grave. Louisa Whitman, his widow, joined him in 1873. Years later their ailing son, by then living in Camden, New Jersey, devoted his remaining energies to designing a granite tomb for himself and his family in a leafy rural cemetery like the Evergreens called Harleigh. After his death in 1892, following his instructions, his parents' remains were transferred there from the Evergreens.

The Seaman's Grounds

For Whitman and other Brooklynites, the unity in diversity in Brooklyn's landscape mirrored the unity in diversity in its people and history. As Ralph Foster Weld later wrote in his celebration of everyday life in Kings County, *Brooklyn Is America*, "There is no deliberate plan to promote unity. It is a democratic process which began in this western tip of Long Island three hundred years ago and has continued with the growth of Brooklyn from its Dutch infancy to its present giant stature." He added, "The threads of race and culture were woven in and out." Naturally, this variety would eventually be reflected in many Brooklyn cemeteries, but the Evergreens adopted diversity as an unstated policy.

There was no elaborate dedication day ceremony with eloquent speeches by local politicians and lengthy prayers by famous clergymen. Rather, the Evergreens opened with its first burial. The first dated interment recorded on the Evergreens' ledger is that of a four-year-old boy, Henry Northall, the son of a dentist, who was interred on February 20, 1850. Where he was buried was not noted in the cemetery's massive burial ledger, but it may well have been in the plot called Path Side, located on the down slope toward Jamaica Pass, near the then main gate on the cemetery's western border and with a good view of Bushwick, Williamsburg, and, on the horizon, Manhattan. That was where the second recorded burial took place on Sunday, July 1, 1850. The deceased was James Dickson, a thirty-five-year-old Irishman who had accidentally drowned in a mill pond in New Lots. Almost all the fifty-eight burials in 1850 took place on the Evergreens' western and southern borders—at Path Side, or at Ocean View or Sylvan Dell, with their even more dramatic views of Jamaica Bay and the Atlantic. In the fall of 1850 the first family plot was sold (it was a large four hundred–foot lot acquired by trustee William Bedloe Crosby), and the first funeral service in the new

chapel, designed by the famous architect Alexander Jackson Davis, was held for William Furman, a farmer whose family's Bushwick property bordered the Evergreens.

Individual burials gradually increased to a rate of five or ten a day. In the meantime the Evergreens became a haven for large numbers of some of the most rootless and abused individuals in history. Actors, African Americans, Chinese, suicides, and other social pariahs would come, but first there were merchant seamen who happened to die in New York. The first large group plot, the Seaman's Grounds, is dedicated to them. Besides risking their necks on a regular basis—mortality rates in some fishing vessels exceeded those of Civil War brigades in combat—sailors suffered infamously exploitative and often brutal treatment by ship captains and their recruiting agents ashore. "The captain was God and his order was law," writes the historian of New York's Seamen's Church Institute, "and if the chief mate beat a few sailors black and blue while carrying it out, well, good discipline made for a smart ship. Life in the forecastle was bleak: damp and unheated, without amenities or rights." Usually illiterate, often known only by nicknames, and always pulled unpredictably hither and yon by the next ship, rootless seamen personified the words "stranger" and "lost" many miles beyond the stabilizing tug of home. When they were lost overboard at sea, shipmates would do anything to recover them, dead or alive. On the belief that loud noises would raise a body, guns were fired, horns blown, drums banged, and bells rung. Many seamen believed that a bundle of straws, or a loaf of bread in which some quicksilver or mercury was inserted, would "swim" directly to a body. To not recover a body was extremely unsettling to sailors. In his book *Two Years Before the Mast*, Richard Henry Dana Jr. described the desperation in the crew after a shipmate fell from the rigging into the sea. "Death is at all times solemn, but never so much as at sea," Dana observed. "A man dies on shore; his body remains with his friends, and 'the mourners go about the streets'; but when a man falls overboard at sea and is lost, there is a suddenness in the event, and a difficulty in realizing it, which give to it an air of awful mystery." That was not all. "Then, too, at sea — to use a homely but expressive phrase —you miss a man so much."

When seamen died in New York aboard ship or on shore, until the 1850s they ended up in the potter's field. At the time the Evergreens was opened, however, the New York Chamber of Commerce decided to arrange for a special burial ground for seamen. The effort was headed by William H. Macy, president of the Seamen's Bank for Saving. In their petition to Congress asking for funds, the committee wrote that dying seamen were so anguished by the prospect of interment in a potter's field "that they often gave utterance to their feelings in the most impressive language." The government funding came and was added to by Macy and his friends. "Jack is now to be buried at least like a gentleman" announced the *Eagle* when the four-acre Seaman's Grounds was opened in 1853 on a broad south-facing slope. The owner of a boarding house described the procedure this way: "When a seagoing man dies at my house leaving no money, I go to the undertaker, give him money enough to pay for opening a grave,"—at that time $2—"and he attends to the rest of the business without another word. The next day the poor sailor is at rest in the prettiest part of one of the loveliest cemeteries on Long Island." Some 1,200 sailors were buried there by 1870.

The first American plot for foreign seamen, the Seaman's Grounds remain striking in their simplicity with just nineteen markers, most of them representing nations or geographical regions providing merchant seamen. Beginning near the gate and working clockwise around the periphery of the Seaman's Grounds are these countries or regions: Mexico, South America Pacific, Mediterranean, Prussia, Asia, Netherlands, Turkey, South America Atlantic, Germany, Spain, Africa, France, Sweden and Norway, Austria, Russia, and Portugal. (Strikingly for an American institution in that period, black sailors from Africa and Chinese sailors from Asia were buried equally with whites.) At the top of the slope, on the treeless promontory of Howard Point,

Seaman's Grounds with Seaman's monument. Hickory Knoll in background.

stood a tall, marble spire rising fifty feet from the base to the top of a two-ton sphere representing the globe. It was so clearly visible from the sea that fishermen used it as a beacon to locate their favorite fishing ground, called "Cholera Banks" because it was discovered in 1832, the year of the worst of the city's many cholera epidemics that, as we will see in the next chapter, played a part in the great New York burial crisis that helped bring about the founding of the Evergreens.

CHAPTER THREE

NEW YORK'S BURIAL CRISIS

N INETEENTH-CENTURY BROOKLYN had three nicknames. Thanks to the burgeoning middle class, it was the City of Homes. The large number of faith traditions arriving in the wave of European immigration made it the City of Churches. And the creation of Green-Wood, Cypress Hills, the Evergreens, and other large new burial grounds on the sandy Long Island moraine made Brooklyn the City of Cemeteries. "Brooklyn stands unrivaled," Kings County's main daily newspaper, the *Eagle*, boasted at the end of the century, when the remains of 2.7 million people were interred there (three times the county's living population). The cemeteries "have girdled it around. They have occupied all the high ground about here."

The City of Cemeteries was created by a burial crisis in Manhattan and Brooklyn between 1820 and 1860 involving public health and land. The solution to this crisis involved three steps. The first was barring new interments in old downtown burial grounds and churchyards. In the second step, the Evergreens and other cemeteries so they would not be covered by new buildings. As straightforward as these steps seem, they did not pass easily or without protest, for as a historian of Brooklyn remarked, "Eternal slumber was not guaranteed in an urban grave." The underlying cause of all the turmoil was the greatest population explosion in New York history. The opening of the Erie Canal in 1825 provided the only direct shipping link to the Midwest through New York and up the Hudson River. The city (which then meant Manhattan) quickly outgrew Philadelphia and Boston to become the country's largest, busiest port and financial center. At mid-century, New York's one hundred ten wharves handled half the country's imports and a third of its exports, as well as the great waves of refugees from an Irish famine and several unsuccessful central European revolutions (in 1855, one-half of Kings County's residents were foreign born). Between 1830 and 1850, the population of what we now know as the City of New York almost tripled, from 242,000 to 696,000. By 1870 it would be 1,478,000, six times greater than the population forty years earlier, leaving New York and Brooklyn as the first and third largest cities in the United States. All this placed unprecedented pressure on essential services, including clean water, real estate development, and public health.

One symptom of the problem was the ancient, crowded, and neglected churchyard in terminal disrepair. As they filled up and were dwarfed by new buildings, and as many families of the dead moved uptown, these once bright places took on the sorry appearance of the "bleak place overgrown with nettles" that Charles Dickens presented at the opening of *Great Expectations*. These unhappy plots were vandalized by criminals, robbed by medical students seeking corpses to practice on, and allowed to crumble. No wonder, then, that many old churches were eager to sell out and follow the northward-advancing population frontier. Some of these problems were characteristic to the United States. In Europe, crowding by the dead had long been eased

through the practice of placing enormous cemeteries outside the city walls and then renting the graves (and even the caskets) for a period of time, often between six and twenty years. When the tenant's remains were disinterred and placed above ground in ossuaries or charnel houses, the grave was available for a new corpse. Americans, however, were inclined to own or at least take permanent leases on lots. Such policies faced no objection so long as open land remained available. Otherwise, Americans were forced to confront the same crowding problem that Roman cities had faced two millennia earlier, and that affected European cities in the Middle Ages. Their solution was to bury only emperors, heroes, martyrs, the wealthy, and other prominent people inside the city walls, leaving the remains of common people in vast, remote civic necropolises—true "cities of the dead." Today a wanderer in a European city will in time come across a plaza or street whose name indicates a previous use related to burials, like the Paseo de los Tristes along which mourners once walked in the shadow of the Alhambra, in Granada, Spain, toward the site of an ancient cemetery. Another solution to the crowding problem, cremation, was rarely utilized in America. Ancient Greeks and Romans practiced it, as did (and do) many Asians, but after it was banned by the Roman Catholic Church and other faiths, cremation was scarcely employed in the United States until very recently when, after decades of hovering at less than 3 percent of all burials, cremations reached 20 percent at the end of the twentieth century.

Shaking Hands with Death

If urban land availability was a serious concern in the 1840s, public health presented a frightening threat. Every few years an epidemic of yellow fever, cholera, or smallpox swept through New York and Brooklyn. Due largely to these epidemics, New York's death rate rose by almost 30 percent (from 21 per thousand to 27 per thousand) between 1810 and 1857, but the impact is vividly seen on headstones. In the Brick Church plot on Church Hill there are inscriptions listing the cause of death as "pewtred fever," "prevailing malignant fever," "the raging epidemic," and "the then prevailing epidemic." Survivors could be less terse. After the 1798 yellow fever epidemic, which reportedly killed 5 percent of the city's population, one said, grimly, "Death and we shook hands so often in those times." Thirty-six years later, as cholera killed 2,996 New Yorkers in less than two months, another survivor, John Pintard muttered, "The face of heaven appeared to be obscured with a somber shroud of death." In 1849, the year the Evergreens was founded, cholera killed six hundred fifty-two people in Brooklyn alone.

This was not just a New York phenomenon. Down in New Orleans, as yellow fever hit in the summer of 1853 and mortality rates skyrocketed to almost 70 per thousand, locals sought solace in the Louisiana habit of dispensing dark humor. Soon, they said, they would be forced to dig their own graves because everybody was dying too fast to have the job done for them.

Trinity Churchyard exemplified urban cemetery crowding at the time the Evergreens was founded.

These regular and terrifying assaults of sickness were like battles in an endless war. When the middle class parishioners of New York's Brick Presbyterian Church honored the long tenure of Gardiner Spring as their leader, their official testimonial told how over "a long series of years, during which at all times, in season of plague and pestilence, of personal peril and public danger, they have observed and marked your devotedness to the cause of your Master." In a war, people know how to defend themselves, but that was not the case with New York's and Brooklyn's many seasons of plague and pestilence before the 1840s. Before quarantine was finally established in New York Harbor, passengers went

ashore from contagion-ravaged ships without either inspection or hindrance. On shore, at the same time that citizens were fumigating incoming mail with sulfuric acid and attempting other useless home remedies, "The streets were coated by 'mud' made by animal droppings mixed with rainwater," historian Andrew Delbanco has noted, adding, with no exaggeration whatsoever, that "without a sewage system, the city was literally flowing with both animal and human shit." Corpses played a part, of course. But when Dr. Samuel L. Mitchell of Columbia College studied 1798's "Pestilential Fever," he properly recognized the public health hazard of "Human carcasses, buried and accumulated for a long series of years," before proceeding to completely misjudge just how that risk became a fatal reality. The real agent, of course, was polluted drinking water. Mitchell was sure the danger lay in "miasmic vapors" suspended in the air that people breathed. Human remains "have poisoned the air in many parts of Christendom."

Some people claimed they could actually see the vapors rising from graves. An early proponent of cremation (whose main selling point was that it eliminated the deadly miasma) swore that on calm mornings, Manhattan's potter's field at Fourth Street (now Washington Square) lay beneath "a dense blue haze several feet deep." The 1822 yellow fever epidemic was blamed on a miasma rising from a single, shallow grave in the intensely crowded churchyard of Trinity Church, at the head of Wall Street. Taking the complaint seriously, the vestry arranged to have the entire churchyard layered with the contents of fifty-two casks of lime. Mitchell's solution in 1798 to the miasma problem was simple: "on account of the horrid mischiefs occasioned thereby," American cities should follow the lead of the ancients and Europeans and inter their dead outside their walls in vast necropolises. His advice fell on mostly deaf ears. Americans much preferred to bury their dead near their homes.

It was not that New Yorkers denied the existence of polluted water. A large stream-fed pond known as the Collect, lying just north of Manhattan's City Hall, had once been so pure that it was fished, but by 1800 it was referred to as "a very common sewer." Filling it in 1813 ended the local stink, but so long as the miasma theory held sway, the true risk of the seepage of human waste and human remains into the thousands of private wells and springs (the only sources of fresh water on Manhattan Island) went dangerously unnoticed. The theory of miasmas gradually gave way, however, and in the 1830s the city undertook to replace outhouses with sewers, to close local wells and springs, and, in its first immense public works project, to import water from upstate through a forty-one-mile aqueduct from the Croton Dam.

"Our Fathers, Where Are They?"

By the time the new water system was completed in 1842, New York was well on the road to addressing the problem of crowded churchyards. In 1822 new burials were barred in lower Manhattan, and as the population frontier advanced northward, so did the line below which interments were illegal without costly special permits. The initial restrictions on downtown interments made no exception for family crypts, so some

Old burial grounds were lucky if a clothesline was the only indignity they suffered. When Nagel Cemetery in upper Manhattan was closed in 1927, 417 graves were transferred to Woodlawn Cemetery.

seventy-five New Yorkers every year willingly choose to pay a $250 fine (the equivalent of $5,000 today) so that a relative could be laid to rest with her or his ancestors. Rising public outrage over what was in effect a legalized bribe eventually forced the city to allow routine interments in existing family tombs.

The aim was dual: solve the public health crisis; and open up land for redevelopment. In the 1840s came more laws shutting down local churchyards and burial grounds and moving remains to new cemeteries in remote Kings and Queens counties. Brooklyn's concerns ran about twenty years behind Manhattan's, but it, too, was eventually forced to deal with the twin problems of population density and public health. In 1847 the town required that new burials be at a depth of four feet. Two years later—the same year that the Evergreens was founded—Brooklyn barred new interments in its most densely crowded wards. As Cypress Hills and the Evergreens joined the older Green-Wood as Brooklyn's new big cemeteries, many old downtown churchyards were shut down. (Public health worries did not end with the formation of rural cemeteries. When Kings County's first reservoir was planned in the 1850s for the south slope of the Green Hills at Ridgewood, a proposal to lead the pipes through the Evergreens stirred up tremendous community opposition, and in the end the pipes were laid around the cemetery's perimeter.) In Brooklyn and Manhattan, old downtown cemeteries were being shut down by the dozens, and remains were disinterred and transferred by the thousands. In 1820, Manhattan had one hundred active burial grounds, twenty-three alone in the one mile between City Hall and the Battery. In 1850 there were only twenty-three active burial sites on the entire island.

The price of all this was the acute distress, even trauma, felt by families. In any ranking of human needs, not far behind knowing that one's own corpse will not be dumped into an anonymous grave in a potter's field is the concern for accessibility to the graves of one's ancestors. Not everybody feels that way. A century ago, a highly respectable American magazine, *North American Review*, published an article saying not only that cemeteries were "a menace to the commonweal," but that nobody cared for what lay there: "it takes more time for the flesh of a body to decompose than its memory is apt to live." That is a decidedly minority view. Seated upon a grave in his family's old burial plot on Long Island, Walt Whitman reflected in 1881 that this "gray and sterile hill" was the repository of the entirety of his clan history, "with its succession of links, from the first settlement down to date, told here—three centuries concentrate on this sterile acre." Such feelings do not depend on such a sweep of time. Philip Roth expressed the same yearning for continuity in his 2006 novel, *Everyman*, through the voice of an aging, ill man who, at his parents' graves, reflects that, though "they were just bones, bones in a box," when near them "he could not leave them, couldn't not talk to them, couldn't but listen to them when they spoke. He couldn't go. The tenderness was out of control. As was the longing for everyone to be living. And to have it all over again."

"Overturn, Overturn"

Grief, memory, and the hope for permanence are too intermingled to be separated even in the most stable of times, but their violation by outside forces can trigger the most intense feelings. The radical rebuilding of Manhattan in the mid-1800s did just that as historic buildings, monuments, and burial grounds were dug up and discarded at an unsettling rate. "Overturn, overturn, overturn!" former New York Mayor Philip Hone all but shouted into his diary on April 7, 1845, upon hearing

that some Revolutionary War artifacts had been discarded during the construction of a new house. From there he slid easily into the burial crisis. "The very bones of our ancestors are not permitted to lie quiet a quarter of a century, and one generation of men seems studious to remove all relics of those which preceded them." Likewise, an anguished congregant of an old Manhattan church, facing the transfer of his family's remains to a remote cemetery, confessed that "The bare thought of their being disturbed, or their once lovely and expressive features being marred by any power but that of natural and appointed decay, is a wound inflected on our affections." Over in Brooklyn, when the trustees of the churchyard of St. Ann's Episcopal Church decided in 1860 to sell the grounds and transfer the remains to the Evergreens, a protestor voiced a fierce jeremiad against "unholy speculators": "Cursed be he who removeth his neighbor's landmark, and may all the people answer, Amen!" In Manhattan, John Pintard could not comprehend the removal of the bones of his ancestors from the churchyard of Manhattan's French Protestant Church, L'Église du Saint Ésprit. Usually a factual sort of man (he had established the city's vital statistics department), Pintard was devastated by the opening of the tombs of his relatives in clear view of passersby. "It was difficult to suppress my tears, amidst a number of spectators all anxious to see the exhumations that are going on in our ancient cemetery."

Some families went beyond tears, ordering gravediggers to stop work, even instigating fistfights and riots. A court hearing concerning the closing of an old Methodist churchyard and transfer of remains to a remote cemetery was interrupted by a man's cries that the behavior of the trustees was "scandalous," "illegal," "illogical," and "avaricious." "Great excitement was manifested by the audience," a newspaper reported, "and many of the ladies gave expressive tokens of their indignation at the action of the Trustees." In 1863 (according to the *Times* in an article headlined, "Our Fathers, Where Are They?"), as remains were being removed from the Baptist churchyard on Amity Street in

Manhattan to be taken to Cypress Hills Cemetery, "One gentleman pronounced the proceeding disgraceful, unchristian, inhuman, and barbarous. Another said that if he acted on his own natural impulses, he would shoot the first man who attempted to unearth his mother's remains; while a third declared the Board of Trustees to be a soulless, godless corporation, in which no sentiment of honor or humanity existed."

"The burial ground excitement," as this highly emotional failed rebellion was sometimes called, could have a long life. A Manhattan Baptist congregation sold its old churchyard to land developers and had the remains transferred to a new one on a farm in Bushwick. On their hopeful first visit, the parishioners were horrified to discover pigs, chickens, and wild children roaming around the headstones. "The place assumed the look of the most desolate place on earth—a neglected graveyard," reported the *Eagle*. The remains were transferred a second time, to Cypress Hills, where they finally rested.

The typical ill-kempt, frightening churchyard was portrayed with exquisite creepiness by the famous illustrator Harry Fenn, who is buried at the Evergreens.

The Rural Cemetery

People needed assurance that if their dead could not rest nearby, at least they would rest in dignity. Churches lobbied the state government in Albany to write new laws encouraging and regulating new cemeteries. In 1847 the New York State Legislature passed the Rural Cemetery Act to permit corporations to be created specifically to establish nonsectarian burial grounds outside the city limits in adjoining counties.

The key terms here are "cemetery," "rural," and "nonsectarian." They identified the Evergreens and the other rural burial sites as new and unique. Replacing "burial ground" and "burial yard" as the generic term for a place of burial, "cemetery" (derived from a Greek word, *koiman*, meaning a sleeping place) reflected a new, gentler American view of death, very different from the old one of judgment and torment. "Rural," as a geographical term, did not mean "agricultural" or "remote," but something closer to what we call "suburban," that is to say near but not in the city. "Rural" also had another meaning, as a place in nature, and this is how many people came to interpret the word.

The Chaplains

"Nonsectarian" does not seem all that unusual today, when the idea is often expressed as "ecumenical," but in the 1840s inter-faith dialogue, much less activity, was a novelty. The hundreds of churches of New York and Brooklyn, which had a total of more than 100,000 active members, were not in the habit of sharing burial grounds or much else for that matter. Roman Catholics, of course, had their own distinctive rites, but so did the many Protestant sects. "The lines between denominations were then rather sharply drawn," wrote the historian of American religion Robert T. Handy. Baptists, Presbyterians, Congregationalists, Methodists, Dutch Reformers, and Episcopalians might exchange greetings, but, as Handy put it, they all "were quite certain that their doctrines and polity were closest to the teaching of the Bible, and they were determined to win converts to their particular ways." A man who grew up in Brooklyn in the 1840s recalled in a memoir, "In the old days each sect regarded

the other as 'lost souls.' 'Our church' was the only one to be saved in. In fact, unity of effort in the cause of religion, based on the Fatherhood of God, was unknown." Hermetically sealed off from each other by differences in theology, polity, ritual, politics, and ethnicity, most American Protestants worshiped then much as they do in our contentious present day, which is in exclusive groups. And they buried their dead in groups, in churchyards that had been blessed and sanctified in particular ways. Some efforts at dialogue were attempted. In 1815 Gardiner Spring of the Brick Presbyterian Church joined clergy of other churches in founding the American Bible Society to distribute bibles to the poor, but the effort quickly stumbled over disagreements about which translation of Holy Scripture to distribute. (As we will see in the next chapter, there was one exception to these ecclesiastical barriers, and that was a widespread feeling among many nineteenth-century Protestants that God could be found in nature. This sublime conviction helped inspire the uniquely naturalistic design of rural cemeteries.)

Burial in sanctified ground was a burning issue. In 1879 a Roman Catholic cemetery on Long Island barred Denis Coppers, a firefighter, from burial in a family plot that contained the remains of his wife, mother, and two children because he was a Protestant and a Freemason. Freemasons were reputed to be anti-Catholic because they qualified for advancement, called degrees, through service to their lodges, but not to any church. Coppers' family went to court and succeeded in getting a stay. Subsequently, a Protestant widow who was related to Coppers, Mrs. E. J. Chovey, died and her family requested that she be buried in that same Catholic cemetery in a plot that she had picked out between the graves of her two deceased Roman Catholic husbands. On the morning of the burial, the grave was dug and the other preparations were being completed when a cemetery trustee informed the family that the interment could not precede. A great many Freemasons were buried at the Evergreens, some in plots controlled by lodges, others in graves or tombs displaying the Masonic symbol of the eye and compass. The trustees there had no objection to burying Mrs. Chovey (or, for that matter, either of her Catholic husbands). After months of litigation, an appellate court ruled that a cemetery had a right to establish restrictions, so long as they were explicit, and Coppers and Mrs. Chovey were later buried in Protestant cemeteries.

Surrounded by the possibility of such contentiousness, the founders of the Evergreens had to step gingerly. They appointed six chaplains—one each from among the Baptists, the Episcopalians, the Methodists, and the Dutch Reform church, and two Presbyterians representing the Old and New Light factions that were then feuding over revivalism—to advise the cemetery but more important to represent it in the sometimes bitterly disputatious world of 1850s Protestantism. One of the two Presbyterians was Dr. Spring, who would bring John Berrien's remains over from the Brick Church's Manhattan churchyard, and would himself be buried at the Evergreens. The Episcopalian was Samuel Roosevelt Johnson, an uncle of the founder, Samuel E. Johnson. The Methodist was an elderly, legendary preacher named Nathanial Bangs. Described as "majestic of structure, voice, and brain," he had been a pastor at the oldest of Brooklyn's many Methodist parishes, on Sands Street, had served as president of Wesleyan College in Connecticut, and at this time headed the denomination's large, aggressive publications operations. The historian of the Sands Street Church would observe, "No man in Methodism wielded a more potent and permanent influence than Dr. Bangs."

Those three and the other chaplains helped attract transfers to Church Hill and other plots at the Evergreens from old churches. The traces of these and other churches may be found throughout the grounds. While most of these plots can be identified by gravemarkers (a lot in Ocean View, for instance, contains the remains of Presbyterian clergymen from Newtown, Queens, some from Colonial times), some look like open lawns with no visible monument. Often at the time of the transfers the stones were laid flat to protect them from damage,

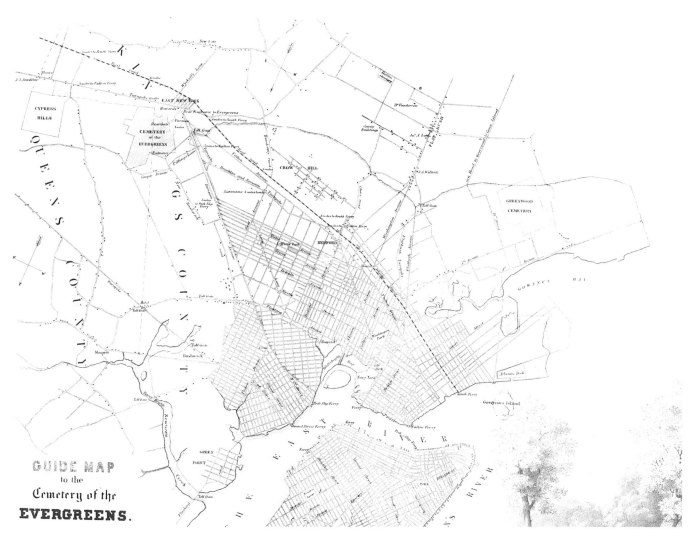

GUIDE MAP
to the
Cemetery of the
EVERGREENS.

Accessibility was a key concern for city families accustomed to nearby churchyards. This unusual map published by the Evergreens in 1852 suggested that it
was closer to Manhattan (at the bottom) than Green-Wood Cemetery.

and the grass had been allowed to grow over them for protection, indirectly enhancing the cemetery's rural appearance.

On the Border

If the Evergreens' founders considered any other site for the cemetery except the Green Hills, nobody mentioned it. The place's advantages were clear. Samuel E. Johnson summarized them simply as "its central position and natural beauties." We have touched on the latter point and will say much more about them. The first one came down to its accessibility from Manhattan via the East River ferries, from downtown Brooklyn, and especially

from the booming town of Williamsburg.

Originally a ferry slip within the town of Bushwick, by 1849 Williamsburg was an industrial and residential center of 30,000 citizens, with a rapidly growing population of recently arrived Germans. It soon became an independent city and in the 1850s was annexed by Brooklyn along with the still largely rural Bushwick. When the cemetery's marketing materials were drawn up, the founders were careful to include special maps suggesting that the Evergreens was more accessible than the older Green-Wood Cemetery, in the Bay Ridge area in south-central Kings County. In addition to providing easy access from Williamsburg, the Green Hills offered a

NEXT PAGE, THE LAWN

way to get around a provision of the 1847 Rural Cemetery Act limiting the size of a cemetery in any one county to two hundred acres. By straddling the boundary between Queens and Kings counties, the Evergreens could always be expanded to as much as four hundred acres, although its maximum size has never been more than two hundred sixty acres (it now has two hundred twenty-five). The Kings-Queens border is settled now, but for over a century in colonial days, its location was the subject of a prolonged dispute. The eventual settlement left the line zigging and zagging for twelve miles between landmarks established by arbitration. Since then, distinct cultures have developed on both sides. Queens people and Brooklynites have no dispute about who is who, but visitors can be astonished by the cultural jumble in one large parcel of land cutting across the boundary. "The border cuts through one large tract that is the most peaceful neighborhood in the entire city," observed a *New York Times* reporter who traced the borderline in 1993. "This is so because all the residents are dead, buried in a cemetery ridge that straddles the two boroughs where the glacial moraine stopped during the ice age."

But even among the dead the reporter was surprised to find extreme variety. In one portion of the Evergreens, on the Queens side he came upon gravestones with markings in Chinese, and, on the Brooklyn side, stones with markings in English. The reporter seemed amazed that, besides being peaceful, this hallowed ground was as diverse as the city growing around it—even though the Evergreens had quietly been burying people of all races, nationalities, and religious beliefs for well over a century.

IN THE NORTH SECTIONS

CHAPTER FOUR

DESIGNING A CEMETERY WITH ANDREW JACKSON DOWNING

"RURAL CEMETERY" WAS A new legal term describing the location of a burial ground in a city's outskirts, but it also meant much more. The Evergreens and other rural cemeteries had a distinctive scenic design and a dual purpose that extended far beyond their fundamental mission as sites for the burial of human remains. Here was a place for burial, yes, but it was also a public center— "a museum, arboretum, bird sanctuary, park, historical archive, and landmark," to quote cemetery historians Blanche Linden-Ward and David C. Sloane. To accomplish all this and still remain an active and respectful cemetery required a novel landscape design that placed the graves and monuments in a picturesque, parklike setting that did not compromise the institution's fundamental calling.

PAGE 54 AND LEFT, THE SUMMER HOUSE AND DAVIS CHAPEL, NOW THE ADMINISTRATION BUILDING

The place itself had to be appropriate, and that was the case with the property selected to be the grounds of the Cemetery of the Evergreens. An early visitor characterized it as a "high rustic enclosure." Rustic the place certainly was after generations of farming. And high this enclosure was, too, its head peaking at over two hundred feet above the flatlands of Brooklyn that sprawled out from its feet, south to the sea. When the glacier retreated more than 10,000 years ago, its moraine formed a forested, spring-fed, and lake-dappled ridge almost the entire length of Long Island. This "knob and kettle country" (to quote Elizabeth Barlow Rogers, a historian of landscaping) impressed visitors with its eye-catching terrain and easily drained sand, gravel, and clay soil. There are times when the knobs and kettles, the hills and swales, appear in a mesmerizing way to roll along easily like an ocean swell in mid-Atlantic, meeting no obstruction that would froth them into steep, white water.

But what first attracted settlers were the thick foliage and rich blooms. "The old island here that flowered once for Dutch sailors' eyes—a fresh, green breast of the new world"—that was F. Scott Fitzgerald's graceful bow to Long Island in *The Great Gatsby*, and it strikes to the heart of its natural richness. Reportedly, the dense forests were so aromatic that sailors downwind of the island would smell the foliage of its hills before seeing the sand of its beaches. When the Dutch acquired Jamaica, Queens, from the Jameco Indians in 1656, the deed included the following stipulation: "One thing to be remembered, that noe person is to cut downe any tall trees wherein Eagles doe build theire nest." There were tall trees aplenty. Long Island then had some seventy species of them—oaks and pines towering sixty feet, tulips more than twice that height, and all those willows, walnuts, chestnuts, maples, cedars, birches. That arboreal splendor (now being approached in the early twenty-first century in the cultivated woodlands of the Evergreens and other old rural cemeteries) has been honored in many ways, but none so telling as the names the Dutch chose for two of their five Long Island vil-

lages—*Boswijck*, "heavy woods," is now Bushwick, and *Vlackebos*, "wooded plain," is Flatbush. (The other Dutch villages—*Breuckelen* (Brooklyn), *New Utrecht*, and *New Amersfoort* (Flatlands)—were named for towns back in the Netherlands.) The foliage was not limited to Dutch areas. When General William Howe's aide-de-camp, Ambrose Serle, came ashore at Kings County's only English settlement, Gravesend, on the eve of the Battle of Brooklyn, he was startled by "Scenes that the Imagination can Fancy or the Eye behold," including "The Green Hills and the Meadows after the Rain and the calm surface of the waters." Marching inland, his soldiers were as "Merry as in a Holiday" as they "regaled themselves with the fine apples, which hung every where upon the Trees in great abundance." Serle saw more such abundance as Howe's forces made their famous flanking maneuver to William Howard's tavern and then along the Rockaway Footpath.

Except for the halting development of East New York, the area around the Green Hills was mostly farmland in 1849, when the Evergreens was established. Census takers around that time discovered that for every three residents in Bushwick, there were six acres of land and one cow. Eastern Kings County served as New York City's farm, providing vegetables and fruit to send across the river in the ferries, and sweet hops and pure water to be gathered by German brewers who quickly made Brooklyn into a center of lager. Long before today's broad Bushwick Avenue was laid, there was a narrow wagon trail called Bushwick Road winding up into the Green Hills. Probably the route that the visitors to the grounds took in October 1849, this trail lay inside the Evergreens' boundaries for several years (its traces are still visible at the cemetery's southwest extreme).

The Open Air Church

A reporter for the *Brooklyn Eagle* in the spring of 1884 climbed up into the cemetery and there found "a cluster of wind-swept hills, with green valleys and winding ways in between." He went on, "Though the wind was bleak and the air chill in that high region, large plots

There scattered oft
    the earliest of the year,
By hands unseen,
    are showers
    of violets found.

The redbreast loves to build
    and warble there,
And little footsteps
    lightly print
    the ground.

A REJECTED VERSE.
REPRINTED FROM THE EARLY EDITIONS.

"Beneath those rugged elms, that yew-tree's shade,
Where heaves the turf in many a mouldering heap."

Before the 1840s, "rural cemetery" suggested sorrowful images like these Harry Fenn illustrations for Thomas Gray's
"Elegy in a Country Church-Yard." The term was redefined by the Evergreens and other bucolic cemeteries.

were abloom with beautiful hyacinths and many colored tulips, showing careful cultivation." This natural garden setting was steadily improved by one strong idea and many hands. The *Eagle*'s observation that "the improvements already made are many, and in good taste" signaled that this was not one of those depressing old burial grounds that were dominated by what one critic colorfully referred to as "sepulchers, melancholy, and ruins."

Some people were disoriented by this rapid shift from gloomy to bucolic burial settings. "The idea of a rural cemetery thirty years ago was one to which the public mind was in no ways educated," recalled an official at Cypress Hill cemetery, the Evergreens' slightly older neighbor on the Green Hills, looking back from the 1870s. When most people first thought of a rural burying ground, they focused on a small, rude plot on a remote farm. Walt Whitman recalled the hillside family burial ground near his childhood home in central Long Island as a "sterile acre" of more than fifty "depress'd mounds, crumbled and broken stones, cover'd with moss." Some graves in old burial grounds were identified by wooden markers that quickly rotted away, others by a tiny slab of crumbly slate or a rock that would soon be overgrown or washed off by the spring rains.

That was the old, bitter style of a rural cemetery. The idea behind the Evergreens and other rural cemeteries flew against American experience. "Charm" was the last word anybody would have used about a typical burial site before 1800. If most old churchyards were austere, their headstones were downright terrifying with those harsh words and images promising doom to all who looked upon them. A "preoccupation with mortality" is how a cemetery historian, Richard E. Meyer, characterizes the purpose of a traditional tombstone, with its skulls, scythes, skeletons, bony hands, hourglasses, and harsh epitaphs sometimes called "holy texts." These messages were hardly cheerful. A famous one reads, "Ye living men, come view the ground, / Where you must shortly lie," and another,

Remember man as you pass by
As you are now so once was I
As I am now so must you be
Remember man that you must die.

Coming across one of these mordant messages from the dead to the living, the American writer Washington Irving complained, "But why should we thus seek to clothe death with unnecessary terrors, and to spread horrors round the tomb of those we love?" Irving had a better answer. "The grave should be surrounded by every thing that might inspire tenderness and veneration for the dead; or that might win the living to virtue. It is the place, not of disgust and dismay, but of sorrow and meditation."

Irving represented a sweeping new attitude about how death should be regarded and represented. Out went the skulls and pedantic pessimism. In came consoling images of angels and nature, and epitaphs like the one in the Evergreens from 1904, on the stone of William Laws and Mary J. Laws:

When I can read my title clear
To mansions in the skies,
I bid farewell to every fear
And wipe my weeping eyes.

And this on the memorial stone at the cemetery for Jean Oigg, who died in 1888:

You asked for rest
You'r freed from pain.
GOD knows what's best
We'll meet again.

The idea of a good death as a bridge to a celestial heaven was expressed even more simply in two words on the stone that a widow named Ellal Stevenson put over the grave of her husband, John: "My Pal"—a thought that surely must have comforted Mrs. Stevenson through her remaining thirty-five years. Death is

not the fearsome thing it first appears, and therefore a burial ground is a welcome place to visit. When an employee of the Evergreens started keeping a scrapbook of news clippings about the place in the late 1800s, he placed on the cover the words "Death is Birth" and, below them, a quote from an American poet, George Spring Merriam, that includes these lines: "To us here death is the most terrible word we know. But when we have tasted its reality, it will mean to us birth, deliverance, a new creation of ourselves."

That era's leading American writers and religious figures believed that this "new creation" came through nature, which they worshiped. "In the woods, we return to reason and faith," the Transcendentalist philosopher Ralph Waldo Emerson wrote in his widely read essay "Nature." "There I feel that nothing can befall me in life—no disgrace, no calamity which nature cannot repair." William Cullen Bryant's poem about death and nature, "Thanatopsis," instructed readers to approach their graves "Like one who wraps the drapery of his couch / About him, and lies down to pleasant dreams"—words that were memorized by several generations of schoolchildren.

The worship of nature directly influenced the design of new burial grounds. After the poet Emily Dickinson strolled through America's first rural cemetery, Mount Auburn, in Cambridge, Massachusetts, she wrote a friend (quoting a popular poem of that time), "It seems as if Nature had formed the spot with a distinct idea in view of its being a resting place for her children, where wearied & disappointed they might stretch themselves beneath the spreading cypress & close their eyes 'calmly as to a nights repose or flowers at set of sun." Founded in 1831 by the Massachusetts Horticultural Society, Mount Auburn was America's first cemetery laid out in a carefully landscaped naturalistic style that had been introduced a quarter century earlier in Paris, France, at Père Lachaise. The simultaneous appearance of this plan and the new, romantic theology of nature inspired the designs of other cemeteries between 1838 and 1849, including Green-Wood in Brooklyn, Laurel Hill in

Philadelphia, Spring Grove in Cincinnati, and both Cypress Hills and the Cemetery of the Evergreens along the Brooklyn-Queens border. When a speaker at Laurel Hill's dedication ceremony described it as a place where men and women could "weep and mourn the loss of beloved friends, but . . . not despond," he spoke for the founders of them all.

Sometimes called "garden" or "picturesque," but widely referred to as "rural," these new cemeteries were designed as beautiful sites where the dead could lie surrounded by beauty, and where the living could visit in contentment outside the increasingly crowded, dirty city. As a writer in Cincinnati observed at the time a rural cemetery was opened there in 1845, "Our citizens have long felt the need of a cemetery that should be located beyond the reach of unhallowed purposes, and where the repose of the dead shall not be disturbed by the incessant turmoil and bustle of the world." Struggling to find a positive definition of the new school of cemetery design, people came up with "open air church," a place "planned with reference to the living as to the dead," and similar phrases reflecting Emerson's romantic understanding of the relationship between life and death, joy and grief, and humankind and God and nature (whose unpredictability and occasional dangers were conveniently forgotten). Here are some notes by a sentimental visitor to the Cemetery of the Evergreens in 1851: "A fit spot is this for man's last resting place, so mournfully beautiful, so solemnly eloquent, so sadly musical. . . . Ah! Let me be buried here, where the thoughts of life cannot jar with those of death; where the sublimity of the scene drowns sorrow and every earthly emotion." Even the stiff Victorian language cannot disguise the depth of feeling.

Nature's Gardener

The rural cemetery was based on two concepts. It was a holy ground for the burial of human remains, and it was a natural retreat for spiritual connection and recreation for the living—in other words, a park. The concept and the look came from two of that era's most noted profes-

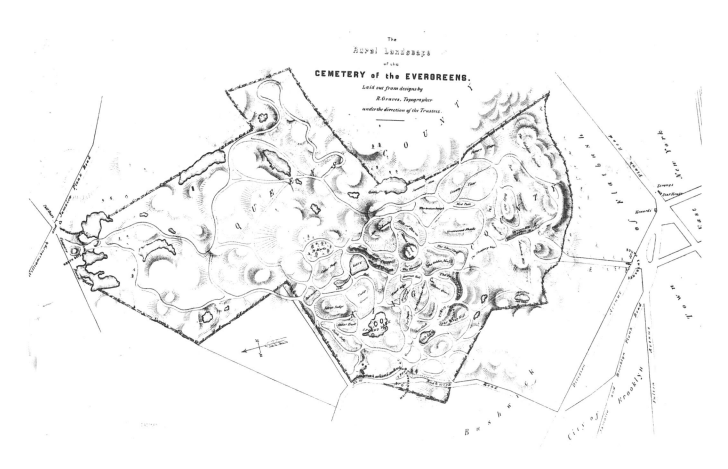

The very first roads and paths circle through the Evergreens in this 1852 map. The hilly southern area (right) was developed first, with the northern sections following in the twentieth century. The main entrance originally was through the road to the left of the lower right-hand corner. Today it is about halfway up the straight boundary above the corner.

sional architects, Andrew Jackson Downing and Alexander Jackson Davis. Downing, who was retained by the founders with the titles of Rural Architect and Landscape Gardener, was the most prominent American landscaper then and perhaps for all time (the mention of his name in a gathering of architects tends to make small talk disappear). Davis, a prominent architect in his own right, served as the architect of a Norman-style gatehouse and a Gothic Revival chapel with one hundred forty seats, a towering six-and-a-half-foot-tall pulpit, and an adjoining Sunday school room. Later, a rustic wooden shelter called the Summer House was built across the street from the chapel to serve as a gathering place for mourners. As the new buildings went up, extensive landscaping was done according to Downing's principles, including laying out eight miles of winding roads and

trails that were described in a brochure as lying "over, around, and through their grounds in the most picturesque and substantial manner."

Such a look was characteristic of Downing. During his brief, hyperactive lifetime (he died in 1852 at the age of thirty-six), as a writer and designer he was the country's leading exponent and practitioner of landscaping in the style alternately called romantic, picturesque, garden, and rural. He aimed to counter the degradations of the crowded, dirty modern city by providing what he called "a green oasis for the refreshment of the city's soul and body." That oasis might be a park, an esplanade, or a cemetery. Whichever, it offered a green retreat from the urban world's dark, bleak woes. This notion that a proper landscape offered a sacred space reached back to the origins of the profession of landscape architecture. In ancient times, land was shaped and structures were arranged to provide settings for worship, burial rites, and the commemoration of heroes. The buildings on these sites were important, but the crucial step was the arrangement of topography and plantings into what Elizabeth Barlow Rogers has called "a contemplative landscape." She explained, "The spaces in which these ceremonies took place were theaters for religious expression within a larger landscape."

The agent of this spiritual-architectural tradition in America in the mid-1800s was Andrew Jackson Downing, who at once was America's national tastemaker, the father of the country's public parks movement, and the major figure in reshaping the American land-

MAIN ENTRANCE.

The distinctive Norman gatehouse guarded the original main entrance.

scape in a way intended to make it look unshaped. "Nature's gardener," as he has been called, Downing won his fame not so much by actually gardening but by writing about the land and enhancing it in his designs. He was a propagandist for taste. In 1841, when he was twenty-six, this self-taught, effusive manager of a nursery in Kingston, New York, produced a nearly five-hundred-page manual on how to make a property beautiful and fruitful (in his nursery, he grew more than two hundred species of pears and one hundred fifty species of apples). The book's title was as exhaustive as his coverage: *A Treatise on the Theory and Practice of Landscape Gardening Adapted to North America; with a View to the Improvement of Country Residences.* Half-technical, half-inspirational, Downing's *Treatise* went through seven editions in its first twenty-one years and has since been reprinted numerous times, most recently in 1991.

Downing put aesthetics at the service of egalitarian politics, which in his day and for many years thereafter

was called "Jacksonian"—referring to President Andrew Jackson, whose name was carried by both Downing and his frequent collaborator, Alexander Jackson Davis, who with Downing designed the Evergreens' buildings. "Every laborer," Downing declared provocatively, "is a possible gentleman." Like Walt Whitman, Downing was buoyantly democratic and optimistic—he spoke of "Nature's Smiles"—and his optimism and ambition carried him to the very top of his profession. The son of a wheelwright, Downing understood the ambitions of average Americans for comfortable, practical, yet stylish living, a life that he identified with the rural countryside and that he believed could be adapted anywhere. He was just about to prove it in the design for Central Park and another one for a national park in Washington, D.C., when he was killed in a steamboat accident on the Hudson.

His colleagues at the magazine he edited, *Horticulturist and Journal of Rural Art and Rural Taste*, memorialized Downing by emphasizing the balance between his democratic political philosophy and his quest for beauty. "The great question with him," they wrote, "was how much of the really beautiful could be made subservient to the public good? How far can elegance and utility be combined?" When the editors added, "Very much of his deserved popularity is owing to his ability to popularize whatever he wrote upon," they were describing a forerunner of American stylesetters. His students—acolytes, really—included architects who, after his premature death, spread the word across America. One of the people who found his voice writing for *The Horticulturist* was Frederick Law Olmsted, Downing's successor as the country's leading landscape architect and the man who, assisted by Calvert Vaux,

A TRADITIONAL
FAMILY LOT

JOSEPHINE GANS

CHAS. M. DA...
NO...

RUTH DAHLBENDER
NOV. 15, 1977

ROSA C. DAHLBENDER

HAYES

made good on his dream of a great park in the middle of Manhattan.

Downing's blended role as cultural critic, propagandist, egalitarian, and fine artist made him one of American history's foremost tastemakers. Like Martha Stewart (with whom he has often been compared in both their emphasis on country things and as a measure of their influence), almost singlehanded he changed what many Americans expected from the world around them both as consumers and as citizens. For Downing, Elizabeth Barlow Rogers observed, the park was "the fundamental civilizing institution in American democracy in the 1840s." And many of the ideas he developed for parks came from his ideas for rural cemeteries, which he called America's "first really elegant public gardens or promenades." Impressed by the throngs who came on foot or in carriages to visit Mount Auburn and Green-Wood, Downing (at around the time he accepted the Evergreens commission) described the idea of the rural cemetery as "One of the most remarkable illustrations of the popular taste, in this country." The rural cemetery signified a triumph, even a revolution. "Twenty years ago, nothing better than a common grave-yard, filled with high grass, and a chance sprinkling of weeds and thistles, was to be found in the Union."

Overhanging all of this was his belief in rural things, which he sometimes called "country living," although the rule seems to have applied to urban parks and cemeteries as well as to truly rural estates. Country living for Downing might be a relatively small feature, say a path or lane gradually curving through a swale and up a hill. All would be beautiful—both the hilltop destination as seen from the lane, and the lane as seen from the hilltop.

Here shown in the 1920s, the Summer House was just one indication of the influence of Downing's ideas of "country living" on cemeteries.

In a home, the key might be a simple front porch, which he believed distinguished a livable country residence from a mere farmhouse. As his biographer David Schuyler put it, in Downing's scheme the porch functioned as a "transitional space between the private world of the family and the public realm of the street." In Downing's words, "The development of the Beautiful is the end," and his fundamental principle was "the preservation of the natural character of the scene." Elizabeth Barlow Rogers has summarized the approach as a triad of "unity, harmony, and variety." He believed that a landscape should not be abrupt or too dramatic. "Scenes abounding in natural beauty were chiefly characterized by gentle undulations of surface, and smooth, easy transitions from the level plain to the softly swelling hill or flowing hollow."

All this can be said about the Evergreens and its topography. "There are no abrupt passages, no rugged hills, but an incessant variety as you pass through it," observed the reporter who accompanied the first visitors in October 1849. Roads and paths, similarly, should be curvilinear as they link different parts of the property, highlight the landscape, and frame the property's hilltops before returning back to where they started. One of his regular themes was the circle, a symbol of renewal that makes his plans look like immense mandalas. At the Evergreens, traces of circular paved paths can be seen looping around the tops of hills, offering grand vistas from many standpoints. Not one to employ one word when three would do, Downing called such vistas "various beauties, peculiarities, and finest points of prospect." By keeping graves on the hills and out of the low spots Downing's design ensured proper drainage—an essential with cemetery layout—but he was also following his rule that a high point should be beautiful to look at, as well as provide a beautiful view.

One of his rules was that roads should fit the terrain by following the land's depressions in "an easy curvilinear manner through various parts of the grounds, farm, or estate" until they approach a hilltop building, where they should make a dramatic last-minute, sweeping turn to the front steps. Another of his stylistic touches was to establish large areas of somber colors on interior walls or, outside, by planting clumps of trees, and then set them off with nearby splashes of light with flowers, and even by carefully locating oak trees so the sunlight sparkled on the leaves. A Swedish novelist, Fredrika Keller, who visited Downing and his wife, Caroline, in 1849, described the process this way: "It has been done with design, nothing by guess, nothing with formality. Here a soul has felt, thought, arranged." Keller felt empowered by Downing's example: "every one ought to mold himself and his own world in a similar way." The best indication of Downing's contribution, obviously, is the finished project, and though only two plans with his work on them have survived, the Evergreens itself is his signature.

Appearing a decade after Green-Wood, the Evergreens stood somewhat in the older cemetery's shadow. "We think our citizens generally are not aware of the beauties of this rival to Green-Wood," wrote a visitor in the spring of 1856. "The latter has so absorbed public attention, that other places of interest have been comparatively overlooked. The grounds in Evergreens are rolling, abounding in hill and dale, with every variety of tree and shrub, and have been laid out with good taste, and in no parsimonious spirit. The dogwood is beginning to blossom and enliven the scene with its joyous

Guarding what had become a side entrance, the picturesque Davis gatehouse remained a favorite of visiting children.

spring flowers, which contrast so strongly in the dark somber color of the evergreen there so abundant." The reporter went on to encourage visitors to "avail themselves of a delightful stroll through this enchanting ground."

"Engaged with Downing"

Downing's longtime collaborator was Alexander Jackson Davis, one of America's most important architects of the mid-nineteenth century. A landscaper, town planner, designer of furniture, and illustrator of Downing's books, Davis specialized in the Gothic Revival style (also called the "pointed" or "perpendicular" style), with steep, peaked roofs and elegant, intricate decorative details resonating of the Middle Ages. Chairs he designed seem like miniature cathedrals, their elegant backs like flying buttresses or rose windows. He also designed in other styles, and described the two Evergreens buildings as "Norman" and the chapel as "Lombard." Like Downing, Davis had a flare for providing dramatic views. When a newspaper reporter climbed up into the Evergreens chapel tower and looked out, he discovered that the window was perfectly placed to offer a view that was "inexpressibly charming."

Davis' clients included such wealthy notables as John Cox Stevens, a railroad and steamboat tycoon and the first commodore of the New York Yacht Club, for whom he designed a mansion on the banks of the Hudson in lower Manhattan. A Gothic villa he designed for William C. H. Waddell filled an entire two block in Manhattan's Murray Hill district. Davis also designed two of the first houses in New York's exclusive Gramercy Park. Besides his city houses, he was well known for country estates and community projects, among them a pioneering early planned suburb, Llewellyn Park in West Orange, New Jersey. His affection for the romantic, elaborate Gothic style, however, was controversial. His plan for the first campus for the University of Michigan in Ann Arbor was rejected in favor of a design in the more subdued classical tradition.

Davis and Downing collaborated six times in the 1840s before teaming up for the Cemetery of the Evergreens. Their other projects were country houses and estates (most of which were built), an agricultural college for New York State (not built), and several publications that Downing wrote or edited and Davis illustrated and designed. As lead partner, Downing dealt with clients, took charge of the landscape design, and subcontracted Davis to draw the plans for buildings under his supervision. They corresponded frequently and often met at Downing's office in Newburgh, sixty miles up the Hudson from New York (Davis lived in New Jersey). Downing usually—but not always, and here was a bone of contention— gave Davis credit for his contribution. A charming, charismatic workaholic who was regularly overextended in both time and finances, Downing had trouble admitting how dependent he was on Davis and others to hammer out the details of his grand schemes.

The distinctive "pointed style" Gothic Revival features of the architecture of Alexander Jackson Davis stand out on the chapel and nearby buildings (since removed), and in monuments in the Hickory Knoll section (opposite).

Each man was known in Kings County and had some experience there. In 1848 Downing bid on the design for Washington Park (now Fort Greene Park). Though the *Eagle* hailed him as "the celebrated landscape gardener," he did not win the job. But two members of the selection committee, Mayor Edward Copland and Judge Samuel E. Johnson, were Evergreens founders and they may very well have retained him for the cemetery. In October 1849 Downing was in the area looking at cemeteries during a slow carriage tour of Green-Wood. His companion, Fredrika Keller, reported that he studied the landscape with care. As for Davis, he was working on a large building in Brooklyn at that time. In November 1849, he noted in his diary that he had stopped overnight at "Howard's Brooklyn." If that was the Halfway House, he may have climbed up on the Green Hills to inspect the property.

Hampered by a paucity of documents and plans (probably lost during the cemetery's later financial troubles), Downing's biographers have been unable to say with absolute authority that Downing drew the plans for the Evergreens. Sometimes the sole name on a map sheet is that of a surveyor or Roswell Graves, the land agent who acquired the land and described himself as the cemetery's designer, engineer, and topographer working "under the direction of the Trustees." Downing by then was conveniently dead and in no position to protest. Yet there is solid evidence of Downing's serious involvement. First, the Evergreens described him as its rural architect and landscape gardener; he himself told Davis that he was "allowing myself to be called the Landscape Gardener & Rural Architect of the Cemetery Co." Second, the design itself, with its mandala-like interweaving of curving roads and topographical features, fits his idiom. Third, there is the entry—until now unremarked on—that Davis made in his working diary (now in the New York Public Library's Manuscripts Collection) for December 28, 1849:

HICKORY KNOLL

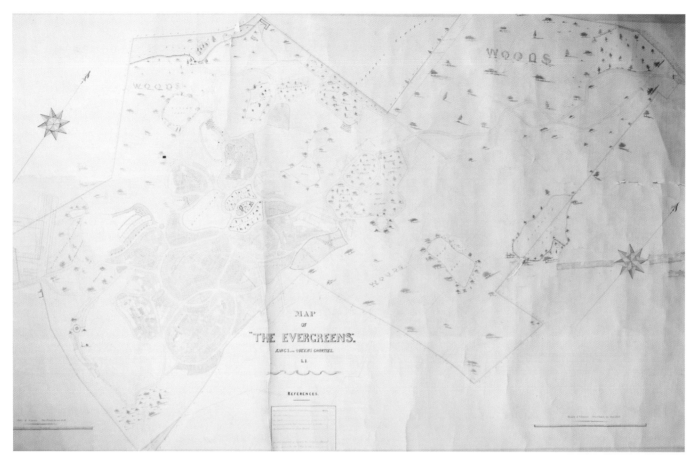

The Cemetery of the Evergreens takes further shape in 1867. This map shows sections filling up with graves, roads, and paths laid out in circular mandala style, and the Seaman's Monument towering above Beacon Hill. One remote section waiting to be developed is labeled, simply, "WOODS." Soon, however, the Evergreens will be on the verge of disaster.

"Engaged with Downing on designs for Cemetery gatehouse, and sepulchral Chapel." Fourth, he made a few careful alterations to Davis' architectural plans. Finally, Downing allowed his name to be associated with no other cemetery.

Relations between the two men were not easy. Alongside the December 28 diary entry, in the column where he noted his fees, Davis scribbled "50.00" with a "*." The most likely explanation for the asterisk is that Downing's check had bounced, a fact he admitted to Davis in a letter on January 13. In the way of people caught in such an embarrassment, Downing claimed that he had inadvertently drawn the check on the wrong account and attempted to calm the waters by praising Davis as essential to the Evergreens project. He himself, he went on, was actually making very little. Apparently

these promises of reform did not work. Davis had already declined an offer by Downing to go into formal partnership. When Downing headed off to England a few months later, he had his eye peeled for a new assistant. He came back with a young architect named Calvert Vaux who, after Downing's death, joined up with Frederick Law Olmsted to design Central Park, Prospect Park, Eastern Parkway, and many other non-classical settings. Alexander Jackson Davis, meanwhile, saw the public taste for Gothic Revival collapse, taking with it his career, which never revived. More than a quarter century after he broke with Downing, when the Evergreens needed an architect to make some alterations to the chapel, the trustees chose Vaux.

Choosing a Name

Whether coming out to the grounds for funerals in the chapel, for burials, or for strolls or carriage rides, visitors were going home impressed. "By the way, we ask the attention of all admirers of scenic beauty to these tastefully arranged grounds" was a typical comment in the *Eagle*. By then the cemetery had a name that suggested visual appeal, respectability, and security. This name took a different path from traditional descriptive ones like Trinity Churchyard (the burial ground next to Trinity Church), the two Marble cemeteries in Manhattan's lower east side (with their marble tombs), and Mount Auburn (on a hill of that name in Cambridge, Massachusetts).

In the 1840s the names of the new rural cemeteries became more comforting, naturalistic, environmentally friendly—literally, more "green." The cemetery we know as Green-Wood started out as Necropolis ("city of the dead"), but the founders decided that was too urban and unnatural. They preferred what they called the "rural quiet, and beauty, and leafiness, and verdure" of Green-Wood. Other tree-inspired cemetery names included Cypress Hills, Oaklands in Yonkers, the two Oakwoods in Troy and Niagara Falls, Beechwoods in New Rochelle, and Vale in Schenectady. The pattern is obvious: trees are natural, nonthreatening, comforting, and hint at the eternal.

The name "The Cemetery of the Evergreens" was chosen for effect, not because the place was full of conifers, which it was not. That was corrected in 1853 when a founder, A. P. Cumings, and one of the chaplains, the Reverend John D. Wells, brought back evergreen plantings from the Catskills. What made "Evergreens" important was that these trees symbolized a particular view of life and of death. An oak's trunk denoted strength and the turning leaves of a maple suggested aging, but an evergreen's pine cone was a symbol of rebirth and immortality. Boughs and wreaths of pine, cedar, holly, and other fragrant conifers became the favorite decoration at Christmas, and also at celebrations honoring George Washington and other American immortals. In the 1830s evergreens became the decoration of choice at funerals, laid on coffins with a few white flowers whose purity was highlighted by the rich dark branches. A bough of evergreen signified a new and better America, not of fancy style but of rural integrity. At mid-century "Evergreen" was found on the covers of magazines, in the names of parks and estates, and on many cemeteries.

While our Cemetery of the Evergreens was not the first cemetery with Evergreens in its name (one in Southgate, Kentucky preceded it by two years), this was an early use, and its fame and location made the name more noticeable. The Pennsylvania cemetery in which Abraham Lincoln was standing when he presented the Gettysburg Address is called Evergreens, and Evergreens or Evergreen was also used in dozens of cemeteries, including ones in New Haven, Los Angeles, Oakland, Bloomington, Illinois, and Bisbee, Arizona. According to one reliable source, today in the United States "Evergreen" or "Evergreens" is in the names for more than seven hundred American cemeteries—each dedicated to the idea of eternal life, or at least to eternal memory.

CHAPTER FIVE

ORDER OUT OF CHAOS AND THE RISE OF WILLIAM R. GRACE

THE NEW CEMETERY'S SURROUNDINGS were changing rapidly. As founder George Hall declared in his inauguration address when he became Brooklyn's mayor for a second time in 1855, in just twenty years a village of 10,000 on the shore of the East River had become a newly consolidated city of 200,000 spread over twenty-five square miles, extending all the way across Kings County to the boundary with Queens. Said Hall, "Hills have been leveled; valleys and lowlands have been filled up; old landmarks have disappeared; and almost the whole surface of the City has been completely changed." The rule of constant overturn applied to Brooklyn as well as Manhattan, and among the institutions that it benefited was the young, struggling Cemetery of the Evergreens. Yet the Evergreens came close to collapsing in a heap of scandal, and was eventually saved by a collection of politicians, newspapermen, and investors who included a remarkable Irish immigrant named William R. Grace. After years of neglect, the cemetery was reinvigorated in the 1870s and eighties in a massive effort to once again "embellish, adorn, and render this place attractive."

That revival would begin in 1872. Fourteen years earlier, toward the end of the cemetery's first decade, many of Bushwick's winding, muddy roads were being straightened and a railroad was stopping at the new Evergreens train station every quarter-hour. The cost of managing the cemetery was surprisingly steep, what with felling old, dying trees, making new plantings, building roads, and filling marshes. With the concept of the rural cemetery still novel for many New Yorkers, interments numbered only 6,493 in the first nine years. Green-Wood Cemetery had suffered its own scares a decade earlier. Founded in 1838, it did so poorly that in 1842 the *Eagle* was speculating that it might be abandoned. Green-Wood did not break even until 1846, and its future was not assured until seven years later when, with great fanfare, Henry Kirke Brown's magnificent bronze statue of Governor DeWitt Clinton, the visionary behind the Erie Canal, was placed over his remains, which had been transferred from a cemetery in Albany. With that Green-Wood began to attract notable New Yorkers and Brooklynites.

Green-Wood's early problems were ascribed in part to public wariness about its remoteness and distrust of its joint-stock financial structure, which was deemed unduly commercial and profit-oriented. In a world that for centuries had depended on nonprofit local burial sites owned by churches, families, or villages, there inevitably was resistance to the requirement that mourners travel several hours to visit a family grave managed by a company that appeared to be profiting from the misery of others. Reacting to concerns about profiteering, the 1847 Rural Cemetery Act imposed a nonprofit structure on cemetery corporations and mandated that investors could draw on no more than one-half the association's annual income to pay off their bonds. While encouraging public confidence, those new rules did not ease the problem of finding investors in the costly and risky enterprise of founding cemeteries.

The only way to guarantee investors a return was to find profit in the initial acquisition of land. This had been the strategy of the Evergreens' founders, and it was almost their and the cemetery's undoing. Between 1848 and 1851 Roswell Graves quietly acquired adjoining parcels of land in Kings and Queens counties at a total cost of about $50,000. He sold the land to the founders, who in turn sold it to the new Evergreens corporation in exchange for bonds with a par value of $350,000. The corporation then issued another $350,000 in bonds to finance the startup. The trustees acknowledged the heavy debt (the equivalent today of about $16 million) but believed the risk was acceptable. What with New York's and Brooklyn's population booms and laws restricting downtown burials, the demand for graves should increase. So would the value of the land, unused portions of which could be sold off.

With that, the Evergreens' well-connected trustees (all of them investors in the enterprise) got to work promoting its services and cultivating relationships with clergymen, undertakers, and editors at English- and German-language newspapers, in which the Evergreens advertised. The company engaged in generally tasteful competition with Green-Wood and Cypress Hills cemeteries, distributing promotional brochures and occasionally slipping to Brooklyn newspapers any sales figures that worked to their advantage. While there were some complaints about commercialism, New York and Brooklyn certainly were seeing far worse hucksterism in other businesses.

James Myers on the Attack

Yet some people were uncomfortable, and they happened to be the very individuals who were potentially the most volatile and the least easy to control. Anybody who had listened with even half an ear to the bitter disputes over the transfer of remains from old downtown churchyards should have been forewarned about which party—the trustees or the families—had the largest emotional stake in a cemetery's development and, in fact, believed it was the true owner, regardless of what the law claimed. Trouble began when the Evergreens cut back on maintenance. A newspaper reporter who attended a noisy meeting in 1858 summarized the families' views this way: "the Trustees of the Cemetery were some of the greatest scamps that ever walked, who had not only robbed the living but robbed the dead." Unprepared to be accused of being crooks, the trustees responded stiffly. Samuel E. Johnson, the new president, wrote a pompous letter to the *Eagle* in which he promised that "Every action shows an entire absence of selfishness, and a regard for the prosperity of the Institution above all other interests."

The truth lay somewhere between these two extremes. The founders wanted to do good, but they also reserved the right to try to do well off their benevolence. They were a little greedy, and the price was paid by the institution's reputation. A dry, precise, and damning summary of the problem was made many years later by one of the cemetery's lawyers: "In the years between 1855 and 1866 the Cemetery of the Evergreens became insolvent, having issued certificates of indebtedness to an amount greatly exceeding the value of the lands and other assets." In short, the place was broke and struggling. The brand that ignited this smoldering fire into a wildfire was tossed by one James Myers Jr. This litigious individual controlled graves held by the Van Voorhis family, local landowners to whom he was related by marriage. In 1858 Myers violated two of the cemetery's rules by hiring his own gardener and allowing him to remove trees without permission. Superintendent William C. Kneeland expelled the gardener and got a court injunction barring him and Myers from entering the grounds. When Myers defiantly returned with the gardener, Kneeland had them both thrown into jail. The gardener and Myers sued, and the mess was plastered all over the newspapers. Under the impression that he owned the lot itself and not merely (as the law said) the right to bury and raise a monument there, Myers launched a furious public relations and legal assault on the Evergreens.

Public and newspaper sympathies initially swept to Myers' side, but as the bitter fight wore on, the David and Goliath scenario dissolved. The Evergreens lost business, neglected routine maintenance, and declared bankruptcy, and it became increasingly clear that Myers was holding not just the board of trustees hostage, but also all the lot holders. The papers characterized Myers

as a man of "constitutional vehemence" and "a little man, with ferret-like features and characteristics." They published his lengthy, vehement letters under headlines such as "The Graveyard Quarrel," "A Good Thing for the Lawyers," and "Evergreens Cemetery Again." The *Eagle* referred to "that unlucky, deeply mortgaged, and incessantly litigated Cemetery of the Evergreens"—the bad luck extending to two destructive fires, one damaging the chapel, the other destroying a stable and several horses.

The trustees were hardly blameless. The heavy debt they had incurred was eroding reserves, which eroded funds for maintenance. Then there was the egregious behavior on the part of superintendent Kneeland. First he was named as correspondent in a sensational divorce case. Then he was found to be selling lots on his own account, declining to issue titles but promising that all would be put to order by a certain "Mr. Meade." When Mr. Meade turned out to be either "mythological" (as the *Eagle* put it) or a six-year-old boy (according to others), Kneeland made off with the Evergreens' official books and records. The cemetery's new president, William A. Cummings, fired him and went to the police, who arrested Kneeland in one of the saloons outside the cemetery's gates. He avoided prison and, changing careers, went into real estate. Amid new charges of malfeasance, Kneeland committed suicide in 1877.

For over a decade the Evergreens was in a doubly cursed freefall of terrible publicity and plummeting revenues. The newspapers that had once fawned over its rolling hills were regularly describing the "execrable disorder," "primitive confusion," and "greenish miasmatic accumulations" of the grounds. This was the worst possible time for such things to be said about a metropolitan area cemetery, what with the boom in population and the aging of the people. Between 1868 and 1874, mortality in Kings County alone increased by 26 percent, from 8,759 to 11,011. The cities of New York and Brooklyn—the country's first and third most populous—became increasingly interdependent. Some 54,000,000 passengers crossed the East River in ferries each year, Augustus John Roebling's great Brooklyn Bridge was under construction, and faster railroads seemingly appeared almost weekly.

The city, meanwhile, was advancing through the old farmlands to the outskirts of Kings County. Gertrude Lefferts Vanderbilt, a descendent of two famous old Dutch families, looked back nostalgically to the 1850s, when there had been "two or three miles of country road between Flatbush and Brooklyn, with farms, meadows and woodland upon the roadside." Thirty years later she was unhappily surrounded by what she called "the ugly pioneers of the advancing city"—"the sunken city lot, with its encampment of shanties, its hummocks of refuse, its open, treeless commons, the resort of goats and geese, its rocks flaunting placards for advertising quacks and speculators." Brooklyn's transformation was not always so crass, though it usually was radical. Inspired by the boulevards of Paris, Frederick Law Olmsted and Calvert Vaux proposed that five new, six-lane roads radiate out from Prospect Park. One of the two parkways that were built, Eastern Parkway, went out to East New York in a massive effort of leveling old hills and valleys, leaving Jamaica Pass not much of a valley at all. In 1893, just a few years shy of the two-hundredth anniversary of the first William Howard's tapping a beer keg, the old Halfway House was torn down to make way for barns for storing and repairing electric trolley cars. As the city quickly overwhelmed old Kings County, one place remained rural, and that was the Evergreens. Someone standing on Eastern Parkway in 1881 looked up into the Green Hills and saw "thick forests, rich fields, and thriving villages."

Recovery

Worn down by James Myers, and seeing no financial return on their investment, the founders began unloading their bonds in the 1850s. One of the second-generation investors was Sylvester M. Beard, an importer of coffee and spices who had done well investing in railroads, life insurance companies, and Brooklyn real estate. A prominent Presbyterian living in Williamsburg, Beard appreciated the implications of both faith and urban development for a nearby reliable cemetery. He spent years trying to extract the cemetery from bankruptcy. In 1866 the state legislature passed a special act

aimed at encouraging the quick liquidation of claims against the cemetery. There were no takers. In 1870 the legislature provided new inducements. The old non-profit Cemetery of the Evergreens would be dissolved and its grounds sold at auction, and the purchaser would create a new for-profit organization. Beard submitted the winning bid of $130,000, a small fraction of the cemetery's debt. He was the cemetery's largest creditor, and having been involved with it for years, knew where the bodies were buried, both literally and figuratively. (Beard also was friendly with the bankruptcy receiver who ran the auction.) The new profit-making corporation had 1,600 outstanding shares of stock with a par value of $100. (In 1891 the Evergreens sold another 3,400 shares to finance improvements.) Now the cemetery was like any other publicly owned business and in a position to attract new investors. Because the public's interest was both large and obvious, with more than 25,000 graves to protect and maintain, everybody proceeded with the understanding that the Evergreens was in fact a quasi-public corporation whose primary purpose was not so much to make money in the short term but to stay in business over the long haul.

"Order Out of Chaos and an Eden Where Once Was a Wilderness" ran a headline over a story about the Evergreens in 1873. Once the company was liberated from the entangling embraces of bankruptcy and debt, it was not hard to find investors. One was Beard's brother-in-law and business partner, William A. Cummings, also a well-known church leader. Cummings was elected as president of the revived board of trustees, Beard as vice president. The new treasurer was a recent immigrant and international businessman with an unusual past and an even more remarkable future, William R. Grace. Also on the board were Grace's colorful former partner, Charles R. Flint, and George C. Bennett, a Brooklyn newspaper publisher. The Grace and Bennett families would be crucial at the Evergreens for more than a century.

The cemetery's core problem was an absence of credibility. No cemetery could survive without public trust. Almost the first words out of President Cummings' mouth in his initial report was a promise to provide "a good reputation for the Evergreens and a spirit of accommodation to our patrons." Those good intentions were promptly put to the test by an unusually harsh winter. Though that time of year saw few funerals and fewer visitors—as Cummings said, "The winter is necessarily a dull season in a cemetery"—the Evergreens, alone among local cemeteries, kept two plows and teams of oxen at the ready to clear roads. That summer the rains were so heavy that the roads had to be repaired three times. Over the next thirty years most of the major roads that looped through the property were provided with drainage, and to encourage walking, many trails were cut over and through the hills and meadows.

An important step in the recovery from the years of lawsuits and bankruptcy was building a first-class receiving tomb to house remains awaiting burial.

A lengthy list of improvements was topped by a new receiving tomb where bodies could lie in dignity while awaiting burial. This was important to undertakers who had a high-class trade and were embarrassed by the poor repair of the old receiving tomb. An architect of Green-Wood Cemetery submitted a bid, as did Calvert Vaux, who had worked with Frederick Law Olmsted on the designs of Prospect and Central parks. Their prices were too high, and the job was done by a Long Island contractor. A landscape gardener, C. W. Bullard, was recruited from Prospect Park to develop the original Downing and Davis plan for the entire cemetery.

While targeting the carriage trade by developing striking new sections like Hickory Knoll, Cummings also had his eye on the average family seeking a modest but dignified grave. "We need to be brought prominently before the great mass of people who have not as yet heard that we exist," he told the board. There ensued a price war with other cemeteries. To make the property more accessible, the main entrance was shifted from the western side of the ground to the southernmost tip, near the main routes of the horsecars and omnibuses coming out from Brooklyn and the East River ferry docks. These reforms and the revived attention to maintenance had an immediate effect. Interments increased by almost one third in 1872 to 3,445, almost 10 percent of the total of 35,266 since 1850. The higher rate was sustained. By the end of the century, the Evergreens had buried more than 150,000 individuals from a very wide range of communities, including several—Chinese, actors, and African Americans—that could not always count on being accepted by New York area cemeteries. Land, meanwhile, was acquired as neighboring farms were broken up and sold off. By 1900 the cemetery had two hundred sixty acres, most set aside for future development. Some open land was planted in corn in order to provide nutrients for the earth. Maintenance was attended to more closely than ever. The payroll during the mid-March spring cleanup in 1886 carried the names of forty-eight men, most of them working six or seven days a week. One year the maintenance budget reached $50,000—four times the cemetery's total income of 1872, and the equivalent of more than $1,000,000 today. Yet the place was making money, with stockholder dividends running between eight and twenty percent annually.

As the finances recovered, so did the reputation. The neighborhood came to be named for the cemetery. "Evergreens" and "Evergreen" became ubiquitous—on an avenue, a railroad depot, a hotel, a park, a post office, an elementary school, a telephone exchange, and even a village. When residents of nearby Ridgewood, Queens, learned that it shared its name with a town in eastern

Long Island, they renamed their village "Evergreen." In a special section on "the city of cemeteries" with 2.7 million residents, the *Eagle* in 1895 proclaimed that at the Evergreens, "great natural advantages have been aided by the skill of the landscape gardener and the constant care and labor lasting through half a century." There had been a time when the *Eagle* hovered like a vulture over the Greens Hills. Now it placed the Evergreens in the top ranks of New York and Brooklyn cemeteries.

Always on the Grounds

If the Evergreens was evergreen once again, it did not happen overnight, and the effort was neither inevitable nor painless. That much can be seen in the lives of the men who brought it about.

The early credit went to the hands-on management of president William A. Cummings. According to the cemetery's advertisements, he was "always on the grounds." He enforced rules aimed at ending the recurring vandalism. Visitors were obliged to obtain passes, and when a security guard caught an eight-year-old girl stealing flowers from a grave to place on her mother's, the cemetery took her to court (after she was assessed a stiff fine, she was heard to declare that the next time she visited the Evergreens it would be in a casket). Flower theft was the most common crime on the grounds, but vandalism took other forms, including theft of metal fences and wire supports for floral displays. In 1876 the indefatigably obnoxious James Myers opened three graves and made new interments without the cemetery's knowledge. Cummings' protests stimulated violent curses, but Myers soon disappeared from the Evergreens, leaving behind a long trail of wreckage and some newly written rules barring bad language and other violations of decorum at penalty of instant removal from the grounds.

Cummings died in the summer of 1878 and was briefly succeeded by his brother-in-law, Sylvester Beard. The rescuer of the Evergreens was a sadder man. The firm of Beard & Cummings went under during a financial panic in 1873, and the same Beard who had long encouraged industrial development in Brooklyn spent his last days suing a factory next door. (Beard and Cummings are buried in a sprawling family plot in the Whispering Grove section. The face displayed on the towering plinth may be Beard's or a logo for one of the coffees he imported.) One of the cemetery's new investors was a metal merchant named Charles Bennett. When he died, his brother, George C. Bennett, took over as the cemetery's president—the first of six top officers in the Bennett-Goodwin dynasty over more than a century. A Bushwick resident who owned substantial amounts of nearby land (a part of Highland Park is on property the Bennett family sold to the city), he was the proprietor and publisher of the *Williamsburg Times*, which became the *Brooklyn Daily Times* when Williamsburg was absorbed into Brooklyn in 1855. He hired Walt Whitman to edit the paper in 1857, but fired him two years later after Whitman—in one of his many bursts of independence—wrote and published editorials favoring the legalization of prostitution and the rights of young women to engage in premarital sex.

One problem he wrestled with was conflict of interest among employees. In 1883 Superintendent W. S. Bullard and his son were found to be hoarding lots and selling them on their own account. Secretary Charles R. Flint noted in the minutes that it would be best if "Both the Messrs. Bullard" would "go back and attend strictly to the business." Apparently that was impossible, because W. S. Bullard was soon working as a gardener in Bridgeport, Connecticut. Charles Pfeiffer was appointed superintendent at a salary of $1,800 and stayed on the job to the satisfaction of all for more than forty years.

William R. Grace, Merchant Adventurer

The Bullard incident motivated the trustees to tighten their control over the management by appointing a small executive committee that often met at the cemetery. The leading figures included two remarkable and very different men, William R. Grace and Charles R. Flint.

The treasurer and majority stockholder (and the Evergreens' third mayor) was a character out of an Horatio Alger story. "Even in this country of self-made men, of great business houses, and of great fortunes, the career of ex-Mayor William R. Grace was a conspicuous one," *The New York Times* editorialized after his death. New York historians Edwin G. Burrows and Mike Wallace have called him "perhaps America's most successful Irish immigrant." Born in 1832 in County Cork, Ireland, Grace emigrated to Peru in 1852 and became the chief storekeeper on a supply ship for vessels carrying guano from the Chincha Islands to North America and Europe for use as fertilizer. Learning Spanish, he rose to partner in an import-export company, then founded his own firm, married the daughter of a shipmaster from Thomaston, Maine, and moved his headquarters to New York. In the 1870s he advised Peru as it created one of the world's largest navies. After its subsequent War of the Pacific with Chile, Grace and his brother Michael forged a settlement between Peru and its international creditors that left *Casa Grace*—as W. R. Grace & Co. was known in Lima—playing the central role in the country's economy through trade, the Grace Bank, and a steamship line that later was a partner with Pan American Airways in opening up South American airline service.

How Grace discovered the Evergreens in the early 1870s is something of a mystery. He may have met Sylvester Beard in bankruptcy court when Grace was the receiver for an insolvent insurance company and Beard was sorting out the Evergreens' problems. The question is why Grace, a Roman Catholic, decided to invest in the nonsectarian Evergreens Cemetery. There is no evidence of his ever explaining it, but his life and personality offer three possible reasons. First, the Evergreens was a safe long-term investment providing a modest but steady income to a man whose other businesses—shipping, real estate, and banking—were subject to wild fluctuations in a boom-or-bust world.

Second, he had a connection with Brooklyn. After Grace and his family arrived in America from Peru in 1866, they lived initially near Coney Island, then in

"Perhaps America's most successful Irish immigrant." New York Mayor William R. Grace played a leading role at the Evergreens in his lifetime and for decades afterward.

Brooklyn Heights, and later in other houses as Grace—an energetic real estate investor—engaged in the practice now known as flipping houses (he eventually settled down in Manhattan and on an estate at Great Neck, Long Island).

The third reason why a large interest in the Evergreens may have appealed to William R. Grace was that it provided a superior outlet for his innate impulse to assist people. At his office he located his desk near the front door so that when visitors arrived, he in his Prince Albert coat and dignified beard was on hand to greet them and inquire about their needs. This served him and others well financially, of course; tips are always important to investors. But his availability was satisfying in other ways, too. The word got around in Catholic circles that whenever a religious order sent nuns through New York, or a South American businessman wanted a Manhattan education for his son, Grace would be there personally at the railroad station or ferry dock to meet the traveler and arrange for housing and further transportation. He took special interest in the preparation of young women for life. He supported a girls' orphanage, the Sevilla Home for Children, and financed the Grace Institutes in New York and Maine as tuition-free training schools to prepare young women for work (the institutes are still functioning on that basis today).

Grace's philanthropy had flare and could be courageous. During Ireland's famine of the late 1870s, he arranged to have a ship carry food across the Atlantic. Late in his life, while riding on the Third Avenue Elevated Train, he offered his seat to a woman but a young man leaped into it. Grace grabbed him by the collar and hauled him out. His best known feat occurred during a ship disaster in June 1880. Grace, his wife, their two daughters, and three hundred fifty other men and women were on board the commuter steamship *Seawanhaka* heading up the East River to Great Neck when

NEXT PAGE, MT. LEBANON
IN JANUARY WHITE

the boiler exploded and the ship was engulfed in flames. Although William Grace and his wife Lillius had no idea where one of the girls was, they calmed hysterical passengers, handed out life preservers, and helped men and women over the side, waiting until almost the last moment before jumping overboard themselves before the captain beached the steamer on Randall's Island. Mrs. Grace was almost lost, but all the Graces survived the calamity. Thirty-two bodies were found and another thirty women and children were reported missing.

Many weeks later, an elderly one-armed man approached Mrs. Grace on the Brooklyn ferry and asked if she recalled him. She did indeed. The man identified himself as Hendrick V. Duryea, a well-known inventor and businessman from an old Brooklyn family that owned the country's largest corn starch factory. He told her he was so grateful for her anonymous help in saving his life that he had appealed through the newspapers for her to identify herself. She told him she had not seen the advertisement. "Plenty of others did," he replied. "Over forty women answered that advertisement."

Grace was as modest as his wife even though he was about to enter electoral politics. He had recently helped his Brooklyn neighbor, Judge Calvin Pratt, in a run for the Democratic Party's Presidential nomination that had collapsed when it was discovered that Pratt had been baptized a Roman Catholic—a distinct liability in American politics in 1880. When Pratt withdrew from the presidential race, Grace was approached about running for New York mayor. Other politicians would have made a campaign issue of his heroism in the time of crisis. Grace did not, but the word spread and enhanced his reputation as he surmounted the prevailing anti-Catholic, anti-immigrant feeling to become New York's first Irish-born mayor. He took a leave from W. R. Grace & Co. and the Evergreens board. After a trying two-year term during which he was badgered by the bosses of Tammany Hall, he stepped down, but then ran and won another two-year term in 1884 as a reformer. He spoke out for honest, efficient government free of the clutches of the party bosses, he accepted the gift of the Statue of Liberty from the people of France, and—an energetic gardener who spent his free time pruning the roses in

his Great Neck estate—he took an extremely active interest in the city's new parks, two of whose architects, Calvert Vaux and Samuel Parsons Jr., he recruited to work at the Evergreens.

It was as a businessman that William R. Grace was and remains best known. His biographer, the Pulitze Prize–winning historian Marquis James, called him a "merchant adventurer"—someone who enjoyed the chase as much as he did the rewards, and a visionary who did not allow his well-honed intuition to substitute for hard work. Among his many slogans was a Spanish phrase that meant "The eye of the master fattens the horse." Among the horses that he fattened were his company and its subsidiary bank and steamship line, plus the International Bank Note Company, the Ingersoll-Sergeant Drill Co. (later Ingersoll-Rand), and The Evergreens Cemetery. One of his few failures was his effort to build a privately owned sea-level canal through Nicaragua—a sensible enough idea that was undone by politics after President Theodore Roosevelt found a way to liberate Panama from Colombia. The sea-level canal scheme was the last of Grace's projects before his death in 1904.

Charles R. Flint, Speculator

A very different man was another Evergreens trustee, Charles R. Flint. Serving on the board for sixty years, he had an even longer direct personal connection with the Evergreens than his one-time business partner William R. Grace. After he was born in Thomaston, Maine (Lillius Grace's hometown), in 1850, the Flints joined the Yankee migration to Brooklyn, where the father acquired some shares in the Evergreens. He graduated from Brooklyn Polytechnic Institute in 1869 and through the influence of Grace became secretary for Peru's Minister to the United States. Flint helped him buy and outfit two Monitor-type gunboats and three transports for the Peruvian Navy. Later, as one of Grace's agents in Peru, Flint imported and sold a wide variety of consumer and manufacturing goods, including Singer sewing machines, canned food, and kerosene. Flint's travels on these and other projects included some colorful activities. He once, he said, dug up an Incan mummy illegally and, to avoid arrest, had its head shipped to New York. He told this and other tales in an autobiography in which the star is Flint's passion for self-promotion.

Flint split off from W. R. Grace & Co. to go into business for himself as what we now call a mergers and acquisitions specialist, though his line of work then carried the somewhat less dignified title of "stock promoter." Concentrating on high-technology companies, he reportedly played a role in founding some twenty new industrial businesses, including U. S. Rubber and International Business Machines (a parent of IBM). Sometimes called a "father of trusts" for his ability to consolidate small companies into mammoth corporations, Flint made sure to look the part, cultivating the portly build, shock of white hair, elegant mustache, and confident air that signified a captain of industry. Once he even backed a New York Yacht Club racing sloop contending for the America's Cup. Whether or not J. P. Morgan actually referred to him as "the phenomenal Flint" and advised, "Give Flint his head and you'll get every dollar," he played the role of a Wall Street prophet, and he liked to tell stories on the great men who made the mistake of disregarding his advice. When he asked Edward H. Harriman to help promote automobiles by sponsoring a road race in 1897, Harriman snapped back, "Come out of toyland."

Flint's habitual risk-taking and the Great Depression eventually ended his string of luck. He spent his last years in reduced circumstances, but always within earshot of financial reporters eager to leaven the day's bad business news with a colorful anecdote from Charley Flint. Why this extravagant character served as a trustee of the Evergreens Cemetery for six decades is a mystery whose only solution lay deep in his soul, which may have been more lonely than he ever let on.

CHAPTER SIX

SOLDIERS AND CONSPIRATORS: THE EVERGREENS AND THE CIVIL WAR

As the new Cemetery of the Evergreens was struggling to remain solvent in 1861, the country was rushing into the event with which it and other American cemeteries would be intimately identified—as shrines to American valor. Traces of the Civil War lie in almost every corner of the Evergreens' older sections. Some are Grand Army of the Republic plots that we will describe in the next chapter, on Memorial Day ceremonies. Several hundred Civil War veterans—all but one from the Union side—are buried at the Evergreens, including two who were awarded the Medal of Honor. Several more people in the Green Hills are connected to Abraham Lincoln. Two were involved in remarkable ways with his assassination—a man whom John Wilkes Booth tried to recruit as a co-conspirator, and Booth's own niece.

Bayard Rush Hall and the Race Issue

The slavery issue had already split New York and Brooklyn. In a city where the textile business and inter-regional trade led many businessmen and politicians to sympathize with the South, the fervently public anti-slavery beliefs of two Evergreens trustees, Luther Bradish and Samuel E. Johnson, were rare at a time when street gangs were known to physically assault abolitionists. One spokesman for the South in the years before the war was a Brooklyn clergyman-educator-writer, Bayard Rush Hall, who is buried at the Evergreens.

If the lure of New York and Brooklyn was great in the first half of the nineteenth century, so also was the appeal of the Western frontier. Among the many New York clergymen who had done missionary work was one of the most prominent of the Evergreens' founding chaplains, Nathan Bangs, who served for years in rural Canada. Bayard Rush Hall went west, too. The son of one of George Washington's physicians, he was orphaned as a boy and worked as a printer before being ordained as a Presbyterian minister. After the death of their two infant children, he and his wife fell into such despair that in 1822 they decided to change their lives entirely and head out to what was then the western frontier in the state of Indiana. Hall was hired as the first and only professor of a new school, Indiana Seminary, which had one building and ten students. The seminary eventually grew into Indiana University, which in 2007 had eight campuses, 99,000 students, and 16,000 faculty and staff members.

Hall loved teaching and rural life, but disagreements with the college president and the state's governor sent him packing. Back East, he resumed teaching and wrote an exciting, slightly fictionalized account of his western travels, *The New Purchase; or, Seven and a Half Years in the Far West*, published under the pen name Robert Carlton in 1843. The book is regarded as one of the best authorities on early western expansion. Hall subsequently wrote books on education and Latin grammar. In the 1850s he was running a school for poor black children, the Park Institute, in his home near Fort

Greene Park, Brooklyn. He joined the slavery debate with a new novel, *Frank Freeman's Barber Shop*. This is a book with an agenda. Apparently attempting to discredit Harriet Beecher Stowe's influential abolitionist novel, *Uncle Tom's Cabin*, Hall's story favored the African colonization movement that aimed to send all African Americans to Liberia. The story's title character is a slave who defends his master against a revolt stirred by up abolitionists. He then runs away, becomes a barber, is freed by the forgiving master, and emigrates to Africa. To his credit, Hall presented one of the first sympathetic literary portrayals of a free African American even though Frank Freeman, like black characters in *Uncle Tom's Cabin* and other books of that period, is childlike, passive, and concerned less with his own welfare than with that of the kindly white folks. This image of black people influenced American attitudes about race for many years. An important participant in three of the most important developments of his time—western expansion, higher education, and the slavery debate—Hall spent his last years in Williamsburg and is buried with his wife and children in Ocean View.

Dutchtown and the Williamsburg Regiment

Many of the Civil War dead at the Evergreens were members of three of New York's most fabled fighting regiments, each of which had a strong identification with Brooklyn. They are the Twentieth Regiment, New York State Volunteer Infantry; the Fourteenth Regiment, New York State Militia Infantry; and the Twentieth Regiment, United States Colored Troops (which will be discussed in Chapter 8).

The Twentieth Regiment, New York State Volunteer Infantry, was known as "the Williamsburg regiment" because it drew on the heavily German area in East Williamsburg called Dutchtown. In Brooklyn, the African Americans had Weeksville, the Irish had Irishtown and Dublin (and other sections with names that the *Eagle* once characterized as "more expressive than polite"), and the Germans had Dutchtown. With some wards more than 80 percent German-born, Williams-burg had a distinctively Teutonic culture. The Deutscher Leiderkranz and other singing societies performed regularly in social halls, the German Lutheran and German Catholic churches and their cemeteries were decorated in the old way, and there were enough brewmeisters among the immigrants to make Dutchtown a center for lager. Two of the most popular fraternal associations were the "target company," which sponsored friendly marksmanship contests, and the *Turnverein*, founded in Germany as both a gymnastic club and an organization of German nationalists.

Many Germans fled to America after the failed revolutions of 1848 and 1849 to avoid being drafted into the imperial army. After the attack on Fort Sumter, their Republican principles led them to support Lincoln and the Union. Organized entirely by volunteers, the regiment raised its own funds and elected its officers. Some of these men became community leaders. Henry E. Roehr would found the German-language newspaper, the *Freie Presse*, and John Rueger (who is buried at the Evergreens) was one of Brooklyn's leading contractors and a colonel in the National Guard. Colonel Max Weber had led a regiment in the 1848 revolution and was running a hotel in New York in 1861, when he became a founding officer of the Twentieth. The unit had so many *Turnverein* members that it was sometimes called "the United Turner Rifles" (although it was so poor that only muskets were issued). Financed largely by donations from German immigrants eager to demonstrate their patriotism as new Americans, the regiment left New York in mid-June 1861 and spent their first night in Washington sleeping in the Capitol building. As the two ironclads, the Union's USS *Monitor* and the

Soldiers model the uniforms of New York's volunteer and state militia units. On the right are the exotically dressed Red-Legged Devils of Brooklyn.

Confederate CSS *Virginia* (the former *Merrimac*), fought their famous duel off the Virginia coast to a draw, the Twentieth protected Newport News against a Confederate assault. The regiment later fought in the Shenandoah Valley, at Harper's Ferry, at Antietam (where it suffered one hundred forty-five casualties and Weber was wounded), and, finally, at the catastrophic battle at Fredericksburg, where Union forces suffered more than 10,000 casualties in a foolish charge. By then the regiment was feuding with the government over the term of the soldiers' commitment. One hundred twenty men who believed their enlistments were up refused to fight at Fredericksburg and were dishonorably discharged (many sentences were later reversed).

Weber was promoted to brigadier general, and after the war served as an American consul in France, and later as New York's tax assessor. He died in his home in Williamsburg in 1901, and went to his grave accompanied by full military honors, joining at least ten other men of the Williamsburg regiment at the Evergreens.

The Red-Legged Devils

As colorful as the Williamsburg regiment was, the Fourteenth Regiment, New York State Militia Infantry, was Brooklyn's star fighting unit, and the price it paid was much steeper. A National Guard unit with reinforcements, on the evening of May 22, 1861, the Fourteenth swung confidently down Myrtle Avenue and Fulton Street to the Fulton Ferry. The soldiers made a vivid sight in their bright red caps and trousers inspired by French Chasseurs. Sometimes called "Brooklyn's Fourteenth," "the Fighting Fourteenth," and "the Brooklyn Chasseurs," the regiment became best known by a name said to have been invented by the enemy—"the Red-Legged Devils." The parade started the 1,100 soldiers off on a confident footing. "There was really something sublime in their mission," the *Eagle*'s reporter exulted before ending his celebration with an ominous reflection: "as their bayonets flashed brightly in the gaslight, thoughts would obtrude as to how soon those bayonets would be crossed in deadly strife, and with no foreign foe." The optimism of that day was tempered by the news that the Union Army's first combat fatality was the young commander of another New York regiment.

Thirty years later, one of those boys of the Fourteenth, by then a scarred veteran in middle age, would recall having the same mixed feelings: "We were all enthusiastic and our minds were full of what we were going to do at the front. We could scarcely get through the street, so full were our ranks. . . . Bull Run soaked up the blood of many of our comrades. Southern prisons took many more who never again saw the North."

Arriving in Washington, the untrained, untested, foot-sore recruits were led across the Potomac and marched seventy miles to the war's initial major battle. Though suffering one hundred forty-two casualties, they performed so capably that when the government attempted to change the regiment's name to the Eighty-Fourth New York Volunteers, the proud enlisted men rebelled. The Union commander, General Irwin McDowell, ruled that even if the new name were used in official documents, "Fourteenth" would be retained in daily use. "You have been baptized by fire under that number," he told the soldiers, "and as such you shall be recognized by the United States government and by no other number." The Brooklyn regiment also left a favorable impression on President Lincoln during a review in April 1863. "'Splendid. That is splendid,' was uttered on all sides and it was a splendid sight." A few weeks later, the Fourteenth was the only Union regiment to fight all three days at Gettysburg, losing one hundred sixty-two men. There were another one hundred twenty-six casualties in the Fourteenth's final fight, at Spotsylvania in early May 1864. During its three years of action, Brook-

Anxious young soldiers posed for photographs to mail home before they shipped out. The photographer, George Lape, is buried at the Evergreens.

lyn's Fourteenth suffered a casualty rate of more than 40 percent.

The regiment's three-year term up, only one hundred forty-seven of the original 1,100 Red-Legged Devils returned to Brooklyn. Their reception was triumphal. As the boat pulled in to Fulton Ferry at 10 P.M., the adjutant general noted, they were greeted by a "roar of cannon and shouts of welcome from the multitudes of people assembled since the morning to receive them. Never, perhaps, has Brooklyn seen such a display." Hanging across one street was a banner that read, 'Welcome, brave Fourteenth, out of the Wilderness.'"

The Brooklyn Fourteenth was the launching pad for

at least two successful careers. Its founding colonel, Arthur Wood, was wounded at First Bull Run, captured, exchanged for a Confederate officer, and discharged for disability. Returning home, he was elected Mayor of Brooklyn in 1864. And Conrad Freitag, while recovering from a wound, produced a painting of the battle of Spotsylvania. It impressed enough people to encourage him to go to art school, where he developed into a gifted marine painter.

A War Photographer

The young men who fought in the Brooklyn and other regiments sometimes stopped off at photography studios so they could send their loved ones what might well be the last images ever taken of them alive. One of these photographers was George T. Lape, who is buried at the Evergreens. Educated as an architectural engineer at Union College, after graduating in 1860 he established a waterfront studio in Manhattan where he specialized in taking small "cartes de visite" of soldiers who were about to board troop ships. His price was $1.50 for a dozen prints. Lape was later assigned to a Union army engineer base in South Carolina. After the war he gave up photography, worked on the Brooklyn Bridge and railroads, and won patents for cast iron arches for bridges and tunnels, a folding stepladder, and other inventions. Permanently capturing the haunted faces of frightened men about to go to war may have been the best work he ever did.

The Fallen of the Fourteenth

In a characteristically Brooklyn way, the fifteen veterans of the Fourteenth Regiment who are buried at the Evergreens and named below tend to be in the middle range of fame and fortune. Many lie under headstones that were recently restored by the Fourteenth Regiment, N.Y.S.M. Living History Association.

Strod Putnam, the Brooklyn Child, best known of the fifteen, was no more than a boy. Throughout the war, regimental recruiters were working the streets of Brook-

lyn. Walt Whitman described their efforts this way:

> *Beat! beat! drums!—Blow! bugles! blow!*
> *Through the windows—through doors—burst*
> *like a ruthless force,*
> *Into the solemn church, and scatter the*
> *congregation;*
> *Into the school where the scholar is studying.*

One of those scholars was Strod Putnam, and he is believed to be the youngest of the Union army's recruits who did not join up as a drummer boy. When he enlisted in February 1864, he was a fourteen-year-old schoolboy taking advantage of an early growth spurt and the low turnout of volunteers after three years of fighting. Claiming to be eighteen, he was promptly handed a uniform and shipped off to Virginia. He fought in half a dozen battles, including the three days of the Battle of the Wilderness, the eight of Cold Harbor, and the five of trench warfare at Spotsylvania in early May. His officers must have been looking after him because he suffered just two minor wounds.

As the tiny remnant of old-timers of the Fourteenth made their way back to Brooklyn, Putnam was transferred to another colorfully attired Brooklyn-based unit, the Fifth Veteran Infantry. Composed of veterans of deactivated units, this largely Irish regiment was called the Duryea Zouaves for its commander, General James Duryea, and its uniform in the style of the French Zouave regiments. In mid-June, in an assault on Confederate positions at Petersburg, Strod Putnam was shot. The bullet was redirected by his pocketbook and missed his heart by a fraction of an inch. He was carried off the field wearing only his underwear, a regimental jacket, and a gray Confederate cap that he had found at Spotsylvania. As he recovered from his wounds, Strod Putnam was assigned to guard prisoners of war in Newark, New Jersey. One day a pistol in his pocket accidentally discharged, wounding him in the leg. Complications set in and after several weeks of declining health he died in his parents' home in Brooklyn on May 2,

1865. "The Brooklyn Child," as he was widely known, was buried in the Falling Leaf section of the Evergreens under a headstone carrying words he had written to his parents after Petersburg: "Tell my friends I was facing the enemy when I was shot."

Wilbur F. Rossell joined up after he turned eighteen in 1862. He was a Methodist preacher's son who, according to his enlistment records, was a typical young white man of his day: height of 5 feet, 7½ inches, fair complexion, blue eyes, and brown hair. When the Fourteenth was sent home at the end of its term, Rossell was transferred with Strod Putnam to the Fifth New York Veteran Infantry. After the war, Wilbur F. Rossell became a bookkeeper and cashier.

Charles A. Bartow rose from private to corporal as he served through the regiment's three-year service. He was wounded twice, breaking ribs at Second Bull Run and, at Gettysburg, taking a bullet that glanced off a testicle. He became Brooklyn's superintendent of sewers and a deputy sheriff. His younger brother, Stephen, was a musician in the regiment.

Peter W. Guinand was a wagoner, an enlisted men in charge of the mules and wagons. Nothing else is known of him.

Evan Davis was nineteen when he enlisted and served throughout the regiment's active duty in the war, from May 1861 to May 1864. He came home to a career as a carver of ornamental objects.

James D. Stafford was another one of the many nineteen-year-olds who signed up as the recruiting drums first sounded in April 1861. His initial ten months were served as a cook, but he saw combat and was wounded in the leg, serving out the term of his enlistment in a unit of invalids. In civilian life he was a hatter.

James E. Eldard was mustered out for disability late in 1862 and is buried at Nazareth Lots. Nothing more is known about him.

Ramon Cardona was a Spaniard who served in the Fourteenth as its armorer. Thirty-three years after the end of the war, he rejoined what was then a National Guard unit, hoping to fight against his native country in the Spanish-American War (he was turned down because of age).

When *George H. Rice* died at age ninety-three in 1936, he was the last living Civil War veteran of the Fourteenth. Rice was visited in a hospital by Lincoln after being wounded in the shoulder at First Bull Run, and he later saved the life of a comrade by carrying him from the field under fire. He fought in all twenty-two of the Fourteenth's battles. After the war he was active in veterans' groups. In 1935 on the sixty-fourth anniversary of the Fourteenth's fabled march down Fulton Street, George Rice was awarded a diamond-studded gold medal by a veterans organization.

Rivers S. Wilson enlisted at the age of seventeen in July 1861, deserted in November, and later had the slate wiped clean and served for three years in the Fifth New York Heavy Artillery Regiment, being promoted to sergeant.

Joseph Heald, having survived three years of the worst possible violence, died as a house painter when a rope supporting the scaffold on which he was standing snapped. He was buried in North Mead.

Aaron Storer was a descendant of an historic Brooklyn family and the son of a prominent Republican who founded the Society of Old Brooklynites. He served in the regiment's ambulance corps and was captured at Gettysburg. Unlike several unlucky members of the Fourteenth, he was not taken to miserable Andersonville Prison but was paroled and returned to the Fourteenth. In civilian life he was a watchman.

Joseph G. Hyer, one of the oldest volunteers at age thirty-two, was appointed a sergeant, probably because he had experience in the National Guard but was mustered out for reasons of disability. Active in Brooklyn politics and charities, he once ignited a controversy by requesting that a female organ grinder not bring her baby along when she worked on the streets late at night.

John F. York was born in England and was a $2.50 a week errand boy in Brooklyn when he enlisted after the assault on Fort Sumter. In a noteworthy military career, he was wounded in battle, rose to sergeant in the Fourteenth, served as an army recruiter in New York, and after transferring to the Fifth New York Veteran Infantry was promoted to captain. When York was mustered out, he was breveted to major and the men in his company presented him with a sword. He fought in a total of twenty-six battles in the two units. After leaving the army he went into the shipping business and lived in Brooklyn for many years before moving to East Orange, New Jersey.

The saddest case is that of *Alfred Lloyd*, who enlisted as a private at the advanced age of thirty-six, and after the Fourteenth's term was up, transferred to the Fifth Veteran Infantry. He was an active member of the Democratic Party, and on a November day in 1866, a year and a half after Appomattox, he washed up in the Atlantic Basin on the Brooklyn waterfront.

After Alfred Lloyd's body was found, the Fourteenth quickly put together an honor guard to escort him to the Evergreens for interment.

The Medal of Honor Recipients

Five recipients of the nation's highest combat award, the Congressional Medal of Honor, are buried at the Evergreens, two from the Civil War. The citation for the first reads, "Through all the din and roar of battle, he steered the ship through the narrow opening of the barricade, and his attention to orders contributed to the successful passage of the ship without once fouling the shore or the obstacles of the barricade." New Yorker Louis Richards was a quartermaster, or helmsman, in the USS *Pensacola*, a ship in Flag Officer David G. Farragut's blockading squadron during the hard-fought but successful campaign to divide the Confederacy by seizing control of the lower Mississippi River. With Richards at the helm, on April 23–24, 1862, the *Pensacola* helped lead the attack of the largest ships in the Union squadron up the mouth of the Mississippi. Through enemy fire from Confederate ironclads and Forts Jackson and St. Philip, he threaded the eye of a narrow passageway in the Confederate barricade and reached

New Orleans, which surrendered to Farragut. "Perfectly heroic" was how one of his officers described him, but Richards was also modest, and there is no mention of his honor on the headstone over his, his wife's, and their child's graves in the Mount Hermon section.

Another Civil War recipient of the Medal of Honor buried at the Evergreens is Private Christopher W. Wilson. Irish-born, he came to Connecticut and spent the war in the Second Regiment of the Seventy-Third New York Infantry Volunteers, known as the New York Fire Zouaves because many of its soldiers were firemen and the uniforms, like those of the Fourteenth, were especially colorful. Fighting in more than two dozen major battles during the war, the regiment was shrunk by casualties from its original complement of 1,350 men in 1861 to fewer than four hundred two years later on the eve of the Battle of Gettysburg, where it suffered another one hundred sixty-two casualties. At Spotsylvania on May 12, 1864, the regimental color bearer was wounded during an assault. Wilson leapt forward and, running through a firestorm so intense that it severed the trunk of a thick oak tree, not only retrieved the flag but captured the enemy's.

Wilson was not awarded the Medal of Honor until many years later, in 1898. By then he had become an important citizen of Brooklyn, running a large Brooklyn lumberyard, serving on the Board of Education, and being seen regularly on the reviewing stand of veterans' parades. Perhaps it was his prominence, or maybe it was the burst of patriotism during the Spanish-American War, but Brooklyn's congressman, James Robinson Howe, nominated Wilson for the Medal of Honor, which was awarded at the end of 1898. In 1911, when Wilson and the other, few surviving veterans of those battles celebrated the regiment's fiftieth reunion in Manhattan's Union Square Hotel, the tattered regimental banner was hanging on the wall. Wilson died five years later and was buried in Tulip Grove.

The Lincoln Connection

The Evergreens is the repository of some astonishing tales of the Civil War. Hannah Perks Butt, who was buried at the Evergreens after her death in Brooklyn in 1904, used to tell how, in the early days of the war, she and her husband, both Union sympathizers, were arrested in Portsmouth, Virginia, and he was sentenced to death. She said he successfully appealed his sentence, and he went on to steal a locomotive and escape to the north.

And then there are the many Lincoln connections to the Evergreens. A few veterans buried at the cemetery met him when he visited the front or hospitals, and, after the war, the Memorial Day ritual often included a recitation of the Gettysburg Address. But it is Lincoln's assassination that provides some of the most startling links to the Green Hills. Two are indirect. Charles Couldock, a famous nineteenth-century actor buried at the Evergreens, made his name acting in *Our American Cousin*, the play Lincoln was watching at Ford's Theatre when John Wilkes Booth put the bullet in his brain. A member of the audience that night, John Y. Culyer later worked as a consulting engineer at the Evergreens.

More intricate is the tangle of supposed conspiracy surrounding two other actors who are buried in the Actors' Fund Plot at the Evergreens. One is Samuel Knapp Chester and the other, six graves away, is Booth's niece, Blanche DeBar Booth. Her ashes lie next to the monument whose dedication she attended in 1887, when the primary speech was presented by her uncle, the great Shakespearean actor, Edwin Booth.

This story begins with Chester. On April 7, 1865, this silent man and his far more talkative friend John Wilkes Booth were drinking in a saloon called the House of Lords, on Houston Street in Manhattan. The city was

"You *must* come to Washington," pled John Wilkes Booth, but Sam Chester never joined the conspiracy. He later provided evidence against Booth.

celebrating the end of the war, but not Booth, who slapped the bar and snorted that a month earlier he had been at Abraham Lincoln's second inauguration, "as close to him nearly as I am to you," and could easily have assassinated the president, "if I so wished." Chester was startled, but not entirely surprised. During their many lengthy conversations over the past months, Booth had become increasing erratic as he had attempted to lure Chester into joining a conspiracy against Lincoln, first through flattery, feigned affection, and appeals to his Southern blood, then through bribes, and finally through threats of violence.

Both men were professional actors from Baltimore. Although Booth was the son of a famous actor, Junius Brutus Booth, the first of the two old friends to go on stage had, in fact, been Samuel Knapp (the stage being almost universally regarded as a disreputable place, he added "Chester" to his name probably to avoid embarrassing his family). In the late 1850s the two men often were in the same plays in Richmond—taciturn Sam Chester specializing in serious roles, and choleric John Booth taking the romantic and heroic parts. Around the time the Civil War broke out, they both came north, although Booth's sentiments (and those of most of his family) lay with the Confederacy. Chester married an actress named Annie S. Hodges, alongside whom he would play many parts until they retired, and next to whom he was buried in 1921 in the Evergreens Actors' Fund Plot.

Chester and Booth acted together in Washington, often in Ford's Theatre. In the fall of 1864 they came up to New York to the Winter Garden Theatre, near Washington Square, which was hosting one of the most famous seasons in American theatrical history. Edwin Booth, who was John's older brother, decided to revive the American theater by producing and starring in

grand revivals of Shakespearean plays, using historically accurate costumes. One highlight was the single performance on November 25, 1864, of *Julius Caesar*, starring the Booth brothers (Edwin, John, and Junius Brutus Jr.) to raise funds to place a statue of William Shakespeare in Central Park. After that came a one hundred performance run of *Hamlet*, with Edwin at his brooding best in the title role. Sam Chester had supporting roles in both plays, completing *Hamlet*'s long run as King Claudius, with Annie as the leader (in this production the Player Queen) of the traveling group of players who, following Hamlet's script, unmask Claudius as his brother's assassin.

In personality, Sam Chester was much less the impulsive, murderous Claudius than another *Hamlet* character whom he would also play, the cautious Polonius. When John Wilkes Booth ranted about "King Lincoln's" aims to found a dictatorship of former slaves, Sam Chester hid his opinions behind a poker face. Booth preferred to believe that Chester was tacitly agreeing with him. "It was a critical misunderstanding," remarks Michael W. Kauffman in his biography of Booth. After a while, Chester sensed that Booth was trying to interest him in one of his projects. Some other men were making fun of Booth, a congenital braggart, for boasting that he was making a fortune investing in oil. Booth turned to Chester and said, "They are laughing at me about a speculation, but I have a greater speculation than they know that they won't laugh at." Not long afterwards Booth offered to help Chester's acting career, and to loan him funds to invest in Virginia real estate.

On Christmas night, 1864, Booth appeared on no notice at Chester's door, dragged him over to the House of Lords, and over liquor and oysters bragged vaguely about this great "speculation." Walking home through Greenwich Village, Booth pulled Chester into the shadows of a side street and told him that "fifty to one hundred" men and women were planning to kidnap Lincoln and his top aides and carry them to Richmond to hold as hostages. "It's nearly made up now, and we

DEAD OF WINTER

want *you* in." The abduction would be carried out in Ford's Theatre in Washington, where Lincoln often attended plays, and it was essential that the escape be perfect. Someone familiar with the theatre must be on hand to open the back door into an alley, where a carriage would be waiting, and that someone must be Sam Chester. Chester said such a thing was impossible. It would surely ruin him and his family. Booth offered to pay him $3,000 or more—as much money, he promised, as Chester would ever require. "It is no compensation for my loss," replied Chester. He would later tell investigators that at this point he was hardly taking John Wilkes Booth seriously. This fantastic plot seemed like another of his ego-inspired, alcohol-induced, and usually transient dreams.

Booth kept returning to the scheme. "You *must* come to Washington. We cannot do without you," he wrote Chester in mid-January 1865. Chester refused. "You *must* come" was the response, accompanied by $50. Booth came up to New York and apologized. Chester was disarmed, but he returned the money all the same. At that, Booth tried to close the trap by threatening Chester. Insisting (as Chester would testify), "You will at least not betray me. You dare not," he promised that if Chester went to the police, he would be fingered as a part of the conspiracy, Chester's career would be destroyed, and he would be hunted down for the rest of his life. He had always been Booth's friend, Chester protested. He had never done him wrong, but he could not do what Booth asked. You *must* come, replied Booth. He was carrying a Derringer and was prepared to use it on anyone who betrayed him. Chester, who was acting in a play about madness and secret murders in *Hamlet*, now was truly frightened. Booth then said that the kidnapping plot was abandoned (in fact, it had failed because Lincoln

Blanche DeBar Booth, the assassin's beautiful, fierce niece, is buried near Sam Chester in the Actors' Fund Plot at the Evergreens.

had not appeared where Booth expected him to be).

Booth's plot would not go away. There they were on April 7, back at the House of Lords, with Booth regretting that he had not shot the President. Seven days later Sam Chester was in New York, still silent, and John Wilkes Booth was in Ford's Theatre, standing outside the door to Lincoln's box with a Derringer in his pocket, awaiting a burst of laughter in the play, *Our American Cousin*, that would cover the shot. Ahead lay a leap onto the stage, the shouts of the audience, and a frantic race to the theatre's back door, which Booth opened without assistance. Twelve days later, Booth's corpse was identified in a burning barn in Virginia.

In late April Sam Chester told his story to a government investigator. Since he obviously was being considered as a possible conspirator, he had to put on the performance of (and possibly for) his life. He carefully led the interviewer through his meetings and correspondence with Booth, adding verisimilitude by citing dates and places. Through verbatim quotes from their conversations and examples of Booth's well-known manipulative ability that blended charm and violent threats, Chester presented a persuasive picture of an ordinary sane man who could not shake off the attentions of a lunatic. Chester's only outburst of frustration came at the end of the interview. Asked if he had been a member of a secret organization, he forcefully insisted that at no time in his life had he belonged to *any* organization except a group of actors in his youth.

In May the government called Sam Chester as a witness in the trial of the accused co-conspirators. His secondhand testimony was so effective that four of the defendants were executed, and the others received stiff sentences.

The Evergreens' Booth

Another character in this extraordinary story was John Wilkes Booth's twenty-one-year-old niece, the daughter of his brother Junius Jr. "This tall and graceful young girl with the brilliant, black eyes characteristic of the Booth beauty," as a Booth biographer described her, Blanche DeBar Booth was then living in St. Louis with her uncle and guardian Benedict DeBar, a theatrical producer and theatre owner there and in New Orleans, and she performed in some of his productions. Outspoken sympathizers with the Confederacy, they were closely watched by Union military officials. When John Wilkes Booth came out to perform in a play in 1862, he was arrested for making derogatory remarks about the Union and released with only a fine after signing an oath of allegiance. After the assassination, Blanche was interviewed by a Missouri state law enforcement officer who, in his report, described her as "an unmitigated rebel" and "possessed of considerable personal attractions, of a vigorous mind and marked histrionic ability."

Following her father and his two brothers, she went into acting, dropping her last name to dodge her uncle John's infamy and her uncle Edwin's fame. She retained her striking looks—"Blanche DeBar is called the handsomest woman on the American stage," declared a theatre critic. Making her New York debut in 1869, she enjoyed a career boost when Uncle Edwin selected her to play Ophelia and Desdemona opposite his Hamlet and Othello. She created a sensation in Chicago in 1871 when she put on the first play there after the city was all but destroyed by fire. As she settled into supporting roles, she took one surprising leading part. In what surely was an effort to put her political notoriety behind her, she smeared on blackface and played the slave Eliza in a New York production of *Uncle Tom's Cabin*. No less bold in her personal life, when her father disinherited her Blanche took the estate to court and won. And then, after retiring from the stage in 1900, she and her actor husband, George Washington Riddell, moved far north to Minneapolis to run an acting school, returning in the 1920s to Brooklyn, where she died in a nursing home.

Before she died, in 1925 at age eighty-one, she bolstered the long-rumored conspiracy theory that it was not John Wilkes Booth who died in the barn. As evidence, she announced that he had visited her in St. Louis in 1865. Back then, she said, the man had struck her as an imposter, but on reflection, sixty years later, she was convinced that he was indeed Uncle John.

Bizarre as this tale was, many people wanted to believe it. In 1936, Hannah Mary Allen, a widow from Garden City, Long Island, told a startling story at the national convention of the Grand Army of the Republic. Her late husband, William C. Allen, who was buried at the Evergreens and whose rank, she claimed, was colonel, had told her the following: he had known Booth, he had been a member of the Secret Service detail in pursuit of the assassin, and the corpse in the burning barn was not his. Booth's hair was black, the corpse's red. Mrs. Allen's story made headlines around the country. Later careful accounts of the hunt for John Wilkes Booth, like *Blood on the Moon: The Assassination of Abraham Lincoln*, by Edward Steers Jr., discount Mrs. Allen's story. The corpse's hair was not red, Allen was far from the burning barn, his highest rank was lieutenant, and the only person who made these claims was talking years after his death. While all this was not encouraging to the tale's veracity, the story survived. Mrs. Allen must have had second thoughts because her obituary in 1958 (when she was buried at the Evergreens with her husband) makes no mention whatsoever of the "wrong corpse" claim. It seems that in her last years she was content to tell people that her husband had merely helped the investigation into the ever strange, rumor-rich, and often perverse story behind the assassination of Abraham Lincoln.

CHAPTER SEVEN

COVER THEM OVER: DECORATION DAY AT THE CEMETERY

OUR
BROTHERS
CLARENCE
1883 — 1934
ARTHUR W.
1879 — 1947
MAY C.
1881 — 1965

NEVER HAVE CEMETERIES been employed in as many ways as they were after the Civil War. Besides places for burial, private mourning, and recreation, they also were patriotic monuments. "There are soldiers' graves everywhere," someone observed in 1884. "Humble mounds and monuments, the resting places of our Union heroes are found in scores." By then, the most crowded of all the crowded days on Evergreens Cemetery's calendar was Decoration Day, the thirtieth of May, when tens of thousands processed into the Evergreens to lay flowers on those graves, reflect on those men's valor, and renew their own patriotic spirit.

Today, May 30th (generally known as Memorial Day but sometimes still called by its original name) is a national day of mourning for all the dead in all American wars, and is one of the more popular days for cemetery visits (after Mother's Day and Easter). But from its founding in 1868 by the Grand Army of the Republic (G.A.R.) until the early 1900s, it was reserved for the Civil War's Union dead. The South had Memorial-Decoration days at other times of the year, with whites honoring the graves of Confederate soldiers, and African Americans those of Union soldiers (a reported 10,000 black men and women took part in Decoration Day in Charlestown, South Carolina, in 1865). But Memorial Day was the North's most sacred patriot holiday. Abraham Lincoln pointed to Decoration Day's purpose in his brief speech at the dedication of the first soldiers' national cemetery, at Gettysburg, when he said that this day was set aside to honor "a final resting place for those who here gave their lives that that nation might live." The idea of national cemeteries caught on quickly. Like the Gettysburg Address itself, the design of the national cemeteries by Frederick Law Olmsted was simple, with a sea of small, identical, white headstones stretching across a field or gently sloping hillside. By 1870 there were seventy-three national cemeteries holding 300,000 remains, 58 percent of which were identified.

At a time when very few Americans did not know a casualty of the Civil War, any cemetery containing the remains of a Union soldier was a place of pilgrimage. Arranging that pilgrimage was the G.A.R., the major veterans' organization for the Union Army with more than 400,000 members (called "comrades") in 5,000 local organizations ("posts"). Throughout most of the year, G.A.R. posts were men's clubs providing the entertainment and relaxation promised by their motto, "Fraternity, Charity, Loyalty." The G.A.R. also followed a political agenda—at first "waving the bloody shirt" at Democrats (many of whom had been unenthusiastic about the war), and later lobbying for veterans' pensions and leading the first "Americanism" patriotic program that included distributing American flags to schools.

A Culture of Character

In his history of how Americans have preserved the Civil War in memory, *Beyond the Battlefield*, David W. Blight has described a "culture of character" shared by Union veterans. "Old soldiers tended to measure each other as preservers of an older, more wholesome society, uncorrupted by materialism and rooted in individual honor." The form of the ceremony was to decorate graves with flowers. It was hardly a new idea. During the war, communities in both the North and the South set aside "decoration days" for that purpose, but the connection between flowers and death stretches so far back that it can be termed instinctive. When archeologists opened the graves of Neanderthals who were buried more than 45,000 years ago in a cave in Kurdistan, among the remains they discovered the remnants of bowers of hyacinth, hollyhock, yellow flowering groundsel, and other wildflowers, many of which have medicinal powers. In some traditions a floral crown was placed on the head of the corpse before interment, and cemetery angels sometimes are shown strewing flowers on graves. Muslims have long marked the last day of Ramadan, Id al-Fitr, by visiting cemeteries at sunrise, placing palm fronds over the grave, and planting myrtle in the grave itself before going off on a round of family visits. "The dead are expecting their families at this hour," explained a Lebanese participant in 2007. Some American Mennonites also come out to their burial grounds at dawn on Easter Day to scatter flowers on the graves while singing hymns of resurrection.

Besides an honor and a symbol of hope and eternal life, a flower in a cemetery may recognize the brief span of human existence—for example, the short lives of young soldiers cut off by war. The Scots song "The Flowers of the Forest" commemorates the calamitous losses in the Battle of Flodden Field of 1513 by referring to wildflowers that are "both pleasant and gay" but "now they are withered away." Revised after World War I to take into account the slaughter in the trenches, "The Flowers of the Forest" (sometimes called "The Lament") is sung and played on Remembrance Day, Britain's version of the American Memorial Day. The flower symbol is profound in Pete Seeger's antiwar song "Where Have All the Flowers Gone?" with its well-known couplet, "all the graveyards gone / Covered with flowers every one." Andrew Jackson Downing and his followers broadened the practice. "A handful of fresh flowers scattered over a grave—the planting of a bunch of Violets, or a Rose bush—never fails to impress us as a sincere and delicate tribute of affection," advised *The Horticulturist* after Downing's death. A modern, carefully gardened rural cemetery was just such a living monument.

By 1870 May 30th was an informal New York holiday, an important one because, as the *Times* said, it had arrived "not by any enactment of Congress, not by any enactment of Legislature, but by the general consent of the people." By the time it was made an official state holiday in 1873, New Yorkers had invented many of Memorial Day's rituals, which then spread across the northern part of the country as state after state in the old Union followed New York's lead. Nobody was more enthusiastic about the day than Brooklynites. The City of Churches and the City of Cemeteries was also the City of Civil War Veterans. The Soldiers and Sailors Memorial Arch was completed in 1892, and in 1926 the nearby entrance to Prospect Park was named Grand Army Plaza.

At a time when most Americans had personal connections to the Civil War, Decoration Day, known as "the festival of our dead," was an occasion for a mass pilgrimage to the cemetery.

"The Festival of Our Dead"

As distinguished as these monuments were, they were outdone by the energies of the comrades of Brooklyn's two dozen G.A.R. posts. The veterans were of course not what they once were. When the Fourteenth Regiment celebrated its twentieth reunion in an armory on Portland Avenue, much of the old jauntiness had disappeared. "The boy soldiers of the twenty-third of May, 1861, those who survive, have become gray-bearded veterans," noted a reporter from the Brooklyn *Eagle*. Yet spirits always revived on Decoration Day, whose exercises were as well planned as one of the battles they

commemorated. After weeks of raising money for flowers, comrades gathered twice—first on the Sunday before May 30th and then again on Memorial Day itself—for church services, and then boarded street cars or marched, sometimes for miles, through the streets to the Evergreens or another cemetery, or to the Tomb of the Martyrs at Fort Greene Park to honor the remains of the thousands of sailors who died in British ships during the Revolution. "Decoration Day was more generally celebrated in the Eastern District today than on any previous occasion," the *Eagle* reported in 1877. "The rush to the Cemetery of the Evergreens and Cypress Hills, and the pushing and scrambling to get on the cars, beggars description." Once at the cemetery, they distributed yew branches, flowers, and small American flags on the graves, some of which were already capped by beds of ivy or flowers.

Some 95,000 graves in New York State were decorated in 1881 alone. The flowers distributed, there came the hymns and the speeches. Typically, a veteran read Lincoln's Gettysburg Address, a pastor said prayers, and a quartet or choir performed "Nearer My God to Thee" or another hymn (one favorite was the joyful Christmas carol "*Adeste Fidelis*"). An honored guest then lauded the honored dead and implored the mourners to follow their example. Then all gave voice to army songs like "Tenting on the Old Campground," and to special Memorial Day hymns like "Our Heroes Graves We're Strewing" and "Cover Them Over with Beautiful Flowers."

> *Cover them over, yes, cover them over*
> *Parent and husband and brother and lover;*
> *Crown in your hearts those dead heroes of ours,*
> *Cover them over with beautiful flow'rs!*

By then the veterans and their friends were dissolved in tears. After singing "America," and after a bugler played "Taps" and an honor guard gave a rifle salute, they slowly broke up for the long walk home.

No wonder Memorial Day was likened to a secular version of All Souls' Day, called "the festival of our dead," and described as "sacred operatic drama, solemn, impressive, pathetic, every way beautiful."

The G.A.R.

A gauge of how completely American life was woven into the memory of the Civil War is the variety of names of G.A.R. posts. Many Brooklyn and New York posts honored celebrated war heroes like George Washington, Alexander Hamilton, the Marquis de Lafayette, and Ulysses S. Grant. After retiring as President of the United States, Grant paid a visit to the U.S. Grant Post in Brooklyn in 1881, and four years later the post provided an honor guard at his funeral, which itself was a Civil War memorial, with a procession of 60,000 moving up through Manhattan to the site of his temporary grave overlooking Harlem and the Hudson. When Grant's Tomb opened in 1897, the Grant Post again provided an honor guard.

A few of Brooklyn's forty-three G.A.R. posts were named for abolitionists, like Henry Ward Beecher. The William Lloyd Garrison Post, named for the publisher of antislavery tracts, was one of the few predominately African American G.A.R. posts. Many German-American Civil War veterans gravitated to a post named for Barbara Hauer Frietchie, a Union sympathizer in her mid-nineties who was legendary for, reportedly, waving the Stars and Stripes in Stonewall Jackson's face from her Virginia home. Another post for Brooklyn's large German population was named for Lt. Col. Germain Metternich, a veteran of the European revolution of 1848 who died in battle in Georgia in 1862.

Several posts carried less famous names. A post that was well represented at the Evergreens every Memorial Day was the one based in nearby East New York named for Louis McLane Hamilton. A grandson of the founding father Alexander Hamilton and Louis McLane, a U.S. senator and secretary of state and the treasury, Louis Hamilton was seventeen when he volunteered in the New York State militia. He received brevets (promotions) for service at Chancellorsville and Gettysburg. After the war, the youngest officer in the Regular Army, he went west to Kansas Indian Territory in George Armstrong Custer's Seventh Cavalry and was killed in a battle. Why Hamilton's name was adopted by a post in East New York is a mystery; there was a rumor that he was buried at the Evergreens (his grave actually is in Poughkeepsie). Veterans of the Indian Wars are interred in the Green Hills, however. Alexander B. Bishop served in Custer's Seventh U.S. Cavalry and was wounded in one of the skirmishes around the time of the Battle of the Little Big Horn. In February 1895 an Iroquois Indian named American Horse died in his bed in an apartment on Broome Street in Greenwich Village. According to a woman friend, Drooping Bough, American Horse had fought the Mohawks, been a canoe pilot on the Ottawa River, and served in the Union Army in the Civil War. His Native American friends conducted an emotional mourning rite that ended when they placed a tomahawk in the casket. American Horse's remains were taken to the Evergreens and buried in a G.A.R. post's lot.

Two G.A.R. posts were named for men killed in the Civil War who were buried at the Evergreens. When the first call for volunteers went out in April 1861, Harry Lee was one of the many Kings County firefighters who stepped forward. After serving his three months' obligation (all that was demanded in the war's early optimistic days), he reenlisted in the One Hundred Seventy-Third Regiment that had been organized by Brooklyn's and New York's police departments. Lee rose to the rank of captain and was mortally wounded in the Battle of Cane River, Louisiana, in 1863. His Sunday school wrote the army to ask that his remains be returned to Brooklyn. He was buried at the Evergreens and honored in the traditional Brooklyn way, which was as a common man. "A leaf in the laurel that adorns the immortal Grant, a stone in the triumphal arch of liberty" was how he was described by Brooklyn's most prominent G.A.R. leader, George W. Brown (who is also buried at the Evergreens). "He was one of the great army of martyrs who helped to make the names of our noted generals what they are today."

Another Brooklyn G.A.R. post honored a father and son who lie side by side at the Evergreens. Abel Smith Sr. was a colonel in a New York National Guard coast artillery unit on temporary duty upstate to recruit troops for a new unit. In October 1851 a horse-drawn passenger wagon ran him down. He was the first soldier buried with full military honors at the Evergreens. Colonel Smith's son, also named Abel, enlisted in a New York volunteer unit as soon as the first shots were fired and by August 1861 had risen to the rank of major. On May 27, 1863, Lieutenant Colonel Abel Smith Jr. of the One Hundred Sixty-Fifth New York State Volunteers was leading a charge on a Confederate fortification at Port Hudson, Louisiana, when he was wounded. He died a month later.

These postcards commemorated the role of cemeteries in one of the country's most profound civic rituals. Ironically, the publisher, Raphael Tuck & Sons, was English and many cards were printed in Germany.

The double tragedy deeply touched New York. The progress of the son's body back to the north was followed daily in the newspapers, and the Common Council of the City of Brooklyn arranged to have him interred with appropriate military honors alongside his father at the Evergreens. Such coincidences were rare and long remembered. Walt Whitman's poem "Dirge for Two Veterans" was written for another double loss, but the words are appropriate:

> Lo, the moon ascending,
> Up from the east the silvery round moon,
> Beautiful over the house-tops, ghastly, phantom moon,
> Immense and silent moon.
> I see a sad procession,

> And I hear the sound of coming full-key'd bugles,
> All the channels of the city streets they're flooding,
> As with voices and with tears.

Mrs. Parker and the Savior of Little Round Top

A fierce controversy over proper credit surrounded the G. K. Warren Post, whose large burial ground lies in the North Mead section of the Evergreens. Brigadier General Gouverneur Kemble Warren, who was born near West Point in Cold Spring, New York, was a topographical engineer turned infantry commander. His career was not a complete success (Grant and other generals considered him unduly cautious), but he did enjoy a moment of triumph during the second day of the Battle of Gettysburg. Surveying the Confederate lines from the round, rocky crest of an undefended hill at the far end of Cemetery Ridge, he noticed glints of metal in the nearby woods. Warren raised the alarm, and troops arrived in time to charge down the steep slope into the heart of the attack. With that Warren gained the nickname of "Savior of Little Round Top."

In 1883, a year after Warren's death, a statue showing him standing on its granite peak, field glasses in hand, was placed on Little Round Top. The G. K. Warren Post of the Grand Army of the Republic was formed that same year in Brooklyn and acquired a plot at the Evergreens for its members. Although G.A.R. membership was limited to Union veterans, the wives in the post auxiliaries were assigned many responsibilities, including beautifying the property of post burial plots. After installing a fence, an arbor, a bench, and trees, Mrs. Benjamin L. Parker and her committee decided in 1890 that what the plot needed was what was described as "a heroic size bronze statue" of Warren in his moment of triumph, similar to the one at Gettysburg. She formed a committee of women and men and raised more than half the $2,200 cost. But the post commander withheld his donation, insisting that credit be taken from the women's auxiliary and given to the Warren post. When Mrs. Parker refused, her committee was shoved aside, and the post successfully lobbied Brooklyn's mayor to have the city commission a larger version of the statue and place it in Prospect Park.

The aggrieved Mrs. Parker became infuriated by newspaper reports that the whole project was entirely

East New York's St. Michael's High School Band prepares to march down Eastern Parkway to Grand Army Plaza (below). Brooklynites were as enthusiastic for Memorial Day as any Americans.

the idea of "Grand Army men." She granted a newspaper interview of her own in which she set the record straight and hinted that she and her friends would picket the ceremony. Feelings cooled when the Warren Post agreed to give the women public credit. The Evergreens' loss was the park's gain. The Savior of Little Round Top, an eighteen-foot-tall bronze statue of General Warren, has been keeping a lookout over Prospect Park for over a century.

George Eggleston and the Road to Reunion

As Civil War veterans grayed, they saw Memorial Day broaden from its original purpose. Some Northerners were sympathetic enough with the men who had long been scorned as "Johnny Rebs" to encourage regional reunion and national reconciliation. One of the key figures in this revival was George Cary Eggleston, the only former Confederate Army officer buried at the Evergreens. Born on the western frontier of southern Indiana in 1839, he taught school (his experiences were later turned by his brother, Edward, into a popular book, *The Hoosier Schoolmaster*) until he inherited a plantation in Virginia, where he practiced law and later fought in the war.

After the war, he moved to New York and worked as a journalist and newspaper editor. Eggleston also wrote books, including romances and histories of the South and the Civil War with titles like *A Carolina Cavalier*. In his memoir, *A Rebel's Recollections*, published in 1875, he blamed the rebellion itself on the popularity in the South of romantic, chivalric novels written by Sir Walter Scott. "Our ideas of the life and business of a soldier were drawn chiefly from the adventures of Ivanhoe." Eggleston portrayed the bitter consequences of Southerners' shattered dreams in a portrait of General Robert E. Lee in defeat: "I saw him for the last time during the war, at Amelia Court House, in the midst of the final retreat, and I shall never forget the heart-broken expression his face wore, or the still sadder tones of his voice as he gave me the instructions I had come to ask. The army was in utter confusion."

His upbeat writing about the former enemy found an audience in the North, where many people, exhausted by postwar sectional bitterness, set out on what was called "The Road to Reunion." Toward the end of his life Eggleston produced a two-volume history of the Confederacy that the *New York Times* praised as a "just and penetrating study," with Eggleston's "fearless and pungent criticisms of some of the leaders on both sides." As history it may be wanting, but Eggleston's writing met a public demand for the end of regional hostilities. Nostalgia about the old Confederacy became a popular theme in books and large-circulation newspapers, and also among some politicians.

Still, the idea of a North–South reconciliation was anathema to many Americans, including African Americans and most members of posts of the Grand Army of the Republic. When an effort was made in 1891 to honor Confederates at the G.A.R.'s national encampment, the Harry Lee Post in Brooklyn voted to bar the "obnoxious emblems" of Confederate war relics from G.A.R. events. Gradually, however, the focus of Memorial Day in Brooklyn shifted away from sad ceremonies at

In this classic Memorial Day scene (from the *Brooklyn Eagle* in the 1920s) a grizzled Civil War soldier marches down Eastern Parkway with veterans of the Spanish-American and First World wars.

Union soldiers' graves to spectacular parades down Eastern Parkway, where all citizens, in and out of uniform, marched to the cheerful thump-thump rhythms of John Philip Sousa. The general orders for Brooklyn's Memorial Day parade past Governor Theodore Roosevelt's reviewing stand in 1899 filled two columns in the *Brooklyn Eagle.* There were so many fife and drum corps and buglers that parade marshals were advised, "when bands are very close together, they must not both be playing at the same time."

Memorializing began to be generalized. In 1895 a group critical of the trolley monopoly in Brooklyn laid red geraniums on the graves of people who had been killed in streetcar accidents (two were at the Evergreens, Henry Havemeyer in Pisgah and Josephine Zeiser in Evergreen Hedge). A year later Mrs. Edwin Knowles, the wife of a well-known actor and theatrical producer, led a group of women to the Actors' Fund Plot at the Evergreens and laid wreathes on the plots of actresses. If there is no record of what the local G.A.R. posts thought about that one, it is probably because their members were too apoplectic to speak.

Where once all sports and games were banned on the day, May 30th was transformed into a true citizens holiday, with family picnics, baseball games, sailboat and horse races, performances of *The Arabian Nights*, and ferry trips up the Hudson accompanied by brass bands and barrels of beer. By 1940, newspapers would be devoting columns not to the G.A.R.'s general orders for the parade of thousands through the streets of Brooklyn, but to anticipating traffic jams on the roads and bridges to Robert Moses' newly constructed beaches.

NEXT PAGE, NORTH MEAD,
G. K. WARREN POST, G.A.R.

BYRON
MORGAN
CONNELL
MUSTERED
1882.
PLOT DEDICATED
1886.
SERSON
1865 PETER 1938
1874 JULIA 1946

From Drummer Boy to Grand Marshall

These changes are exemplified by the life of one G.A.R. comrade who is buried at the Evergreens. George R. Brown was a fourteen-year-old bugler in a New York regiment when he was wounded and captured, and he subsequently spent eleven months in Confederate prisons, including the infamous Andersonville. An engraver, in his spare time he threw himself into veterans' activities, serving as a comrade and commander of the Harry Lee and U.S. Grant posts, and appearing at schools to hand out American flags. He served as grand marshal for Brooklyn's Memorial Day parades and was G.A.R. Officer of the Day at a Memorial Day at Grant's Tomb. During the 1920s Brown and two hundred fifty other old soldiers were among the 10,000 veterans and Boy Scouts parading on foot or in automobiles down Eastern Parkway and through the Soldiers and Sailors Arch to Grand Army Plaza. One year, Brown broke his right arm soon before the parade but insisted on taking his usual position in the head car and saluting with his left hand. In 1932, at age eighty-three, he again served as grand marshal then went up to Albany for the annual encampment of the state G.A.R. After returning to Brooklyn, he had a brief illness and died.

Five Days at the Evergreens

"Memorial Day is a religious day, the day of sweetest memories," proclaimed a speaker in a New England cemetery on a May 30th in the 1930s. This uniquely American blend of religious faith and secular remembrance came to be shared by the four other great holidays, when people in droves go out to the cemetery. What the sociologist W. Lloyd Warner wrote in the 1950s about Memorial Day in his fascinating study of mourning in America, *The Living and the Dead: A Study of the Symbolic Life of Americans*, applies also to Christmas, Easter, the Chinese family day of Ching Ming, and Mother's Day. "For one day the cemeteries were a place for all the living and all the dead," Warner wrote, "and for this one day the bright-colored flowers and gaudy flags gave them almost a gay appearance. Death declared

a holiday, not for itself but for the living, when together they could experience it and momentarily challenge its ultimate power." On those ceremonial days, Americans were united and equal.

Near or on Christmas, thousands of families went to the Evergreens to "spruce" the graves with sprays or boughs of spruce and lay wreathes. To entertain the many children who came out, the Evergreens sometimes set up Christmas displays, with a tree and electric trains in the old Alexander Jackson Davis chapel, which had been converted into the administration building. Four or five months later came Easter and the Chinese ancestor day of Ching Ming. Then in mid-May came Mother's Day, founded in 1905 and made a national holiday in 1914. Finally, almost at the beginning of summer, came Memorial Day, which many Americans continued to call Decoration Day into the 1950s. While Mother's Day eventually became the most popular of the five, Memorial Day remained the most profound even as the parade of men in old uniforms shortened. "I remember the old-timers saying that Memorial Day was the biggest day at the cemetery," said Evergreens president Paul Grassi, who started work there in the late 1960s. Although volunteers continued to distribute American flags on the graves, the marches to the grounds and the twenty-one-gun salutes at the flagpole ended. The day's uniqueness was diluted when it was shifted from May 30th to the last Monday in the month, bundling it into a three-day holiday.

Contributing to the decline of Memorial Day's uniqueness was the extraordinary power of a memorial to a more recent war, the Vietnam Veterans Memorial, on whose black wall are inscribed the names of almost 60,000 war dead. After opening in 1982 with 150,000 people on hand, it became one of the country's most visited monuments, standing as another reminder of the hold that America's war dead have on the nation's heart.

CHAPTER EIGHT

AFRICAN AMERICANS IN PEACE AND WAR

FOR ALL ITS CLAIMS of inclusiveness, the Grand Army of the Republic did not always invite black Union Army veterans to participate in Memorial Day ceremonies. But there were African American and integrated G.A.R. posts that sponsored burial plots, and of the Civil War regiments represented at the Evergreens, none has a more painful history than the Twentieth Regiment, United States Colored Troops. Several of its veterans—John J. Jackson, Elijah White, W. H. Hasbrook, and others—lie in the plot of the Frederick A. Douglass G.A.R. Post, in the spacious Cedar Vale section. The open spaces between and among their headstones indicate that there are many more burials there, the number and identity of which awaited the conclusion of an ongoing census.

Considering the hostility of the many antiwar and pro-Southern New Yorkers to Lincoln, the Republican Party, African Americans, and the Civil War, it was noteworthy that the black regiment was

PAGE 116, LILACS AND ANGEL

LEFT, EARLY SPRING

even formed. Across the North, black Americans lobbied Washington and their state capitols to be permitted to join the Union Army, preferably in integrated units but, if not, in what were called "colored regiments."

"Treated Like a Parcel of Rebs"

The country's first black regiment was the Fifty-Fourth Massachusetts Infantry, formed in February 1863. The enlisted men were mostly former slaves, and the officers were white men under the command of Colonel Robert Gould Shaw. At the battle of Battery Wagner in South Carolina on July 18, the regiment took its objective and then was driven back with a loss of almost three hundred men, including Shaw. The subject of the 1989 film *Glory*, starring Denzel Washington, Morgan Freeman, and Matthew Broderick, that collective act of heroism and sacrifice spurred African Americans across the Union to demand that they, too, be allowed to fight against slavery. As a few regiments were integrated and several black regiments were formed by a few states, the 70 percent–enlistment rate of eligible black men was far above that of eligible whites. And yet, before 1864, the only way for a black New Yorker to help preserve the Union was to travel to another state or serve as the personal servant of a white officer.

Racial violence was notorious in the streets of New York. In August 1862, four hundred white men attacked and tried to burn down a tobacco factory on Sedgwick Street in Brooklyn where fifty African Americans were employed. The next July, the federal government's imposition of the military draft triggered violence across New York. White rioters invaded the campus of Columbia College and destroyed the home of its president, Charles King. There were at least one hundred deaths, many of them lynchings of African Americans. Appalled by the draft riots, prowar New Yorkers founded the Union League Club and set about forming a black fighting unit. With New York State still unwilling to integrate its militia, the club made an arrangement with the Lincoln administration to raise a federal black regiment. As a committee headed by Union Leaguer George Bliss Jr.,

a hero of the battle of Gettysburg, collected $20,000 to fund the regiment, recruiters fanned out across the state. "Men of Color to Arms! To Arms!" read one recruiting poster, echoing a famous cry of Frederick Douglass. Within a few weeks more than 1,000 black men were recruited from Long Island, Brooklyn, New York City, and upstate, and under the command of white officers went into training on Rikers Island (today a prison near LaGuardia Airport). When the commanding officer, Colonel Nelson B. Bartram, was asked if his troops were prepared to face down hostile New Yorkers and go to war, he replied, "Give me room to land my regiment, and if it cannot march through New York, it is not fit to go into the field."

The Twentieth Regiment made good on Bartram's word. In one of the most famous parades in New York history, on March 5, 1864, the Twentieth marched through Manhattan to the Union League's clubhouse, where it was presented with the regimental banner. "A vast crowd of citizens of every shade of color, every phase of social and political life, filled the square and streets," reported one newspaper, "and every door, window, veranda, tree, and house-top that commanded a view of the scene was peopled with spectators." Self-congratulation swept through the city. "Eight months ago the African race in this City were literally hunted down like wild beasts," the *Times* editorialized. "How astonishingly has all this been changed! The same men who could not have shown themselves in the most obscure street in the City without perils of instant death, even though in the most suppliant attitude, now march in solid platoons with shouldered muskets." Even the unsentimental lawyer George Templeton Strong was impressed, confiding to his diary, "It is among the most solemn memories of my life thus far." In the main address at the Union League Club, Columbia president Charles King told the soldiers, "when you put on the uniform and swear allegiance to the standard of the Union, you stand emancipated, regenerated, and disenthralled—the peer of the proudest soldier in the land." With the praise of white New York ringing in their ears,

PRESENTATION OF COLORS TO THE 20TH U. S. COLORED INFANTRY, COL. BARTRAM, AT THE UNION LEAGUE CLUB HOUSE, N. Y., MARCH 5.

"It is among the most solemn memories of my life so far," noted a white New Yorker after watching the 20th Regiment, U.S. Colored Troops, march through the streets of Manhattan in 1864 and receive its colors outside the Union League Club. The black soldiers then went south, but not to fight.

the men of the Twentieth Colored Regiment boarded a ship and sailed to New Orleans, ready and willing to go to war.

The rest of the story is nowhere near as glorious as its first chapter. It was hard enough that black soldiers were tortured or even massacred when captured by Confederates. In their own Union camps their treatment was abominable. "We are treated Like A Parcel of Rebs," a soldier of the Twentieth, George Rodgers, observed bitterly. Black soldiers' pay was half that of whites', punishments were unusually severe, and, most humiliatingly, despite fighting heroically and skillfully in a few battles, black troops were often barred from going into

combat (General William T. Sherman refused to issue weapons to many black soldiers). Black volunteers dug latrines, drained swamps, stoked fires, and buried the dead after battles from which they were barred from fighting. A partially literate soldier, Nimrod Rowley, sent a letter of protest to Abraham Lincoln: "My Dear Friend, Instead of the musket, It is the spad and the Whelbarrow and the Axe cuting in one of the most horable swamps in Louisana stinking and misery Men are Call to go thes fatigues wen sum of them are scarc Able to get Along Before on the sick List. . . . the Colored man is like A lost sheep." A black regimental chaplain, the Reverend George W. LeVere (of a Brooklyn Congregational church), appealed to a higher authority in a letter from a Louisiana backwater: "We have been endeavoring to find out for which of our many sins we have been sent here to be punished."

After Appomattox, many survivors of the Twentieth Regiment remained in the South to try to start their lives over among the freed brethren. When John J. Jackson, Elijah White, W. H. Hasbrook, and the others returned to New York, there were no public welcoming parties or parades up Broadway.

An Heroic Clergyman

In August 1879, the pastor of a prominent New York African American church, the Reverend James H. Cook, acquired a plot at the Evergreens not for his or his family's use but for a thirty-three-year-old illiterate mulatto cook from Virginia named Chastine Cox, who had been condemned to the gallows. After breaking into a Manhattan house where he had done odd jobs, Cox was groping around in a dark bedroom in search of valuables when he awakened the owner's wife. His efforts to silence her with a gag led to her suffocation. Cox fled to Boston, where he was arrested while leaving a church where he had just taken in a sermon titled "The Horrors of Hell." He eventually confessed to the robbery and to his part in the death.

The trial started less than a month after the arrest and was completed after four days, in scorching weather under a national deluge of headlines. Though the woman's death clearly was accidental—Cox had splashed cologne on her face in an attempt to awaken

The astonishing, sad story of the 20th Regiment ended for some of its veterans in the Cedar Vale section of the Evergreens, in the plot of the Frederick A. Douglass G.A.R. Post.

her—he was convicted of capital murder and sentenced to hang. The legal justification was that the death occurred while the hapless Cox was in the act of committing a felony. There were other considerations. One was the assumption that he had wanted to rape the woman, another that he presented his testimony with an air of informality, and a third that, in fleeing, he had cast suspicion on her husband, a white man. And, of course, he was black—worse than black, a mulatto. A phrenologist (a specialist in the pseudo-science of gauging character from the shape of heads) determined that Cox's mixed blood made him especially dangerous. On one side his white father made him prideful, and on the other an American Indian grandfather introduced even more pride, plus streaks of treachery and cruelty, while a black grandfather instilled in him an overweening love of display. In the eyes of much of the world, this man was destined to perform (to quote a headline) "A Negro's Bloody Work."

Cox's lawyers filed appeals on grounds of mitigating circumstances, a prejudiced juror, and erroneous testimony. As the appeals ran their course, Cox was jailed in the Tombs, Manhattan's grim, damp old prison on the site of the old Collect Pond, the source of so many of old New York's epidemics. After he lost his appeal, he predicted that everybody, white and black, would stare at him as though he was "a hyena." A small number of clergymen disagreed. One was James Cook, the black rector of the Union African Methodist Episcopal Church on Fifteenth Street in Manhattan. Cook believed that if anything good were to come out of this tragedy, it would be Cox's conversion before he went to the gallows. Cook was excoriated in the press, the *Times* sarcastically suggesting that one route to divine grace is to commit a murder.

As execution day neared in July 1880, Cook remained committed to his prison chaplaincy and was determined to provide Cox with a good and respectful burial. He acquired a lot at the Evergreens, a new suit of clothes for Cox, and a first-class casket with a white satin lining, silver handles, and a silver plate with Cox's name. He did all this without the support of his congregation, who refused to allow the funeral to be held at his church on the grounds that Cox's sins were too great and the case was too notorious for them to become involved. Assisted by one of his vestrymen and a clergyman from Queens, Cook conducted the service in the Charles A. Benedict funeral home on Carmine Street in Greenwich Village. (A year later, Benedict would make the funeral arrangements for the assassinated President of the United States, James A. Garfield.) Standing over the open coffin, Cook shushed the mostly African Americans who filled the room and crowded the street outside the door. After praying that he and they would reach the end of their lives in the same state of peace that Cox demonstrated, Cook proceeded to conduct the complete funeral service, from "I am the resurrection and the life" through the Lord's Prayer. The "Amen" said, the casket followed the hearse to the Evergreens.

At that time a simple burial cost less than $50, including a plain pine coffin, the services of the undertaker, a hearse, and a simple plot at the Evergreens, but James Cook spent a total of $85, the equivalent of $1,700 today. At odds with his congregation, Cook soon left New York for a parish in Massachusetts, but returned several years later, when he was elected as a bishop.

Integrating Cemeteries

Racial burial policies mirrored local racial policies, which in nineteenth-century Brooklyn were unusually tolerant. For example, segregation was barred in trains and street cars. "Brooklyn was indeed something of a paradise for the African American middle class," write the authors of *Gotham*, a history of New York. Still, a few nonsectarian cemeteries barred African Americans outright, and most (if not all) others, including the Evergreens, had a section for blacks called the "colored grounds." The Evergreens was well-regarded by Brooklyn's African Americans because its "colored grounds" were located in the center of the main grounds, not (as at many other cemeteries) shoved out to the border, along the fences. "One would think that at least in the grave, all such distinctions would be laid aside," a frustrated African American told the *Eagle*, but the temptation to found an all-black cemetery was not followed out of fear of inviting even more discrimination. At the Evergreens, in fact, African Americans were regularly buried outside the "colored grounds." Some were freed slaves. On July 29, 1907, Robert and Sarah Nash, two former slaves, came out to the Evergreens and purchased a plot in the Nazareth Lots section for themselves and their nine children. (Nineteen people were interred there over the following century, and on July 29, 2007, the Nashes' descendants held a centennial family reunion at the plot.) In the spring of 1908, the United Order of Tents, an organization of African American women founded by former slaves, arranged for a burial in the Mount Grace section. Surrounded by tombstones for German-Americans, there stands a small stone that says this:

Erected by Order of Tents
No. 4 Naomi Tent
To the Memory of Our Leader
Fanny Richards
Who Departed This Life
March 2, 1908
In God's Care

The Sands Street Church

One of the most provocative stories in The Evergreen Cemetery's history concerns the transfer in the 1880s of the remains of one of Brooklyn's oldest racially mixed congregations, Sands Street Methodist Church.

John Wesley's "rule and method" of adding warm piety to chilly old Anglicanism was introduced to America by a British army officer, Thomas Webb, in the 1760s. Methodism caught on quickly and permanently, especially in Brooklyn and among African Americans. Henry Ward Beecher put his finger on the reason when he observed, "They had the good sense to go out among the common people, and they had a habit of exhibiting their feelings." The egalitarianism crossed gender and racial boundaries. In 1794 the First Methodist Episcopal Church was built near Fort Greene on a street owned by the Sands family, with a congregation membership of seventy-six, a third of whom were black and almost another third of whom were women.

Here is the Douglass Post plot in 1935. The invention of gasoline lawnmowers after World War II made maintenance much easier.

Like most churches then, the Sands Street church was surrounded by a burial ground maintained by the sexton. For almost a century burials of congregants, white and black, were conducted in the churchyard and under the altar, with occasional transfers of remains to other cemeteries to make way for new buildings. In 1885, reeling from the noise and disruption of heavy traffic to the new, nearby Brooklyn Bridge, the congregation decided to sell out, build a new church in Brooklyn Heights, and transfer the remains in the churchyard to the Evergreens. There were concerns; one church member worried that the "sacred dust" of the old churchyard's tenants might not be properly identified and reburied "with tender care."

When the contractors started digging, there were three surprises—one shocking, one embarrassing, and the third suggesting an insight into the relationship between race and cemeteries. The shocking discovery lay under the church. The thirty remains found under the altar were no surprise, but nobody expected to find twenty coffins under the Sunday school. The bodies had been unknown or ignored when new structures were built. (Such a lapse in judgment is sometimes called "a poltergeist" in honor of the horror movie of that title whose plot hinges on a callous real estate developer's decision not to move bodies before building new houses.) The second surprise and the embarrassment came when a workman digging under the altar came up with the nameplate for the coffin of one of the church's most celebrated preachers, the Reverend John Summerfield, who everybody presumed was interred in Woodlawn Cemetery in the Bronx (it turned out that the wrong coffin had been removed).

And then there was the very large number of remains in the churchyard's African American section. The burial ground was divided into two sections, one reserved for whites, the other for blacks. In the white section the workers found enough loose bones to fill twelve pine boxes, approximately ten people per box. In the other section, where four or five African Americans were buried in each grave, there were enough bones to fill twenty-five boxes. All the remains were taken across Brooklyn to the Evergreens and buried there in an attractive west-facing slope near the area called Tulip Grove. Interestingly, the boxes were arranged according to the traditional Brooklyn theme of unity in diversity. The remains believed to be of whites were laid in one trench of one side of the plot, and those thought to be African American were placed in another trench on the other side. And then the two groups were brought together by laying the headstones and footstones flat in the earth around the two trenches, in the pattern of a hollow square.

"ONE OF THE GAYEST ORNAMENTS OF OUR NATIVE WOODS" (ANDREW JACKSON DOWNING ON THE DOGWOOD)

The Hornes of Brooklyn

A few minutes' walk from the veterans of the Twentieth Regiment and other black and white Civil War fighting men is the plot of a family of African Americans so formidable that they were called "the Hornes of Brooklyn." The best known are the singer and actress Lena Horne and her daughter Gail Lumet Buckley, an author, actress, and filmmaker. Several of their ancestors were remarkable in their own way. Among them were a slave on a Maryland plantation who could read and write (a rare accomplishment for a female slave), a Native American who married a sea captain, an inventor, many professionals, and several social activists. Lena Horne herself was well known for her talents and her independence; she declined opportunities to "pass" for white in order to win roles and, while entertaining troops during World War II, refused to perform before segregated audiences.

Buried in the Horne plot in Cedar Vale are Lena Horne's paternal grandparents, who raised her in a Brooklyn brownstone while her mother, an actress, was on tour. Edwin Fletcher Horne was a teacher, journalist, and an editor who mastered six languages. Cora Calhoun Horne was a pioneer female graduate of Atlanta University, a social worker, an early member of the National Association for the Advancement of Colored People, and a proud member of Brooklyn's black upper middle class, known as the black bourgeoisie. Interred with them is one of their four sons, Frank Smith Horne. A graduate of City University, where he lettered in track, he had one of those careers for which the usual adjectives, like "varied" and "energetic," can only seem tepid. At first an optometrist who published poetry in his spare time, he went on to be a teacher, college administrator, and an official in the United States Housing Authority and Office of Race Relations. He was a member of the "Black Cabinet," the informal group of African Americans who advised President Franklin Delano Roosevelt and first lady Eleanor Roosevelt, and also executive director of the New York City Commission on Intergroup Relations—all this despite suffering from painful degen-

erative arteriosclerosis. Such a career should not be surprising in a man who once wrote a poem on the subject of determination, titled "To James," in which he likened life to a track race:

> Live
> as I have taught you
> to run, Boy—
> it's a short dash. . . .

When a relative showed Frank Horne's great-niece Gail Lumet Buckley a trunk full of family artifacts, she was inspired to write a book, *The Hornes: An American Family*, which was published in 1986 and became a bestseller. Guided by the insight that the story of a single community can increase our understanding of the world around it, she traced the history of the American black bourgeoisie and their struggle to share in the American dream through the experiences of six generations of her family. She wrote on the first page, "Family faces are magic mirrors. Looking at people who belong to us, we see the past, present, and future. We make discoveries about ourselves and them. Forms, faces, skin, stature all form a circle of existence. If you spin us we become a glittering chain of life."

She skipped one relative, Frank Horne's brother Errol, a career army soldier. Born and educated in Brooklyn, when he joined the army he was assigned to one of the mostly black Buffalo Soldier regiments in the American West. By 1916 twenty-six-year-old Errol Horne had risen to the rank of sergeant, which was about the best that most African American soldiers could hope for until the 1940s, when President Harry S. Truman ordered the racial integration of the military. But after taking part in General John Pershing's punitive expedition into Mexico in pursuit of the bandit-revolutionary Pancho Villa, Errol Horne was promoted to officer and given command of a platoon of black laborers in the American Expeditionary Force during World War I. A few months after he arrived in Europe, he died from influenza in the terrible pandemic that will be described in Chapter 14. "Everything possible was done for him, and he was buried with every military honor," his mother wrote the family, "but O, it is a deep, deep sorrow." Decades later, that anguished letter and a photograph of Errol Horne inspired Gail Lumet Buckley to write a second book about African American history—*American Patriots: The Story of Blacks in the Military from the Revolution to Desert Storm.* That story, of course, led her deep into the accounts of the free black men of the Twentieth Regiment, United States Colored Troops, who marched so bravely through New York's streets on that day in 1864, several of whom were buried a short walk from the Horne family's plot.

CHAPTER NINE

CROOKS, COMPETITORS, WRITERS, AND CONGRESSMEN

T HE WHOLE, COLORFUL range of New York and Brooklyn life is here at the Evergreens: Tammany Hall crooks and their enemies, murderers, temperance fanatics and barkeeps, a world-famous bibliographer and a dime novelist, a handful of Congressmen—not to mention a corrupt baseball player and a world chess champion.

I. TALES OF TAMMANY HALL
Christian W. Schaffer, Gambler

Christian W. Schaffer was a soldier in the corrupt army of Boss William M. Tweed, the monarch of Manhattan's Democratic Party in his castle, Tammany Hall. For over a quarter century Tweed and his ring enriched themselves by tens of millions of dollars through corruption of all kinds. Schaffer's name first appeared in the 1850s, when he ran on the Tammany ticket for the city offices of Alderman, Commissioner of Streets and Lamps, and City Inspector. Fortunately for the general welfare, he

PAGE 128, SUMACHS, LOOKING TOWARD BEACON HILL

LEFT, EASTERN SLOPE

did not win, but he was well enough regarded by Tweed to be admitted into the Boss' personal benevolent association, the Americus Club, which met at his mansion in Greenwich, Connecticut.

This was the time of the vicious political-ethnic wars portrayed in Martin Scorsese's 2002 film *Gangs of New York*. Old New Yorkers formed gangs with names like "the Dead Rabbits" and "Plug Uglies" to fight recent German and Irish immigrants. One nativist leader, Bill Poole, was nicknamed "the butcher" because that was his trade and because he used a butcher's tools in street battles. One day in a New York bar called Stanwix Hall, Schaffer witnessed a brawl between Poole and a Tammany operative that ended with Poole taking three bullets. Poole hung on for two weeks before finally expiring with the words, "Good-bye boys, I die a true American," on his lips. Six thousand people in one hundred fifty-five carriages followed his casket to Green-Wood Cemetery.

After being caught thanks to William S. Copland's undercover work, Boss Tweed (in the white vest) and his partners in bribery and skimming plead poverty to Lady Justice.

Schaffer's enthusiasm was gambling, and he pursued it energetically and not very successfully for most of his life. In one twenty-seven-hour period at the racetrack in Saratoga, New York, he succeeded in losing $43,000. He briefly resurfaced in the 1890s to testify that he had regularly made protection payments to policemen, among them a few high-ranking officials. By then the former prince of the Tweed ring was a pathetic character. "He was shabbily dressed and does not in any way come up to the generally accepted picture of a gambler," went one report, which described him as a walking anachronism—"an old-time gambler and doubtless the oldest living gaming-house keeper in this city or neighborhood." Penniless and friendless Christian Schaffer died in 1901. Following a funeral that was far less popular than Butcher Bill Poole's half a century earlier, he was buried next to his wife, Elizabeth, in the Ocean View section of the Evergreens Cemetery.

William S. Copland, Undercover Agent

Schaffer was largely responsible for his own ruin, but he also was the victim of the Tweed ring's breakup decades earlier, thanks in part to the efforts of one of his Evergreens neighbors. In 1873 a coalition of reformers succeeded in tossing Tweed out of office and into jail, thanks in large part to an undercover agent, William S. Copland, an accountant who worked in the city's Comptroller's Department. "A smooth, smiling fellow, bright, clever, and quick," was how Copland (sometimes spelled Copeland) was described by ex-Sheriff Jimmy O'Brien, the Tammany Hall operative who got him his job in 1870. Going over city accounts, he noticed that some payments were made from public funds without invoices and solely on the approval of three men, Mayor A. Oakley Hall (known as "The Elegant One"), Comptroller Richard B. Connolly (a.k.a. "Slippery Dick"), or William M. Tweed (always "the Boss"), whose job as public works commissioner put him in the middle of all construction projects. Copland would testify, "There was something wrong." Purchases for one new building, including awnings costing $18,000, were enormous enough to cover a dozen buildings. He estimated that favors to Tweed's friends cost the city $11 million.

Copland brought the story of the awnings and other discrepancies to Jimmy O'Brien, whom Tweed had recently cashiered as city sheriff after making a show of independence. O'Brien advised Copland to take notes, which he did, and which he gave (or perhaps sold) to O'Brien. With that proof in hand, the former sheriff attempted to blackmail Tweed for $350,000. When Tweed turned him down, O'Brien took Copland's documents to the newspapers. With the assistance of Thomas Nast's famous cartoons of bloated, arrogant Tweed in *Harper's Weekly,* the Tweed ring was broken and the Boss himself went to jail. Copland went on to expose corruption in the U. S. customs operations.

Oliver Cotter, Temperance Man

"At one time one of the best hated men in Kings County" (to quote an obituary), Oliver Cotter was an Irish immigrant who fought for the Union and ended the war with the more than honorable rank of brevet colonel. He proceeded to run saloons in Brooklyn until he experienced a crisis of confidence in 1870 and took the temperance pledge. At that he went to war on his old friends in the liquor business.

Not the oddity that it seems today, the temperance movement was an arm of a broad, progressive, proto-feminist movement for social betterment—an effort opposed by liquor distributors, corrupt policemen, and any number of politicians. Cotter's energy was seemingly limitless. "Oliver Cotter's Sunday Harvest," ran a headline in September 1876 over the names of sixteen saloons that he had found open on the Lord's Day. Three more excursions came up with thirty-seven more violations by the end of October. For ten years he dodged repeated attempts to entrap him with bribes as well as threats to his life (he carried a pistol) until, worn out, he retired to the calmer life of managing a cigar store. He died in 1900 and was buried at the Evergreens.

II: THE COMPETITORS

Bad Bill Dahlen

The Evergreens is the permanent home of the first world champion of chess and two star baseball players—one famous, the other infamous. The ballplayer with the good name is Bill Dahlen, the son of German immigrants who in his career as a shortstop between 1891 and 1911 assembled such a record that some baseball scholars wonder why he has not been elected to the

Baseball Hall of Fame. Just before the 2007 Hall voting period, the sports statistics columnist for the *New York Times,* Dan Rosenheck, argued persuasively that Dahlen "has a strong claim to be the best player not in the Hall of Fame—including Joe Jackson and Pete Rose."

As of 2007 Dahlen still has the fourth longest hitting streak—forty-two games in 1894, when he batted .362 and hit fifteen home runs. (Ironically, the streak ended on a day when his teammates had twenty hits but he was unable to get even a scratch single. The next day his luck returned and he started a twenty-eight game streak.) Dahlen also holds the Major League record for chances by a shortstop, 13,325, and he played on two pennant winners and the world champion 1905 New York Giants. The only thing anybody held against Dahlen was a quick temper that showed itself in razzing umpires so aggressively that he was nicknamed "Bad Bill." He managed the Brooklyn Dodgers from 1910–13 under various team names before being replaced by Wilbert Robinson. He went off to work in construction and then run a Brooklyn gas station, but late in his life Bill Dahlen returned to the game as an attendant in Yankee Stadium's left-field bleachers, where he held forth for fans and reporters on baseball's colorful history. He is buried in the Redemption section at the Evergreens—sadly, in an unmarked grave.

Greedy George Hall

George W. Hall did not have a nickname, but "Bad George" would have been a more than suitable one because he was a cause of one of the worst scandals in the game's history. Born in England, George Hall spent most of his life in Brooklyn or in nearby Ridgewood, Queens. His father was an engraver who specialized in preparing steel plates to print currency—an irony considering his son's behavior. He grew up with baseball, which was first played in Hoboken in the 1850s and quickly spread. When he was nine, in 1858, the *Eagle* listed him as a member of one of Brooklyn's first organized neighborhood ball clubs. A decade later he was playing for one of the city's top teams, the Brooklyn

Excelsiors, in the city's first big ball park, Capitoline Grounds, in Bedford. The game then was in flux between cricket and the one we know. There were strikeouts but no walks, the pitcher had to throw stiff-armed, batters could request a pitch in a favorite location, and there were eleven players in the field.

Professional ball gained new status in 1870 just as Hall was developing into a star left fielder and batsman. On June 14 that year he was in left field for the Brooklyn Atlantics in one of the most famous games in early baseball history. Playing before a Capitoline Grounds crowd estimated at 15,000, the Atlantics broke the nearly two-year, eighty-four-game winning streak of the Cincinnati Red Stockings, the first successful professional club, coming from behind in extra innings to win, 8-7. With that the Red Stockings departed Cincinnati and moved to Boston, where they came to be known as the Red Sox. In 1871 Boston and other cities were represented in the country's first professional baseball league, the National Association. Although his hometown team, the Atlantics, joined the league, Hall got a good offer from the Washington Olympics and became one of the new league's most promising young players. "As good a thrower as ever stepped on the ball-field," another player said about him, adding, "he could bat, too, as well as the best of them." In 1874 Albert G. Spalding, the father of modern baseball, invited Hall to join a team that was touring England. The young Brooklynite was on the way up.

Things were not quite right, however. Although play in the new professional league was faster and more skillful than anything most amateur teams could produce, the National Association stank of corruption. Home teams were allowed to name the umpires, baseballs were

The gifted George Hall of Brooklyn might be enshrined at Cooperstown were it not for the fact that he went on the take in the early days of professional baseball.

doctored, and players bet on games and even threw them at the bidding of gamblers who assembled huge nationwide betting pools linked by Western Union's telegraph system. The National Association timidly responded to these outrages with mere slaps on the wrist.

"A certain prejudice has been created against the existence of this class of ball players," advised *Spalding's Baseball Guide* for 1876. That year many teams and players fled the National Association for the new National League, which promised to clean up the professional game. George Hall became a star with the Philadelphia Athletics, and later with the Boston Red Stockings. In June 1876 he became the first professional player to hit for the cycle (a single, double, triple, and home run). Two days later he attained another first—two home runs in a single game, a wonder in the dead-ball era. That year he batted .366 and set a new season home-run record with five. Had he kept his nose clean and played anywhere near this level, George Hall would be in the Hall of Fame today.

But Hall got greedy. Jumping contracts yet again to his fifth team in seven years, he joined the newly formed Louisville Grays of Kentucky. In early August 1877 he was the star left fielder of the league's first-place team, which enjoyed a seemingly safe three-and-a-half-game lead over Boston. When the third baseman was injured, at Hall's urging the Grays hired one of his Brooklyn friends, a utility infielder named Albert H. Nichols who, it turned out, was very friendly with some gamblers. Soon after his arrival the Grays went on a long eastern road trip and proceeded to fall apart. Making errors and hitting poorly, they won only four of thirteen games and fell permanently into second place behind Boston. One morning the team president received a warning that the Grays would lose that afternoon's game, which they did in a spate of errors. There were rumors that Hall and other players were flashing diamond stickpins. Hall's wife, meanwhile, was confiding to other players' wives that he had received cash windfalls from betting on games.

All this remained a Grays family secret until a hard-working reporter for the *Louisville Courier-Journal*, John A. Haldeman, began sniffing around. He quickly concluded that "four unprincipled black-legs" on the team had sabotaged the Grays' season. His bombshell revelations forced the league to order the Grays to initiate an investigation. Like a modern-day investigator gathering records of telephone calls and contents of e-mails, the team demanded that players, on pain of instant dismissal, instruct Western Union to release copies of telegrams they had sent or received. There was clear proof of regular contacts between gambling interests in New Jersey and Brooklyn, at one end, and Nichols, Hall, and Jim Devlin, at the other. A fourth man, Bill Craver, probably was innocent, but circumstantial evidence swept him up in what was called "the crime of '77." All four were barred for life from professional ball. Their punishments, declared the *Courier-Journal*, were "the fruits of crookedness."

Just twenty-eight years old and a national disgrace, George Hall quietly returned home to Brooklyn. While Devlin pleaded his innocence for years with no success other than a small handout from his old team, Hall moved on. Although stories circulated that the true culprit was a brother-in-law who had badgered Hall into

The first chess world champion, William Steinitz, lies under a headstone showing one of his favorite games, donated by Kurt Landsberger.

taking the payoffs, Hall sought no sympathy. He followed his father into the engraver's trade, and later was employed by an art museum. He played in the occasional local ball game, but by the late eighties, as the *Eagle* put it, George Hall was nothing but a "once noted outfielder." He lived out his old age in Ridgewood, dying in 1923, and was buried in the Hall family lot in the Orient Hill section at the Evergreens.

The Grays' reputation was so compromised that Louisville never again fielded a major league ball team. Professional ball itself survived because the scandal of "the crime of '77" was marked indelibly on the country's memory. A baseball-loving boy in nearby southern Ohio, Kennesaw Mountain Landis grew up to pass judgment on Shoeless Joe Jackson and the seven other Chicago White Sox who threw the 1919 World Series, and he later became a tough commissioner of baseball. "Gambling is the one thing that can bring sports to its knees," said a later commissioner who ruled on the Pete Rose and other betting scandals, Fay Vincent. "It's naïve not to recognize the threat to corrupt sports through gambling and naïve not to think gamblers aren't looking for an advantage. They're there, they have a lot of money, and in the right circumstances, they use it on vulnerable people." One of those people was George Hall.

"Bohemian Caesar"

Chess was one the most closely followed international competitions in the nineteenth century. Games that were played then are studied today, especially ones involving the first official world chess champion,

William Steinitz, the "Bohemian Caesar," who is buried at the Evergreens in Bethel Slope. For three decades he was a great champion of chess and, as an editor and writer for chess magazines, an influential missionary for the game. As a player, he was one of the first to realize that genius and finesse may be less important in competition than avoiding mistakes, and from that insight he developed a strategy of applying ruthless pressure until his opponent cracked. His understanding of the board and the pieces seemed random, even chaotic. As one authority described it, "Place the contents of the chess box in a hat, shake them up vigorously, pour them on the board from a height of two feet—and you get the style of Steinitz." Sometimes Steinitz's life seemed just as messy.

Born in 1836 in Prague, then in Bohemia, he was raised in Vienna, studying and playing chess from childhood. Not naturally gifted except in an ability to apply himself to a problem, he worked himself up the ranks until, in 1866, he beat the best British player in a tight fourteen-game match to become world champion. Steinitz moved to New York but devoted the remainder of his life until his last, sad days on a perpetual international tour, playing for pittances and holding onto his title sometimes by his fingertips. When he was at last beaten by a much younger man, Emanuel Lasker, in 1894, he remained optimistic. "I am an old man now, but these youngsters must remember that I can still bite." Steinitz was suffering from gout, insomnia, heart trouble, and—as it became increasingly clear—mental disorders. He broke down during a match against Lasker in Moscow and was hospitalized for a month. Back in New York, he instructed his wife, who was living off the meager returns from a candy store she was running, that electricity was governing the health of their children and providing his means of communication with other chess players. After that he was in and out of mental institutions. The members of the Manhattan Chess Club provided funds for a stay in a private care center, but otherwise he was dependent on meager public services, and in 1900 he died in the Manhattan State Hospital on Ward's Island.

A century later, William Steinitz is even better known than he was during his twenty-eight-year reign as world chess champion. More than a dozen books in several languages by or about him and his games are available. Among them are a science fiction novel—*The Squares of the City*, by John Brunner, whose plot is structured on the moves of a match played by Steinitz in 1892—and a biography by his great-grand nephew Kurt Landsberger, who has donated a sign directing visitors to the great man's grave in the Bethel Slope section of the Evergreens. Suitably, the top of the headstone is engraved with a chess board and pieces showing one of Steinitz's favorite games.

If Colgate is just a kid's cavity fighter, how come Amy Vanderbilt won't brush with anything else?

"I like simplicity in people," said Amy Vanderbilt, who taught good manners to Americans in her newspaper columns and best-selling books.

III. THE WRITERS

Amy Vanderbilt, Etiquette Maven

William Steinitz was one of the most prolific and widely read of the Evergreens' writers. A very different corner of publishing—but one also of vast influence—is represented by Amy Vanderbilt, the nation's authority on etiquette and manners from the 1950s into the 1970s. Her sympathetic yet authoritative magazine articles, newspaper columns, and best-selling *Amy Vanderbilt's Complete Book of Etiquette* brought etiquette into the modern era. She appreciated that Americans in the late twentieth century would no longer accept rules blindly and for their own sake. Etiquette had to be and feel authentic. Her tastes were strikingly modest both for a person of her background (a descendant of the famous old Brooklyn family, she was a distant cousin to the

tycoon Vanderbilts) and for a woman of her authority. "I hate big parties," she once said. "I like simplicity in people and in entertaining. I have met all kinds of people; I like to talk to and hear them talk. I have no use for people who exhibit bad manners." She died tragically in 1974 in a fall from an upper window in her Manhattan brownstone.

Harlan P. Halsey and "Old Sleuth"

Harlan P. Halsey was a very different writer. As Establishment as they come—a descendant of the Colonial leader Robert Treat, a longtime member of Brooklyn's Board of Education, and a prominent banker—he chose as his hobby the writing of boys' books at a rate that is mind boggling. In the years between 1872 and his death in 1898, Halsey turned out some seven hundred novels, most of them serialized mystery-adventure tales aimed at boys. "Old Sleuth" was Halsey's best known pseudonym as well as the nickname of his hero, an energetic and at times super-human young man named Harry Loveland, whose favorite disguise was a white beard. Written at a fast clip—sometimes two a week, occasionally even one a day—Halsey's novels were often based on plots borrowed from newspaper crime stories and given breathless titles like *A Desperate Chance: The Wizard Tramp's Revelation* and *A Thrilling Narrative: Cool Tom or The Sailor Boy Detective.*

Harlan P. Halsey turned out hundreds of popular children's books at a fast clip, many featuring a youthful detective in disguise called "Old Sleuth."

Halsey's language may be stilted—he was, after all, pushing out a new book every few days—but his stories were universal. His lawyer described him as "undoubtedly the most popular writer in the English language" because "his themes are such as have always interested the majority of mankind," and because he presented them in realistic New York settings. "His scenes are laid, not in English country shires, nor in Swiss boarding-houses, nor in the unexplored parts of Africa, but on the Bowery, Broadway and Staten Island. His heroes live, not in the middle ages nor in the times of the Puritans or the Jacobites, but when Fernando Wood or [William R.] Grace or [Abram] Hewitt was mayor."

Scholars and a Hitler Victim

At the other end of the literary spectrum were a few distinguished scholars. Professor William A. Dunning, a political scientist and historian at Columbia University, was the leading authority on the post–Civil War Reconstruction Era until his death in 1922. Wilberforce Eames was one of America's most scholarly bibliographers. Starting out with barely any education as a clerk in a New York bookstore, he joined the staff of the private Lenox Library and moved with it into the great, consolidated New York Public Library at Bryant Park in midtown Manhattan. His life's work, *Bibliotheca Americana: A Dictionary of Books Relating to America from Its Discovery to the Present Time*, was published in twenty-nine volumes in 1936. A monument was erected over his grave at the Evergreens in the Mt. Seir section with contributions from the Pierpont Morgan Library and eleven of Eames' friends and admirers.

Because Alice Salomon spent most of her life in Europe, one of the more remarkable individuals at the Evergreens may not be as well known as she should be. She was called "the German Jane Addams" (after the pioneering Chicago settlement house worker and writer) for her leadership in the field of social work and social reform. Born into a wealthy Jewish family in 1872, she was one of the first German women to earn a Ph.D. (her thesis was on causes of unequal pay to men and women for equal work). In the 1890s she co-founded Germany's first training program for women social workers and over the years was extremely influential in Europe and the United States through her teaching and her more than twenty books. The regime threw Jews out of teaching positions, and demanded that social workers care only for the strong. Salomon protested what she called this "reversal of humanitarian thought and moral codes." A convert to Christianity, she joined the anti-Nazi Confessional Church. The Nazis forced her out of her institute, had her Ph.D. rescinded, and in 1937 expelled her from Germany.

Salomon made the best of her exile. On arriving in New York in September 1937, she announced that she was proud to be one of the "enemy aliens" who were "born to become Americans." She became a U.S. citizen at the age of seventy-four. Honored by American social scientists—three hundred of whom attended her birthday party at the Biltmore Hotel in 1942—she got to work on her autobiography, *Character Is Destiny*, which was eventually published in 2004. There she wrote, "Everything I had done during my life had one object: to help bring about a social order with more justice, more equality of opportunity, and a deeper sense of solidarity and brotherhood." At the time of her death in 1948, her work was beginning to be rediscovered in Germany. Today the Alice Salomon University of Applied Sciences offers bachelors and masters degrees in Berlin.

A founder of social work in Germany, Alice Salomon was expelled by Hitler and emigrated to America, where she was much honored.

IV: THE CONGRESSMEN

Of the former Congressmen buried at the Evergreens, the best known was Charles Goodwin Bennett, in part for his public service in Washington, and in part because of his and his family's long involvement with the management of the cemetery. The son of the newspaper publisher who was the Evergreens' president, George C. Bennett, he was born in 1863 and raised near the Evergreens in the family mansion at the corner of Bushwick Avenue and Palmetto Street. After attending Brooklyn schools, young Bennett became a lawyer, was active in Brooklyn's Republican Party, and joined the Evergreens Board of Trustees at the age of twenty-three (he later was president for several years).

Bennett first ran for public office while in his twenties and in 1894 was elected to the House of Representatives representing Brooklyn's Fifth District. The *Eagle* would praise him as a man of vigor—"no namby-pamby in politics, but a hard hitter, and one for whom the Pharisaical vice of hypocrisy was as hideous as ingratitude"—molded on the image of that rising star of American politics, Theodore Roosevelt. Bennett looked after Brooklyn's interests well enough, backing the construction of the Williamsburg Bridge and the dredging of stagnant Newtown Creek, but in 1898 the Republicans were thoroughly out-organized by the Democrats, and with the exception of the new governor, Roosevelt, basking in his Spanish-American War Rough Rider celebrity, almost all Republicans were beaten. In 1900 Bennett returned to Washington as secretary of the United States Senate, responsible for maintaining the Senate's minutes and records, supervising the reporting of debates, and transmitting official messages between the Senate, the House of Representatives, and then-President Roosevelt, in whose informal "tennis cabinet" he served. His thirteen-year tenure as secretary is the third longest in the Senate's history.

Three other Congressmen at the Evergreens were from a family of Democrats who represented Brooklyn districts almost continuously between 1901 and 1935—George H. "Pop" Lindsay, his son George W. Lindsay, and his son-in-law Steven Andrew Rudd. Charles Tappan Dunwell, a Republican, represented Brooklyn's Third District from 1903 until his death in 1908, during his third term, and William Forte Willett Jr. represented New York's Fourteenth District from 1907–1911 and was noted for his opposition (even though he was a Republican) to Roosevelt's attempts to reorganize and centralize the federal government.

Then there was a very determined reformer named Robert Baker. A founder of the Citizens' Union, he chose as his main cause a relentless assault on the power of American railroads. When he criticized the railroads' currying favor with legislators by providing them with free passes, he was nicknamed "No-Pass Baker." A socialist and a pacifist, he went so far as to refuse to appoint any cadets to the U.S. Military Academy at West Point. Scorned as a "comedian" who "would rather be different than right," he lasted just one two-year term, from 1903 to 1905. Baker spent the remainder of his working years selling Brooklyn real estate.

That totals seven members of the House of Representatives at the Evergreens. There may be an eighth from a much earlier time. James Lent started out as a merchant in Manhattan and moved to Newtown, Queens, where he served as a judge and in 1828 was elected to Congress as a follower of Andrew Jackson. Lent proposed that a lighthouse be built on Long Island Sound, he chaired a committee that oversaw the finances of the State Department, and he may have been destined for greater things, but when he died in 1833, just eleven days before the expiration of his second

Congressman and Secretary of the U.S. Senate Charles G. Bennett was an Evergreens President. Other congressmen lie in the Lindsay plot.

term, the only thing anybody could say about him was that he was unusually modest. "This gentleman was an honest, faithful Representative," said the *Washington Globe*, "and was the more useful public servant, because he was altogether unpretending as a politician." In other words, James Lent had come and gone unnoticed. The same could be said about him after his death. Lent was buried in the Congressional Cemetery in Washington, and was later disinterred and moved to the churchyard of the First Presbyterian Church, in Elmhurst, Queens. In the 1950s the cemetery was vandalized so often that the church sold it and transferred some two hundred remains to the Evergreens. Whether James Lent was among them, nobody can say.

AROUND A CORNER
OF A WINDING LANE

CHAPTER TEN

THE POETRY OF THEIR EXISTENCE: ARTISTS OF THE EVERGREENS

PAGE 142,
SILVER CORD

LEFT, NEAR
THE ADMINIS-
TRATION
BUILDING

O F THE WELL-KNOWN ARTISTS buried at the Evergreens—who include the noted painter Martin J. Heade, the prolific illustrator Harry Fenn, and the pioneer cartoonist and animated filmmaker Winsor McCay—the one who is most intimately identified with Brooklyn is Francis Guy, whose lively paintings of Brooklyn Village in 1820 are treasures of the Borough of Kings. English-born in 1760, and trained as a tailor and dyer of fabrics, he came to America in 1795 and established a silk-dyeing business in Baltimore, Maryland. He later picked up landscape and seascape painting and in about 1817 he moved to Brooklyn and settled in a house near the East River whose upstairs window looked out on the human comedy of old Brooklyn. During 1819 and early 1820, Guy painted several energetic, humorous scenes of the village and its people, one of which, a winter scene, is reproduced in Chapter 2. He died a few months after finishing this sequence and was buried in the Sands

Street churchyard, from which his remains were transfered to the Evergreens in the 1880s.

Now widely regarded as a master of the Hudson River School after many years in obscurity, Martin Jefferson Heade has been characterized by his biographer, Theodore E. Stebbins Jr. of the Boston Museum of Fine Arts, as "one of America's most productive and inventive artists" who "captures such a variety of moods, from his atmospheric effects, the glory of his light, the sumptuous warmth of his orchids and tropical scenes, and the inexplicable sensuality of so many of his works in every genre." Born in 1819 in Bucks County, Pennsylvania, Heade studied art there and later lived and painted in New York, Brooklyn, New England, Europe, and South America before settling down for good in St. Augustine, Florida. His lifelong subject was nature, and he approached it in several ways, including wildlife (notably tropical flowers and hummingbirds) and the seashore, which inspired several extraordinary paintings of onrushing storms. When public taste turned against the Hudson River School, he stubbornly refused to move on to different styles, explaining that his deepest feeling lay with nature, "the poetry of my existence." Except in his paintings, Heade had difficulty sharing that poetry with others. A quarrelsome, solitary man whose personality prevented him from acceptance by many patrons and artists, Heade had and was not afraid to mention his somewhat radical political views. "I am not likely to be placed in the rank of 'boot lickers' to the rich," he once commented. He proposed that all wildlands be bought up by the government to keep them out of the hands of the wealthy. Further biting the hand that fed him, he crankily objected to the art world's patronage system. All this did not help his

Drawn to nature, both grand and small, Martin J. Heade made gemlike portraits of South American hummingbirds.

fortune. Late in his life, he confessed a sense of failure: "The fact is I doan [don't] know that I ever painted anything that was worth remembering."

The fact is that Heade did leave a great deal that was definitely worth remembering, although it took many decades for the public to realize it. His gemlike portraits of flowers and birds were in a style that was both voluptuous and scientifically rigorous. One series has been called an "outline of the very life cycle of hummingbirds." And there is Heade's series of shorescapes in which blacker-than-black clouds loom over bright, picturesque scenes, triggering in the viewer a mood best summarized in the word "numinous"—meaning the presence of a profound sense of connection with the supernatural. The art historian John Wilmerding has written of Heade's several striking storm paintings that they give a "sense of an almost surreal world held in a tension of oppositions about to shatter in noise and light." The first viewers of these paintings did not know what to make of them except that they were "very peculiar" (to quote a critic for the *Brooklyn Eagle*) in their portrayal of a nature that was anything but pretty and tame. Anybody who has experienced a storm at sea will understand these grand scenes, with their flat sea and small boats about to be hit by a dark squall that can be seen as either demonic or holy. The sky is so broken between light and darkness that these paintings have been interpreted as allegories for the American Civil War, for madness, for spiritual crisis, and for the stages of life that lead inevitably and inexorably to death. Viewers have found graves in the corners of these paintings, or have traced in them a catastrophic Darwinian tooth and claw nature. These images do not show the soothing, romanticized, and

In *Approaching Thunder Storm* and similar numinous paintings, Heade may have been commenting on the approaching Civil War. His postwar, post-storm *Summer Showers* reflects an easier temperament.

completely domesticated nature that Andrew Jackson Downing was trying to present in his landscape designs.

"The poetry of my existence" remained fresh with Heade until the end. In 1903 a visitor found him still painting landscapes and portraits of hummingbirds—"tall and erect and clear of eye at 83, active and strong, and ever ready for action." After his death a year later, he was taken to the Green Hills for burial at the Evergreens (possibly because his wife was from Long Island). Already long in eclipse, his name disappeared completely from galleries and auctions until one day in 1943 *Thunderstorm Over Narragansett Bay* turned up in an antique shop in Larchmont, New York, and caught the eyes of artists who were developing the new style of surrealism. Biographies, studies, and exhibits followed, and by the early twenty-first century Heade was so well established that his works were displayed on U.S. postage stamps.

A Pioneer Photographer and an Unlucky Sculptor

Martin Heade's astonishing seascapes were painted at around the time that photography was developing into an art form. A pioneer photographer is buried at the Evergreens, William H. Guild Jr., who is interred in his father's strange round tomb on Hickory Knoll (about which we will say much more in Chapter 13). He took some of the first photographs of Central Park soon after it opened. His photos emphasize the power of the terrain that Frederick Law Olmsted and Calvert Vaux molded, and the daring of their efforts.

Not every creative person at the Evergreens was so eminent, of course. The spotlight briefly, and perhaps unluckily, shone on a sculptor named John Donoghue. One of his works won a prize at the 1893 Chicago World's Fair, and he was especially celebrated for a statue of the boxer John L. Sullivan. But Donoghue did not take well to celebrity. He lost touch with the marketplace and, alas, his wits. A statue he made of a winged figure was so enormous that it could not be transported and had to be broken up. He fell on hard times and shot

himself. Only one of his friends was at the graveside when he was buried at the Evergreens in July 1903. Several of John Donoghue's statues and busts have been exhibited in a few of Boston's museums and libraries.

Harry Fenn's Picturesque World

Harry Fenn was far more fortunate. Between the Civil War and the 1920s, an American would have to be blind not to see one of his drawings. "He could do it all," observed an authority on the history of American illustration, Paul Giambara—"meticulous drawings, prints and paintings from his extensive travels throughout the world." Oversize volumes about the glories of America, Europe, and the Holy Land, and popular magazines like *Harper's Weekly*, *Appleton's*, and *Century* all overflowed with his finely crafted etchings of frothing waterfalls, delicate Manchu hairpins, downtown water fountains, rustic cabins, Brazilian mountains, and Swiss valleys. A Fenn illustration was instantly recognized for its exotic subject matter and for what one of his many admirers called the "force and beauty" of its bold lines and his knack for "seizing upon unconventional points of view in a scene." If it existed, Harry Fenn drew it, and in a way that instantly caught the eye.

Born and trained in England, he came to America in the 1850s with the professed aim of viewing Niagara Falls (his addiction to waterfalls was total). He first made his name providing engravings and paintings to illustrate Civil War commemorative volumes and special editions of popular books by the rustic poet James Greenleaf Whittier and William Cullen Bryant (the author of the cemetery poem "Thanatopsis"). In 1870 Fenn became the chief illustrator for a magazine and then book series titled *Picturesque America*, edited by Bryant. While some urban sites and buildings were included, the emphasis was on spectacular images—including a total of ninety-five drawings of waterfalls—by Fenn and others based on their travels and other people's photographs and paintings. (One of the engravers who worked on the project was George R. Hall, the father of the then-star but soon to be disgraced

baseball player George W. Hall.)

Picturesque America caused a sensation. No longer did Americans have to feel that their landscape was playing second fiddle to Europe's. The two-volume book sold more than 100,000 copies and was kept in honored places in parlors across the country as a patriotic emblem of the country's centennial in 1876. For similar publishing projects on Europe and the Middle East, Fenn traveled abroad, spending the better part of two years in Palestine, the Sinai, and Egypt. The understanding that Americans had of what was then called the Holy Land was largely shaped by the drawings of Harry Fenn. Cemeteries always caught his eye, and the special "Harry Fenn Edition" of Thomas Gray's poem "Elegy Written in a Country Church-Yard" captured the look and spirit of England's and America's old local burial grounds, down to the tilting of headstones by the upthrusting roots of "those giant rugged elms, that yew-tree's shade, / Where heaves the turf in many a mouldering heap. . . ." Fenn proved a master of the profound mood as well as the profound landscape when in 1887 he illustrated a special edition of the poem that best marked the break

Envisioned by Andrew Jackson Downing, Central Park and its graceful structures were photographed by W. H. Guild Jr., who is buried in one of the Evergreens' most unusual tombs.

from Victorian certainties, Tennyson's "In Memoriam." The last illustrations that he drew (the topic was a somewhat more tame than his old haunts, *Suburban Gardening*) appeared in print in *Century* magazine the same month as his death, April 1911.

Winsor McCay, Cartoonist and Animator

Although cemeteries are not widely regarded as centers of laughter, buried at the Evergreens is one of the greatest of all cartoonists, Winsor McCay, who among other things created some of the very first animated cartoons and shorts. According to the creator of Bugs Bunny and Road Runner, Chuck Jones, "The two most important people in animation are Winsor McCay and Walt Disney." A *New York Times* cultural critic reviewing a DVD of McCay's work once commented, "After watching this disc, you'll wonder what more, apart from greater technical sophistication, was really left for Disney to add." When the animation industry honors lifetime achievement in its art, the winners receive an award named for this illustrator and artist who almost

This tangled thicket on the bank above
Thy basin, how thy waters keep it green!
For thou dost feed the roots of the wild vine
That trails all over it, and to the twigs
Ties fast her clusters.

Not such thou wert of yore, ere yet the axe
Had smitten the old woods. Then hoary trunks
Of oak, and plane, and hickory, o'er thee held
A mighty canopy. When April winds

Here the quick-footed wolf,
Pausing to lap thy waters,
   crushed the flower
Of sanguinaria, from whose
   brittle stem
The red drops fell like blood.

Many Americans saw nature and foreign lands through the sensitive eyes of Harry Fenn.
These illustrations are from his edition of William Cullen Bryant's poem "The Story of the
Fountain" (above) and a book on the Holy Land (below, *Caesara Philippi*).

one hundred years ago made the cartoon movie an art form.

The son of a lumberyard owner, McCay was born in 1867 and raised in Detroit. He started drawing as a young boy and by age thirteen was earning 25 cents for each portrait he did of a customer in an amusement park's quick-sketch sideshow. He painted signs for a while before finding outlets for his cartoons in magazines and newspapers. As new printing technology made color comic strips possible and popular, McCay developed a dynamic yet detailed style that in 1903 won him an offer to be a staff artist for a New York newspaper, turning out daily and Sunday comic strips at a rate of three or four at a time. One of the first, *Little Sammy Sneeze*, challenged McCay not only to write a funny illustrated story about a boy, but to produce a silly but convincing sneeze in the last panel. He pulled it off by exploiting his talent for showing vigorous action in a static drawing. McCay's world did not concern commonly understood notions of hard reality. His most famous strip, *Little Nemo in Slumberland*, was a fanciful take on children's dreams, and his series *Dream of the Rarebit Fiend* portrayed adult nightmares triggered by eating an excess of the cheese pie called Welsh rarebit. In this way McCay salted his humor with just enough fear to keep viewers from becoming complacent. For a while he was drawing so many comic strips that he signed some of them with pseudonyms like "Silas."

By nature McCay was a solitary workaholic who largely lived for and through his work. Although he found comfort in parenthood and friendship, pleasure in the mystical rites of Freemasonry, and considerable joy living on the Brooklyn waterfront in a large house on Voorhis Avenue in Sheepshead Bay, he was happiest at his drawing board. In 1908 he was persuaded to go on stage as a vaudeville show "chalk talk artist" and found that he loved it. To enhance his show of quickly drawn cartoons on blackboards he started experimenting with a new medium called "moving comics," or what today is known as film animation. Invented a few years earlier, it had not advanced very far before McCay got hold of the concept and developed a new technology and striking style that paved the way for Mickey Mouse, Bambi, and Shreck. McCay's first animated film, *Little Nemo*, appeared in 1911, with thousands of frames hand-drawn by McCay on rice paper. More a novelty than a story, Little Nemo was followed a year later by *How a Mosquito Operates*, a very funny pseudoscientific short whose star, a cheerful but persistent bug, comes equipped with a grinder to sharpen his beak. McCay's most popular film was *Gertie the Dinosaur*, with a leading character who, like that mosquito and many other of McCay's characters, was alternately charming and terrifying.

Outraged by the 1915 torpedoing by a German U-boat of the passenger ship *Lusitania* with more than a thousand fatalities, McCay (who probably did not know that the ship was carrying arms to the Allies) brilliantly applied his new art form to a film that required him to make 25,000 drawings on the new medium of transparent celluloid "cels." *The Sinking of the "Lusitania"* may be a propaganda film, but it is a brilliant and quirky one, with its fish dodging the torpedo. McCay continued to make animated shorts and do vaudeville into the 1920s. He never did finish his last film (sketches for which have Gertie the Dinosaur energetically using the Brooklyn Bridge as a trampoline) because his bosses at William Randolph Hearst's publishing company ordered him to limit his work to drawing editorial cartoons defending Hearst's political whims. A brief escape to revive his *Little Nemo* comic strip proved a failure, and what few challenges came his way were minimal, such as an illustration for a cigarette advertisement and an assignment to produce a drawing of the house from which Charles Lindbergh's baby was kidnapped.

McCay's name and even his contributions came to be taken for granted. Film animation was advancing, though in a way he could not countenance. As the guest at a gathering of animators in 1927, he refused to join the celebration, lecturing them, "Animation should be an art. That is how I conceived it. But as I see what you fellows have done with it, is making it into a trade. Not an art, but a trade. Bad luck!" Still, he was working and

Winsor McCay's comic yet dark dream world appeared first in newspapers, then in early
animated cartoons. At the bottom right is Gertie the Dinosaur, who (as a tribute by one
genius, Steven Spielberg, to another, McCay) has a role in *Jurassic Park*.
McCay lived in Sheepshead Bay and is buried at the Evergreens in The Lawn section.

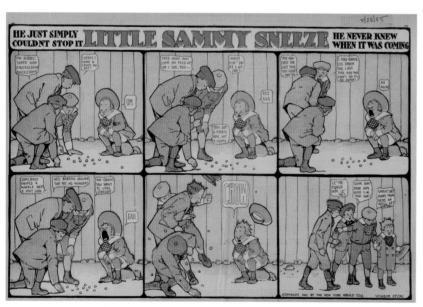

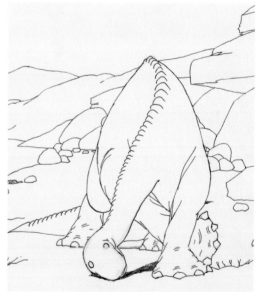

so he remained a contented man of what his biographer, John Canemaker, has called "elfin charm and generosity." America's first master cartoonist and film animator lived out his remaining days in the Hearst offices, in his winter apartment in the Hotel St. George in Brooklyn Heights, and in his summer home in Sheepshead Bay—always working. In the moment that he suffered a cerebral hemorrhage in 1934, as his arm became numb McCay exclaimed that his life was now ruined because he would never be able to draw again. He died a few days later, and after rites at his Masonic lodge, was interred at the Evergreens on the beautiful hilltop called The Lawn, with its sweeping prospect over the cemetery's southern area. His personal logo was replicated on his headstone.

McCay was long forgotten except by Walt Disney, Maurice Sendak, Berkley Breathed, and a handful of other cartoon artists who, in varying ways, sustained his iconoclastic view of the world. "He and I serve the same master, our child selves," exclaimed Sendak, the author-illustrator of *In the Night Kitchen*. When Disney devoted one of his weekly *Disneyland* television shows in 1955 to the art of the cartoon, McCay was shown in reenactments drawing Little Nemo and Gertie the Dinosaur. His reputation finally escaped the shadows in the 1970s, when his films were salvaged from a garage and restored at a Canadian government facility. In 1993 Gertie reappeared on the big screen in a sequence in Stephen Spielberg's movie *Jurassic Park*.

CHAPTER ELEVEN

THE CEMETERY-PARK AND ITS MANAGEMENT

RECOVERING FROM BANKRUPTCY and years of chaos, the Evergreens with a great effort of design skill and physical labor restored the property, altered some of it, and resumed filling it. There were more than 2,000 interments a year in the 1880s, and often double that number after the turn of the century. The grounds, meanwhile, were crowded on weekends and holidays with New Yorkers and Brooklynites who came out by the thousands to the high rustic enclosure, many to mourn and many to stroll among the tombs in the park that was a cemetery, and the cemetery that was a park.

Sometimes a visitor might go a little far. One summer's day in 1881, an Evergreens guard noticed a man standing on the bank of one of the seven lakes, holding an umbrella out over the water. Closer inspection revealed a string leading from the umbrella's tip into the water to a baited fishhook. The only thing caught that day by "the Lone Fisherman" (as he was dubbed by the newspapers) was a $5 fine. He was not the only visitor to forget where he was. In the 1930s the teenage son of Queens shopkeepers, Isaac Asimov, needed a quiet place where he could read his science fiction magazines. After some exploring, he decided that the only place where he was comfortable was the Evergreens Cemetery, which he would later describe in his autobiography as "a lonely Eden. . . , a park without the disadvantages of being full of people." The boy spent his afternoons sitting on one of the cemetery's benches, reading and engaging in his half-conscious habit of whistling.

One day an attendant politely asked him not to whistle. It might offend the mourners. Asimov was shocked. "What could they be mourning? Then I remembered, apologized, and whistled no more." Asimov went on to write *I, Robot* and hundreds of other science fiction classics. The Evergreens may have nurtured his ability and ambition, but after his death, at his request his ashes were distributed to the wind.

The Beautiful Resort

In its newspaper advertisements and press releases the Evergreens sometimes called itself a "beautiful resort" where strollers ambled along "winding avenues," "open glades," and "the deep recesses of the forest." Similar words were used by and about Mount Auburn in Massachusetts, Green-Wood in Bay Ridge, and, in fact, cemeteries everywhere, which were expected to provide the services later offered by public parks. "I tell you that before the days of the park, lovers had no place to walk in but the cemetery," the English writer Arnold Bennett wrote in his novel *Helen with the High Hand*. When Bennett visited New York in 1911, he said that one of the best things about the city was its collection of splendid cemeteries.

Today we take public parks for granted. New York had 1,700 of them in 2007; 75 percent of all New Yorkers now live within a ten minutes' walk of a park. But in 1849, when the Evergreens was founded, the metropolitan area had virtually no land providing comfortable, equal-access recreation. Walkers on the streets and side-

walks dodged roaming pigs, dogs, and horses when they were not stepping around fecal matter. Strollers along river shores tripped over stinking mounds left by emptied chamber pots. Rowers out into the rivers risked life and limb among the many ferryboats and other commercial vessels. Hikers into the countryside might be threatened by farmers and their dogs. About the only downtown properties where nature was allowed to blossom were the churchyards and private cemeteries, but many of them were fenced in, open only to members and families. "In our daily walks, we pass by a beautiful graveyard, which almost invariably arrests our progress for a few minutes," a *Brooklyn Eagle* reporter noted in 1842. "To be sure, there is no access to the public that we are aware of, but we have frequently seen parties in it, wandering about among the grassy mounds, trailing the vines, pruning shrubbery, reading inscriptions upon tombstones, or planting flowers upon some newly sown grave." The envy is obvious.

The new nonprofit, nonsecular rural cemeteries with their typical open-gate policies offered a new alternative. Newspapers regularly ran features titled "Among the Tombs" or "Our Cities of the Dead" in which a cemetery was praised as a friendly place where nature "invites the quiet-minded to stroll and meditate." No attractive public area approximating the size and natural splendor of Green-Wood, Cypress Hills, and Evergreens cemeteries existed in metropolitan New York before Central Park opened in 1859. First envisioned by Andrew Jackson Downing, the great park finally took shape in the hands of Downing's former partner Calvert Vaux and Frederick Law Olmsted, who assumed the "purpose of favoring simple, tranquilizing, contemplative, rural recreation."

Across the East River, Brooklynites were no less desperate for open spaces. "The great need of Brooklyn is public parks," declared the *Brooklyn Star*, and the first places they turned to in order to satisfy it were the big cemeteries. The *Williamsburg Times* (whose publisher, Charles G. Bennett, later invested in the Evergreens and became its president) proposed in 1857 that the Evergreens be officially certified as a park. This new idea gained wide support. A state commission formed in the late 1850s to create public parks in Kings County came up with two proposals. For Brooklyn's Eastern District (from Williamsburg to East New York) and western Queens, there would be a 1,200-acre park on the Green Hills encompassing the Evergreens, Cypress Hills Cemetery, and the land near the new Ridgewood reservoir. For the rest of Brooklyn, the commission proposed a public park less than half that size nearer downtown, on Prospect Hill. Since the Eastern District plan involved complicated land acquisitions, the second idea garnered the most support and so Prospect Park was created and opened in 1868. The Eastern District was left without a park for another thirty years until Highland Park, near East New York, was created in the 1890s.

(Above) Sunday strollers, to judge by their outfits, pose beside an Evergreens lake as boys play on the far side. (Below) A family in more somber mourning dress pause at the original main gate.

People flocked to their own "green oasis," the Evergreens. Its appeals seemed to grow as the advancing city crowded around its borders. "The immediate surroundings were somewhat a commercial aspect," a *New York Herald* reporter noted in 1885 about East New York and the Green Hills, "but the landscape to the north was as lovely as an English park." Simply stepping through the Evergreens' main gate surprised him. "The transition from brick walls and cobblestone pavement to a kind of mortuary paradise seemed too sudden to be real."

Jonathan Reed's Happy Watch

The "mortuary paradise" offered some surprises to visitors, one of the best known of which was a strange little man who all but lived in a tomb.

After Mary E. Gould Reed was laid to rest inside her father's vault on March 19, 1893, her husband, Jonathan, a retired merchant in his sixties, began to stop by frequently. His father-in-law's objections stopped that, but after Mr. Gould died in 1895, Reed purchased another vault in the Whispering Grove section, overlooking the same small lake where the umbrella fisherman had been arrested. Reed had his wife's casket transferred to the vault, where he installed an empty casket in which he would eventually lie. He then settled into what became his second home. Domestic furniture stood in the vestibule, a woodstove provided heat, and scattered about the vault were a clock, some urns filled with flowers, photographs, paintings on the wall, a deck of playing cards, Mary's half-finished knitting, and the family's pet parrot (first alive, later stuffed). One visitor described the place as "furnished just like a living room in a fine house." Jonathan Reed came out early every morning, unlocked and opened the tomb's door, and announced, "Good morning, Mary, I have come to sit with you all day." He did just that, reading to her or gazing at her face through the casket's glass plate until evening, when a guard came to gently announce that it was time for him to return to his other home.

On the far bank, on the right, stands the vault where Jonathan Reed kept his curious vigil over the casket of his wife until his own death in 1905.

As word of Reed's vigil spread, company began stopping by. By his count, 7,000 people visited in the first year alone. "I had seventy priests one day," he boasted. "Twenty-two people came from England, six from Germany, and six from Jerusalem." Seven Buddhist monks appeared to say that they had traveled all the way from Burma to visit the Reeds. The Reed tomb was so popular that the pond it overlooked came to be known as Reed's Lake. An Evergreens security guard, George Bonner, recalled, "People were always coming out to see him, more and more of them all the time, especially on Sundays. They were mostly women, and there'd be as many as a hundred or more in a single day. They'd all want to know what his idea was, and he'd explain it to anybody who asked." He told some people that Mary on her deathbed implored him never to leave her. To others he said that she was not dead at all but merely chilled, needing the warmth of the stove. Occasionally he

sounded thoroughly Gothic, declaring, "I love my wife's dust." The Evergreens' management was at first disturbed by the crowds, and friends tried to talk him into returning to a normal life, but they all threw up their hands and joined the crowds around this gnarled little old white-haired man in a shabby suit, with a large diamond ring on a finger and a contented smile on his lips. One newspaper cruelly described him as "a freak of the town," but that was the minority view. "He lives as he does because he enjoys it," one visitor concluded, "and possessing his theories of life, he could enjoy nothing else."

In May 1905 Reed was found unconscious on the tomb's floor with his arms stretched out toward Mary. After he was laid to rest a few weeks later, the vault door was closed for the last time; there was an unfounded rumor that the keys were thrown into Reed's Lake. When the Evergreens management decided in 1917 to fill in the lake to provide more land for burials, the owners of nearby plots briefly threatened to file an injunction on the grounds that the lake enhanced the value of their property.

The Evergreen Breweries

Tourists also found places to visit just outside the Evergreens gates. The City of Homes and the City of Cemeteries was also a city of breweries. The nearly 1.5 million Germans who came to Brooklyn and New York brought with them a taste for good lager. Some immigrants were experienced brewers and recognized the possibilities in Brooklyn's pure water and fields of hops.

More than one hundred breweries were established in Williamsburg and Bushwick. By one estimate, before Prohibition began in 1920, 10 percent of all beer brewed in the United States came out of Brooklyn, much of that from near the Evergreens. There were so many beer halls among the stone masons on Bushwick Avenue that a funeral procession into the cemetery was described as "turning through an avenue of beer saloons and marble yards."

Trees of the Evergreens rise above Trommer's Restaurant, a subsidiary of the nearby famous brewery.

One of the best known Brooklyn breweries, Trommer's, was right across the street from the cemetery, at the intersection of Conway Street and Bushwick Avenue, where a gas station stands today. In 1897 John F. Trommer arrived from Germany via New England, and bought a failing brewery on that location, renaming it J. F. Trommer's Evergreen Brewery. He died within a year, but his son George took over and for almost fifty years ran one of the few breweries specializing in all-malt beers and ales. With their distinctive Evergreen Brewery labels, Trommer's beers were among the most popular in the city. A marketing genius, George Trom-

mer invested in the Brass Rail and other restaurant chains, and installed a huge beer garden called the Maple Garden next to the brewery. During Prohibition he brewed a legal malt "near-beer" called Trommer's White Label and distributed it through almost a thousand Brooklyn and New York hotdog stands. After the repeal of the Volstead Act in 1933, he pioneered in targeting beer advertising to women and the use of cans and small bottles. In 1940 Trommer had 1,600 employees in two plants, the old one on Bushwick Avenue and a second in New Jersey. In 1948 he sold more than a million kegs of beer. But a year later, during a strike, his proprietary yeast strain somehow died off, taking the distinctive Trommer taste with it. George Trommer sold out to the Piels Brothers, who kept the Trommer brand names alive into the 1960s.

Brewers' Row

The Trommers were one of several families that commissioned mausoleums alongside the main road into the Evergreens. All were handsomely appointed inside and out, like a small house even to the knockers on the front doors. Mausoleums and large vaults became popular in part for their grand appearance but also because wealthy families feared body snatchings. When the corpse of the proprietor of New York's largest department store, A. T. Stewart, was stolen from a churchyard and held for ransom in 1878, the gentry removed the bones of their ancestors to remote areas (as the Vanderbilts did when they created a private cemetery on Staten Island) or built mausoleums as sturdy as small banks. Sometimes called "brewers' row" because the Trommers and other beer barons are entombed there, the row of mausoleums also includes leading figures of the Todd shipbuilding empire and the Jantzen swimsuit company.

Just off brewers' row is a smaller but still substantial tomb for the man behind one of Brooklyn's most famous old-time institutions, the Lundy Brothers Restaurant at Sheepshead Bay. Starting out in 1907 by selling clams from a pushcart, Fredrick William Irving Lundy ran a seafood restaurant on stilts over Sheepshead Bay and in 1934 opened a huge new mission-style restaurant that prominently displayed his initials, "F.W.I.L." Reputedly the world's largest restaurant, Lundy's could handle 3,000 patrons digging into the famous chowders and huckleberry pie. Tragedy stalked Lundy's. In 1972 the restaurant's manager, Lundy's nephew, was pistol-whipped by thieves in the parking lot. When masked men made a failed robbery attempt in 1974, he became so confused that he held the police at bay with a shotgun for three hours before he was calmed down by a hostage negotiating team. A year later Irving Lundy's sister and brother-in-law were murdered in their Forest Hills home during a robbery attempt. Fearing for his own safety, Lundy became a recluse in his apartment in the restaurant, totally dependent on his butler. After his death in 1977, his estate turned out to be far smaller than expected, and an investigation led to the conviction of the butler and two accomplices for stealing $11 million. Rumors of foul play were further excited when Lundy's casket was disinterred and his remains were inspected by government investigators. The restaurant was reopened by others, but eventually failed.

A Personal Touch

As tastes in monuments and landscaping evolved, changes were made to the Andrew Jackson Downing–style, picturesque rural cemetery—but not so many that it was transformed. In 1995 a landscape designer

Sections of brewers' row stretch along the main road in the 1920s (top) and 2007.

and preservationist, Charles A. Birnbaum, reported that "Today the cemetery retains a high level of integrity of its original design." If there was a theme to the alterations, it was toward standardization of design. Since its opening, the cemetery had granted considerable freedom to lot owners to install their own monuments and foliage, within limits. A modest example was Emil Seifert's idiosyncratic grave. For a quarter of a century Seifert was well known throughout East New York as the German-American gentleman in the white top hat who peddled vegetables from a pushcart during the day, and in the evenings sang in a local German-language choral society. His operatic cry of "sooouup greeeeens, sooouup greeeeens" was so familiar that it became his nickname. As Soup Greens Seifert lay on his deathbed in July 1895, clutching a bunch of parsley, he instructed his wife to plant a vegetable garden on his grave. "Let the greens always remain here," he said, gesturing toward his heart. A few days after he was buried in Bethel Slope at the Evergreens, two parsley bushes were planted over his breast. They quickly blanketed the grave. Over time, the

A MAUSOLEUM'S
DOOR KNOCKER

keted the grave. Over time, the Seifert garden became fallow, but one spring, over a century after he died, the Evergreens' onsite historian and tour guide, Donato Daddario, resumed the tradition. When the parsley had trouble taking root, Daddario opted for tulips.

Seifert was hardly the only plot holder to take special interest in a grave. In the 1960s a man would leave his office and come out to the Evergreens for short, regular retreats whenever his work hit a rough spot. "I put my hat on my head and say, 'See you tomorrow,' and walk out the door and go over to my grave and relax." Once or twice a year he had a wreath placed on his headstone with a card that read, "From Me to Me."

Whether eccentric or routine, graves and lots fell under the purview of the superintendents of grounds. The longest serving superintendent was Charles Pfeiffer, a German immigrant who started work at the Evergreens in the early 1870s under the unfortunate William Kneeland. He was promoted to superintendent in 1885 and retired thirty years later. Pfeiffer was responsible for every square foot of the property, where he eventually was buried in an attractive corner lot. His work force numbered about fifty men during the winter and one hundred or more during lawn-mowing and weed-pulling season. Advising him were professional engineers, gardeners, architects, and landscape architects, most of whom had learned their trades during the massive projects to build and maintain Central and Prospect parks. (The problems presented by parks and cemeteries were so similar that they had the same professional magazine, *Park and Cemetery*.)

These consultants included three stars of the parks movement. The consulting engineer in the 1880s was John Y. Culyer, Prospect Park's chief engineer (and a witness to Abraham Lincoln's assassination). He worked on the Evergreens' long-neglected roads, fences, and drainage systems before he was appointed Brooklyn's Superintendent of Parks. The two consulting landscapers, Calvert Vaux and Samuel Parsons Jr., were even better known. Each had served as the chief landscape architect for the New York Parks Department.

PROSPECT HILL, THE ACTORS' FUND PLOT AND THE LAWN PLAN

The Lawn Plan was not popular at the Evergreens. Families much preferred elaborate privacy inside metal railings. By the 1920s rail lots were everywhere, for example, in the areas of Hickory Knoll in these two panoramic views. Shown opposite is one of the last remaining rail lots in 2007.

After working for Andrew Jackson Downing until Downing's accidental death in 1852, Vaux formed the partnership with Frederick Law Olmsted that created Central Park, Brooklyn's Prospect Park, the first park-ways, and some suburban estates. The partnership ended when Olmsted moved to Boston, and Vaux continued his practice with Parsons. William R. Grace, the majority stockholder at the Evergreens, had a keen interest in the city's parks when he was New York mayor, and retained Vaux to make alterations to his New York mansion, do the landscaping for his Long Island estate, Gracefield, and perform some duties at the Evergreens, including making alterations to the Davis chapel and designing a stable built near the chapel.

Vaux's partner, Samuel Parsons Jr., left a larger mark on the Evergreens. Originally a horticulturist—he was a member of one of the families of Quaker gardeners in Flushing, Queens—in his long career Parsons designed or helped design Manhattan's Riverside Drive, Grant's Tomb, Morningside Park, and Union and Washington squares, as well as Brooklyn's Grand Army Plaza, San Diego's Balboa Park, and several cemeteries and estates. A co-founder of the American Society of Landscape Architects, he was an energetic and effective defender of public parks, and a prolific writer about landscape

design. In 1885 the Evergreens hired Parsons to prepare the southern corner of the grounds for development. The result was a very different landscape design than the familiar garden-like, monument-rich scheme that dominated the rest of the cemetery.

In a single paragraph in one of his articles, he condemned the proliferation of monuments as "excessive," "tasteless," "vulgar," and existing "merely for the sake of fashionable display." He added, "If there is a great over-balance of curiosity, then we have the grotesque in everything." He favored a new landscape style called the Lawn Plan, in which individuality was subordinated to a more consistent look. The main element in the Lawn Plan was a sweeping unobstructed expanse of greens-ward, like the great lawns of Central and Prospect parks.

The Lawn Plan's inventor, Adolf Strauch, the super-intendent of Cincinnati's Spring Grove Cemetery, argued that "gaudiness is often mistaken for splendor, and capricious strangeness for improvement." Strauch referred favorably to his layout as the "scientific plan" because it was meticulously planned, though he may also have been proposing emotional coolness. A later landscape architect who specialized in Lawn Plan design, Ray F. Wyrick, criticized old cemeteries as places where people "seem to try to keep grief alive for a long

HOLLY DELL, WITH A
SURVIVING RAIL LOT

time." A *proper* cemetery by Wyrick's lights encouraged people to "try to soften grief and think of the graves of our dead as melted into the peace of a quiet landscape." All should be green, smooth, unobstructed, and unified. Where the Lawn Plan was adopted, decoration and arrangement of lots were removed from the hands of lot holders and assumed by the cemetery's management.

It was too late to change all the Evergreens over to the Lawn Plan, and Parsons made compromises. In the Actors' Fund Plot, which opened in 1887 (and where Blanche DeBar and Sam Chester would be buried), he placed a single, tall plinth in the middle of the field, and surrounded it with simple gravemarkers placed so low to the ground as to be almost invisible. In other sections Parsons applied what he called a "vine-clad border plan," in which each grave was bordered by patches of honeysuckle three feet wide and reaching so high that fences were masked from view. Here his intention was that any mourner standing before a loved one would see only that grave. A glance to the side or ahead should leave only "an agreeable monotone" of a view of "flowing level lines of tossing tendrils."

The Rail Lot Fad

The Evergreens' grounds and monuments were already too dramatic to be shifted over completely to the school of the "agreeable monotone." For instance, there was a program of diversified tree planting at the turn of the century (many of those trees are still standing, though well aged, in 2008). Panoramic photographs taken of much of the grounds in the 1920s provide a prospect that would have pleased Downing, with a lush new-growth forest and gardens among intertwining curved roads and paths, with the hills and hollows almost filled with monuments.

One feature of the Evergreens would not have pleased Downing. This was the profusion of metal around many graves and family plots—so many fences and tubular railings, in fact, that these graves were known as "rail lots." In the 1880s families began to instruct landscapers and gardeners to rip out hedges and

replace them with wrought-iron benches and fences manufactured of brass or iron tubes. The popularity of the rail lot has been characterized by an historian as an industrial age's attempt to bring about "victory over nature." The whole idea of the rural cemetery and landscaping is that nature and humanity are not at war but are allies. Lot owners liked rail lots because they provided a sense of privacy and individuality in a crowded cemetery, and allowed them to do special plantings on or near the grave (an Evergreens president of a later day, Paul Grassi, would describe rail lots as "little farms"). Cemetery officials wanted to please their customers, but they disliked rail lots because the metal rusted and obstructed lawnmowers. As rail lots suddenly became popular, Pfeiffer and the Evergreens trustees imposed new rules on gardeners, landscapers, and stone masons to at least try to keep excesses under control. Here are a few of the fourteen rules and regulations that the Evergreens promulgated in 1890:

4. All posts must be of granite with square butts, and be three feet in the ground, and no posts may exceed two feet above the ground except gate posts. Gateposts must not exceed 2 ft. 4 in.

5. Posts used in the enclosure of lots must not be less than eight inches square. The bars must be inserted into the posts, not less than one and a half inches. If of iron they must be well galvanized.

6. If brass tubes are used they must be annealed and seamless, and from one eighth to one quarter of an inch in thickness, according to diameter of tube. Sills between all gate posts must be laid on masonry three feet deep.

The penalty for nonobservance was extreme: "*14. Any person violating any of the above rules will be prohibited from working on the grounds.*"

The rules did not stop the spread of rail lots. In mailings to lot owners in the 1930s, Superintendent Hasbrouck H. Wright tried to induce families to give up the railings, offering free lawn mowing and perpetual care coverage in exchange. Few families bit. Then came Pearl Harbor. As local governments conducted patriotic drives to gather scrap metal, the Evergreens enthusiastically joined in, and families followed. Photographs taken in the early 1940s show stacks of tubes ready to be picked up and hauled to munitions factories. A few rail lots remained, but today the older sections of the Evergreens are as close to their original appearance as at any time since the 1890s.

Managing the Grounds

Backing up the landscape designers, and performing the work that made the cemetery secure for burials, comforting for mourners, and attractive for the strollers, was the large maintenance operation. The job was a hard one right from the beginning, in 1849. With its forests, lakes, and views, the Green Hills may have seemed beautiful, but the area had been farmed hard for many years and was more than a little ragged. One keen-eyed visitor recalled "A sort of wild abandoned pasture land with stunted shrubs and broken trees and boulders, scattered here and there, with ponds imbedded in its hills." A lot of work had to be undertaken to prepare and maintain these marshy and rocky grounds.

An 1868 inventory of the cemetery indicates the scope and complexity of the job. In the office there were two safes for the cash that was routinely accepted for payment and for the massive ledgers containing the vast and extremely complete documentation required in cases of death and burial. When the family of a man who had died in the 1850s was unable, twenty years later, to identify his cause of death in order to file a legal claim, they asked the Evergreens for assistance. The information was found in one of ledgers, with row after row of entries of the deceaseds' name, age, home

(Above) Some rail lots were so elaborate that they had been called "little farms." (Below) World War II scrap metal drives finally provided a persuasive rationale for disposing of most railings.

address, and cause of death, and the names of the hospital and undertaker.

The list of tools needed by the architects and engineers included many maps, a drawing table, and drawing tools. Moving outdoors, there were four wheelbarrows, two hedging shears, four spades, six hoes, nine rakes, five axes, two crosscut saws, seven scythes, four spades, four sickles, and (to keep a sharp edge on all of those blades) two grindstones. Three pails, two watering cans, and two barrels were available to help with watering the grass and flowers. (Running water was eventually installed and today a truck carries water to remote corners.) For dealing with rocks and other obstructions, there were several implements of removal and destruction, including a stone drag, crowbar, drill hammer, and mason hammer, plus eight hammers of various sizes, two large chains, and a derrick "with appurtenances" (meaning a block and tackle or two). Depending on the soil, it usually took between three and five hours for a man to dig a grave with a shovel. If it clanked on a big rock, several men and maybe an ox or a horse would be brought into action. Some boulders that seemed small and manageable near the surface turned out to be earthy equivalents of icebergs, defying all efforts of extraction.

The heavy work was accomplished with the help of three carts, one spring wagon, one farm wagon, two plows, one snow plow, and (to pull them) three horses and some oxen that were kept at an on-site farm. In 1868 the following notice was placed in the *Eagle*'s Lost and Found section: "STRAYED—$5 REWARD—From the north gate of the Evergreen Cemetery, a dark red, hornless cow, a white spot in the face, a little white under the belly." Cows were not the only problem. "No horse may be left by the driver unfastened" was one of the cemetery rules of 1890. Horses and oxen finally left the grounds in the 1930s, long after the internal combustion engine had taken over the roads outside. Mechanical stone crushers and stump pullers appeared in the 1870s, dynamite in the late 1880s, and gravediggers struggled to dent frozen ground with picks or soften it with wood fires or cast-iron drums filled with hot coals. If the ground still resisted, bodies could always be stored in receiving vaults to wait for spring. Maintenance tools changed little until the twentieth century, when tractors were introduced and, in the 1950s, grounds crews were provided with two new machines that greatly eased their burden—the gasoline-powered lawnmower and the backhoe, which dramatically shortened the time to dig a grave to less than one hour, depending on the terrain.

(Above) Superintendent Hasbrouck H. Wright glares at a tree felled by a storm in 1950. (Below) Cemetery labor has always been intensely hands-on.

Equipment is one part of the story. A first-person view of the human side is provided by the memorandums that were sent to the staff by a longtime superintendent (and later president), Hasbrouck H. Wright, from the late 1930s through the 1950s. Weather was one of Wright's relentless worries. A late Easter and tardy spring in 1943 left Wright with gardens filled with blooming pansies at just the time they should have been fading and replaced by yew branches and other Memorial Day favorites—if only the florists had succeeded in making their deliveries on time. As the flowers and plants finally began to arrive late on May 29, Wright commanded his army of gardeners to be at the cemetery early on Memorial Day morning to start replacing the pansies. He knew there would be problems, and complaints. "The section foremen and their assistants, and the gang of four on the Worthington Tractor, will be on the grounds Sunday as well as Monday, and will be taking care of past complaints as well as urgent ones received over the weekend." A cemetery must be responsive on Memorial Day.

Wright also wrestled with changing styles of burial and remembrance, and with the stubborn survival of old habits. Many rail lots disappeared during World War II, but not all of them. If one family flew the American flag from a four-foot pole, owners of neighboring lots might install a six- or an eight-footer. When trim wooden coffins were supplanted by large caskets, graves had to be dug wider and deeper. Running throughout Hasbrouck Wright's staff memorandums is advice to be hypersensitive to any possibility of family conflict. After one family threatened to sue because an unpopular nephew was buried in the family plot (the undertaker had somehow decided he was a grandson), Wright laid down two laws: anytime someone who might be a relative or in-law was to be interred, at least two trustees of the lot had to approve in writing; and when two or more branches of the family were involved with a burial, both branches must grant approval in writing.

And, of course, there was the not-so-small detail of getting names right: "When taking interment orders, be sure to read back for the spelling of the name of the deceased," Wright lectured his subordinates. You might be able to get away with misspelling a name in a public park, but not in a cemetery.

TEMPLE HILL

CHAPTER TWELVE

BURIED FROM THE HOME

U NTIL AROUND 1930, the typical American burial came at the end of a period of highly ritualized community mourning, almost all of which took place in the home. "Dying was as social as it was somber in the early republic," observe two historians of customs. The importance of the broad community was first acknowledged after death by the ringing of church bells in distinctive patterns—nine tolls for a man, for example, and six for a woman and three for a child, with an additional toll for each year of age. The women of the house and their friends then washed the body and laid it out in the parlor. As the corpse was attended to, a wreath with a black ribbon was placed on the front door, clocks were stopped to show the time of death, mirrors were turned with the glass to the wall, and if the family kept bees, someone might be delegated to knock on the hives and inform them of the death, for otherwise they might fly away.

PAGE 172, THE SUMMER HOUSE

LEFT, BURSTS OF WHITE

Despite the near universality of religious observance, most funerals were held in the home, not in church. Baptists, Episcopalians, and Roman Catholics made a regular requirement or at least a custom of a church funeral, but otherwise this was a thoroughly domestic event, with the deceased (as the saying went) "buried from the home." Services were led by a clergyman the evening before the funeral. The next day there was the main service, again in the parlor, after which food—including a nut and raisin pie called "funeral pie"—was provided by neighbors or the family. Mourners might be served alcohol, though this custom was notorious for being carried to excess (Brooklyn's grand dame, Gertrude Lefferts Vanderbilt, compared the frequency of inebriated funeral processions to "the noxious growth of some poisonous weed").

The coffin was removed (the stairwells of small houses were built with special niches called coffin corners to allow coffins to pass) and placed in the horse-pulled hearse. The procession to the cemetery then commenced. Sometimes it wound through neighborhoods that had been frequented by the deceased, and it might stop at his or her lodge, where the casket would be carried inside for special, often secret, rites before heading off once again to the grave. If the distance were short, mourners might walk behind the hearse to the cemetery, singing hymns or anthems from operas. "It seems we are never out of the sound of the Dead March in *Saul*. It comes and it comes," Mary Chestnut of Richmond, Virginia, told her diary during the Civil War.

Once inside the cemetery gates, the clergyman presided over the third religious service in two days, either in the chapel or at the grave. He might present a lengthy sermon guided by Plato's advice to "laud the

With the vast majority of deaths occurring in the home, the house was the focus of mourning rituals until relatively recently.

dead and lead survivors." As Robert Pogue Harrison wrote in his important book on the cultural significance of cemeteries, *The Dominion of the Dead,* the dead will "come forward and show a way. . . . Some truths are glimpsed only in the dark. That is why in moments of extreme need one must turn to those who can see through the gloom."

When the Evergreens' first sales agent, former Mayor George Hall, died in 1868, he was accorded four of the highest honors any Brooklyn politician could hope for. One was the obituary in the *Eagle* praising him both as a convivial fellow who loved to sing old ballads and as "an honest hater" who "never turned his back on a foe for fear of him or from a friend because he was disinclined to receive him." Another was the crowd of 10,000 mourners who stood outside his home while the funeral was conducted in the parlor. The third was the grandiloquent funeral sermon preached by the most acclaimed orator of the day, Henry Ward Beecher. And the fourth was the grand parade of public officials—from the mayor on down to school principals—following Hall's coffin to Green-Wood Cemetery.

White Scarves and Pale Flowers

The yearning for a good funeral was widespread. After Keziah B. Blackburn died in her bed in late December 1883 and was buried at the Evergreens in a simple grave alongside her father's, her rector belatedly produced a will indicating that she had wanted something far grander. That this spinster lady even had a will was a shock; her impoverished father had been saved from a pauper's grave only by the kindness of friends, and Miss Keziah herself had lived in a walkup just off Broadway in East New York, where her sole means of support was the sewing she did for the ladies of Trinity Protestant Episcopal Church in New Lots. But it turned out that she had an estate totaling $1,200 (the equivalent today of more than $24,000), and that in her will she requested not just a decent funeral but a luxurious one, like Cinderella going to the ball. Her body, she wrote, must be dressed all in white and placed in a rosewood casket with six silver handles, and there must be six pallbearers wearing white scarves and white kid gloves, and the hearse must be pulled to the Evergreens by a team of six horses. The rector explained that this grand ambition originated in her father's disgrace. Ever since her family's brush with shame, she had been saving toward the day when she would be buried gloriously. But her former lawyer went to court and challenged the will, and Miss Keziah remained in that lot next to her father on Eastern Slope.

As those wishes indicate, white lay everywhere at a good funeral as a sign of purity and God's blessing. Lilies, white roses, and white carnations were placed on caskets or displayed in arrangements called "set pieces," portraying crosses, doves, or other inspiring objects. The corpse might be dressed in white, and placed on white sheets in the casket, which might be borne to the cemetery in a white hearse. As tokens of the family's appreciation, white linen scarves, gloves, or rings were presented to the pallbearers, the clergymen, the family doctor, the executors, and other participants to wear during the service and the procession to the grave. When the deceased was wealthy or especially notable, the scarf might be replaced by a six- to nine-foot white sash made of the best Holland linen and worn across the shoulders. Mourners were expected to "go about the streets," wearing the white sash on the day of the funeral and at church the next Sunday. In the case

White was visible somewhere at most funerals, at minimum in scarves and flowers but often throughout, as at this home laying-out.

of the passing of a prominent person, there might be special ribbons or badges to wear.

White was especially called for during the most dreaded funeral of them all, which was that of a child. A popular sentimental poet of the antebellum period, Felicia Hemans, instructed everyone to bring white flowers to spread over the graves of children: "Bring flowers, pale flowers, o'er the bier to shed, / A crown for the brow of the early dead!"

White clothes might even be worn to the funeral itself (for example, by the female attendants at Abraham Lincoln's funeral at Springfield, Illinois), but mourning clothes were black. Only unusually insensitive family members did not wear bands made of black-dyed bombazine—a blend of silk and cotton or worsted—on their hats and arms for several weeks, even months. The conviction that there must be a long formal period of mourning was absolute. Hamlet criticized his mother not just for marrying her brother-in-law, but for doing it after her husband was "but two months dead." In America and Britain, mourning could be a lengthy ritual broken into two segments, the mandatory eighteen- to twenty-one-month period of "deep mourning" followed by a short period of "half-mourning" when the family gradually reentered normal secular life, and could put away their bombazine in anticipation of the next funeral.

Professionalizing the Funeral

In the early nineteenth century, the only people who were compensated for helping out with a typical funeral usually were the clergyman, the church sexton who dug the grave, and the local undertaker—a barber or carpenter who sold coffins on the side and had an arrangement with a stable to provide a hearse. Quick, simple, and dignified was the rule. American death was changed forever in the 1860s with the introduction of embalming. Before then, the funeral and burial had to be held fast before decomposition set in. Undertakers and cabinet-makers (often the same individuals) experimented with special coffins. The "corpse preserver," involving a wooden coffin and a lot of ice, appeared in York, Pennsylvania, in 1847 and was said to preserve a body for eight days "with scant appearance of decomposition." Somewhat higher tech was the Fisk Air-Tight Coffin, developed in 1848 by Almond D. Fisk and William Raymond and manufactured in Newtown, Queens. Custom-built to fit around the deceased, it was made of cast iron and featured an arrangement for pumping out air.

Such experiments were soon outdated by modern embalming. Although the practice dated to the Egyptians, the technique of preserving a corpse by replacing blood with a chemical was not well regarded in America until Dr. Thomas Holmes introduced a new method that he claimed used no arsenic or other poisonous chemicals. He was shading the truth; not until formaldehyde began to be used in 1868 could that claim be made accurately. But Holmes inspired sufficient confidence that when the Civil War began, thousands of army enlistees purchased insurance policies guaranteeing that should they die on the battlefield, they would be embalmed and sent home to their families with a natural appearance. Holmes and other embalmers stood ready at battlefield hospitals. There were reports of fraud, but what won most Americans over to embalming was the twenty-day funeral procession of Lincoln's open coffin before more than 100,000 mourners.

The relatively simple job of the part-time undertaker evolved into that of the full-time funeral director. A leading Brooklyn funeral director of the late 1800s, John Schlitz, started out running a livery stable, but after some training in embalming he was Doctor Schlitz. He managed all the arrangements of the corpse and the funeral, and provided the horse-drawn hearse and car-

riages from his Williamsburg livery stables, Tally-Ho Coaches, that were otherwise busy taking people on excursions. According to an invoice in the Evergreens archives, in 1895 Schlitz charged $4.50 to transport two coffins to the Evergreens, $7.00 to carry three.

When a trade is transformed into a profession, the language takes on dignity, the rules become elaborate, and specialization reigns. Coffins were "caskets," states imposed stringent licensing requirements, professional associations formed, practitioners received academic-style training, and alternative methods of burial were debated. On December 6, 1876, F. Julius LeMoyne, an anthropologist and social reformer, supervised America's first cremation in the crematory he had built in Washington, Pennsylvania. His chief arguments in favor of cremation were that it eliminated most of the risk of contaminating drinking water while costing less and taking up less space than traditional burial. Although cremation is an ancient method for disposal of the dead, there was considerable opposition to it by the Roman Catholic Church and other religious organizations. (It did not help LeMoyne's cause that his first choice for a site was the town's old place of execution, Hangman's Hill.) Over the next twenty-five years, LeMoyne's crematory was used only forty-two times, in each case for friends or members of his family (and for LeMoyne himself). Until the 1960s, cremains—the remains after cremation—were involved in fewer than 4 percent of all burials. Lately, cremation has become more popular as cemeteries filled up and as families dispersed and, therefore, were more concerned about the portability of remains. In 2000, 27 percent of burials involved cremations.

The role of the clergyman changed with the management of funerals. In 1896 several prominent Brooklyn Protestant pastors who were concerned about overwork and their health staged an organized letter-writing campaign against Sunday and multiday funerals, and protested the assumption that they would always conduct graveside burial services regardless of the weather. There was widespread dismay. One supporter

of the old tradition observed, "Time was, years ago, when in city or country, a funeral would not be regarded as a funeral if the clergyman did not go to the cemetery." Another pastor who refused to support the change went further: "The minister christens us, he marries us, and surely it is not too much to ask him to bury us. If he can be with us in a time of joy, surely we need him more on an occasion of sorrow." All that may have been true, but modern life and death were rapidly becoming more complicated and more demanding.

The Tragedy and Romance of Suicide

The custom of the home funeral was followed even in the most wrenching case, the suicide. At a time when the suicide rate was high, such attention was appreciated by families, and also by observers pained by the events. In 1883, in the parlor of his parents' apartment, a mentally disturbed clergyman named James Kemlo slit his wife's throat with a carving knife and then threw himself out the window onto the sidewalk four stories below. Two days after the gruesome murder-suicide, the family held a Christian funeral service in the same parlor whose rugs and walls had been covered with Mrs. Kemlo's blood. The two were carried to the Evergreens and buried in the Mount Magnolia section employing the common practice of turning a single grave into a family plot by placing one casket above the other. The only unusual feature noted by the newspapers was the absence of floral displays in the parlor.

It was a relatively new idea that suicides were owed a tender public burial alongside people who had died natural deaths. Until the nineteenth century, they were barred from burial in sanctified ground, and families felt

As one of artist Charles Dana Gibson's fashionable "Gibson Girls" proves, mourning could be stylish (despite those nasty birds of prey).

such shame that interments often were secretive in remote burial grounds or potter's fields (Judas Iscariot was a suicide). Some suicides were buried at road intersections near signs warning passersby against following their example. By the 1830s the living were more forgiving if not of suicide itself, at least of the feelings of the family and friends. As public funerals of suicides became more common, even an old traditionalist like John Pintard, who had complained so bitterly about the removal of his ancestors' remains from the cemetery of the French Church, realized he could not condemn the new practice. "Such mistaken motives ought not however prevent doing what is right" was his rule.

This tolerance only increased in the nineteenth century. It may have been a pragmatic adaptation to the fact that at no other time in American history were suicides more frequent and more noticed than in the late 1800s. In 1897 the *Eagle* ran a headline, "An Epidemic of Suicide." Given what is now known about waves of copycat suicides, the word "epidemic" not only was appropriate but suggests one reason why there was so much more self-destruction a century and more ago than there is now. In 2006 in New York City, the suicide rate was 5.7 per 100,000. But for the period 1892–1902, the average annual rate in Brooklyn was 17.13 per 100,000, while the one for Manhattan and the Bronx (which then comprised the City of New York) was 21.6 per 100,000. While the national rate then was just 3.5 suicides per 100,000, the average rate for the fifty largest cities was 16.3 per 100,000. All urban America, in fact, was suffering a suicide epidemic.

The compiler of these data, Frederick L. Hoffman, an actuary at the Prudential Insurance Company, made the breakthrough observation that the stress of a wildly

HICKORY KNOLL, AN OLD RESIDENT

unstable culture was the main cause of suicide. A large number of lonely, al-but-destitute people—men, mostly—roamed the country as vagrants, going from boardinghouse to boardinghouse in a constant search for work, unprotected by government social services. The problem of self-destructive itinerant people was so serious that the Salvation Army established an antisuicide bureau in 1905. But Hoffman revealed that the problem lay not only with the poor. The rich and the middle class were affected by frequent financial crashes, easy availability of alcohol and guns, and society's minimal understanding of how to treat depression. (Hoffman also pioneered in finding links between cancer and smoking, asbestos, and industrial dust, and was a founder of the American Cancer Society.)

To these burdens on troubled hearts, add the lurid interest of sensational newspapers relentlessly fascinated by incidents of self-destruction, some of which they even romanticized. One type of suicide received more than special notice. This was the one referred to in a headline that ran almost every year in the *Times* or *Eagle* between 1870 and 1900: "Suicide in a Cemetery." Today few suicides occur in cemeteries, but a century or more ago, when a cemetery made it into a newspaper headline, it was very likely because some poor soul had done away with him- or herself on the grounds. "Suicides in Cemeteries: They are Strikingly Frequent in and around Brooklyn," ran the headline over an *Eagle* story in 1893. Of course there was plenty of speculation as to why someone would choose a burial ground as a site for self-destruction. The *Eagle* writer suggested that people who were "suicidally disposed" wanted "the most congenial surroundings for terminating a tiresome existence." If by that the reporter meant a

The intense sentimentality and widespread personal engagement of mourning affected everything from clothes (like this Victorian era half-mourning costume) to attitudes about suicide to the choice of cemetery monuments.

place that mirrored the person's feelings, agreement can be found in the depressed English poet William Cowper's description of himself as "in a fleshly tomb" and "Buried above ground."

Many cemetery suicides occurred near or on the graves of loved ones. Walking through the grounds one hot July day in 1874, Evergreens President William A. Cummings came upon a distinguished-looking middle-aged man sitting on a bench near a grave and appearing to be taking a nap, with his head on the ivory handle of his cane. Worried that he might suffer sun stroke, Cummings approached him and noticed an empty glass and a phial of sulphuric acid on the bench. It seemed the man had committed suicide while looking down at the grave of his mother. A writer commenting on this incident described it as a "sentimental suicide."

It seemed also that some people wanted to be sure to die in attractive places where they know they would be cared for in a way that, in life, they had been unable to care for themselves. In 1890 a thirty-three-year-old German immigrant came to America hoping for a new life but was unable to obtain permanent work. Without money, shamed by the thought of returning home or accepting assistance, she became depressed and spoke vaguely of doing herself in. An acquaintance heard her say that she had visited the Evergreens and found it "a nice place." She did not know what that meant until a few days later, when the poor woman shot herself on the Green Hills. The best thing anyone could do for Ida Niedmann was to bury her where she last was happy, at the Evergreens.

SILVER CORD, LATE
SUMMER HYDRANGEAS

CHAPTER THIRTEEN

ANGELS BESIDE THE TOMB: MONUMENTS GRAND AND HUMBLE

I N 1873 PRESIDENT William A. Cummings informed the cemetery's Board of Trustees that the Evergreens was about to develop "one of our choicest lots," Hickory Knoll, into the cemetery's crown jewel for "first-class buyers to secure a plot which will gratify the most fastidious taste." With their large size, variety of images, and the recurring Gothic Revival architecture style mirroring the look of the chapel a short walk away, the monuments that were put up on this hill over the next fifty years more than satisfied that expectation. As an authority on cemetery monuments, Dr. Richard Welch has said about Hickory Knoll, "Featuring design elements adapted from archways, cathedral windows, cutaway domes, and spires of the late medieval period, these funerary monuments are at once individual yet typical of the type of funerary architecture favored by the upper and upper middle classes in the late Victorian period."

PAGE 184,
HICKORY
KNOLL

LEFT,
ANGEL
RISING

Other than a Gothic appearance, what most Hickory Knoll monuments have in common is that they are imposing. Tall, wide, or bulky, they offer a grand feast for the eye that can be called Victorian. As an observant student of cemeteries, Robert Woods has written, "The nineteenth was the century in which the dead were glorified. It was the age of dramatic obsequies, of the cult of remembrance and of pilgrimages to graves collected together in new urban cemeteries, the great 'cities of the dead.'" But setting aside their size, these monuments strangely have little else in common because their imagery is so varied. A few are overtly religious with images of Jesus, Mary, or crosses, but the others are only vaguely spiritual, employing different symbolic language. One popular theme on Hickory Knoll and throughout the Evergreens is, in fact, almost secular—the branchless log, called a "stump stone," representing a life cut short. Another frequent symbol is the partially draped urn. As Douglas Keister explains in his guide to cemetery iconography, *Stories in Stone*, this is a universally understood, comforting symbol of the transition from life to the afterlife presented in the classical style that pleased the typical Victorian-era American. The partial drape shows communication between the dead and the living in a kinder, gentler way than the old, harsh, chiding death's-head-and-skeleton motif, in which the deceased warns onlookers that they, too, must die.

But for all the draped urns on Hickory Knoll, there is another figure that dominates the older sections of the Evergreens. This is the angel, that beautiful intermediary between God and humanity that suddenly became popular in America around the time the Evergreens was founded. "What sign could be given so assuring as the very presence of an angel?" asked the contemporary preacher Henry Ward Beecher, and in 1867 another religious leader, Philips Brooks, promised in his Christmas carol, "O Little Town of Bethlehem," that "While mortals sleep, the angels keep / Their watch of wondering love." In 2007 Rowan Williams, the Archbishop of Canterbury, characterized the symbol of the angel as "at the very

The archangel Gabriel sounds the divine message. The angels that became popular in Protestant cemeteries took several forms, all offering comfort to mourners from beyond the grave.

least a sort of shorthand description of everything that's 'round the corner' of our perception and understanding in the universe"—the universe itself being a place of "an overwhelming abundance of variety and strangeness." The angel offers glorious hope in response to our longing for transcendence and immortality, or what the Roman Catholic theologian Charles Taylor calls "the yearning for eternity." We hope that meaning does not end with death. The angel offers that hope as it serves as a messenger from eternity, mediating between the living and the dead.

Angels first burst forth in America in the mid-1800s, when they began appearing in rural cemeteries. According to Elisabeth L. Roark, a scholar of cemeteries

writing in 2007 in *Markers*, the annual journal of the Association of Gravestone Studies, there are as many as eight styles of cemetery angels. Some are triumphant archangels, others tiny putti. They may kneel in prayer or blow trumpets, stand quiet guard over the souls of the dead or transport those souls to heaven, or record their arrival there in the book of life. And—in a motif seen widely at the Evergreens—angels may demonstrate their concern for the dead and mourners by gazing or pointing either aloft to show the heavenly destination, or down at the grave to console the living with the implicit promise, "I care." While angels can be male or androgynous, most of them in rural cemeteries are vaguely feminine; this was the time when the cleaning of the body and other funeral preparations were conducted by women. All angels serve a dual function that Roark ascribed to every cemetery angel, which is to articulate "the hope for eternal life" and help "the bereaved negotiate death." The kindly angel has its wings unfurled and is prepared to fly the soul to heaven, transforming it from an earthly life to a higher life. To quote a popular headstone epitaph of the period, "Immortal hope dispels the gloom; / An angel sits beside the tomb."

Here we have a paradox. Although Protestants historically regarded angels as idolatrous symbols of Roman Catholicism, in the 1850s Protestants were putting up angels by the thousands. The arrival of Italian stone masons in America during the great trans-Atlantic migration may have played a part, but, according to Roark, American families were desperate for a kindly but certain indication of a transformation to heavenly rest. "The angels that filled rural cemeteries in the sec-

Some inscriptions are little more than attacks from the grave. These two young men were killed by machines, and their parents wanted everybody to know it.

ond half of the nineteenth century were not erected to teach history lessons. Instead, an angel monument was a dynamic presence that attended to visitors' emotional needs, revealing a shift in the meaning and function of cemeteries." Thus it was that the angel joined the rural cemetery's role as a park to provide personal renewal to mourners.

The Monument as Accusation

Not all monuments express an angel's gentleness. A few stand as permanent indictments of the individuals, organizations, and forces that brought about the deaths of the people they memorialize. While inept doctors and caretakers were usually let off the hook before 1900, careless handlers of heavy machinery were not always so lucky. On one of the monuments on Hickory Knoll where an angel is absent, an elegantly attired, handsomely mustachioed young man gazes down sadly. The inscription tells us that on November 21, 1888, John J. Mulligan's "bright young life was sadly ended by a rail road train in Orange, New Jersey." We are then informed exactly how old he was when his life was cut off, perhaps by an incompetent engineer, maybe by a drunken crossing guard: "Aged 24 Years, 1 Month & 13 Days." This extreme meticulousness of the record makes the family's anger painfully clear, deepening the pathos of the poem at the bottom of the monument that ends, "A place is vacant in our home / That never can be filled."

A similar sense of rage is expressed on a simple headstone in a low-cost section along a fence in the Evergreens' Mt. Pisgah section:

Henry Havemeyer
Born July 14, 1877
Killed Feb. 7, 1895
By a Trolly Car In
Brooklyn

The spelling of "trolly" may be off, but the bitterness of the message is obvious.

Even at their slow speeds, the electric trolley cars that were introduced to Brooklyn during the summer of 1892 were potentially dangerous. The reason is suggested by their nickname, "street cars." They ran on tracks down the middle of busy thoroughfares filled with pedestrians and horse-drawn wagons. In their first three years of operation, since 1892, Brooklyn's electric trolleys were involved in a total of one hundred four fatalities. Number ninety-seven was seventeen-year-old Henry Havemeyer, an assistant to a coal salesman.

Brooklyn's transit workers were on strike. For three weeks during the deep winter of 1895, the city's trams were in the hands of hardly competent motormen recruited from the police force. Strikers and their sympathizers meanwhile were rioting in the streets. In the middle of a blizzard on February 7, young Henry Havemeyer was sitting on a barrel in the back of a horse-drawn coal wagon slowly making its way up the middle of snowy Myrtle Avenue toward Queens, followed closely by a trolley whose motorman was yelling for the wagon to get out of his way. When the wagonman tugged the reins to the side, the horse veered but a wheel became stuck in the tracks. The

The fantastic Miller monument on Hickory Knoll elaborately combines children, dragons, and Greek mythology.

wagon lurched, throwing Havemeyer under the tram car, which dragged him for half a block, nearly cutting his body in half. Horrified pedestrians gathered around, shouting, "Kill the motorman! Lynch him." Only after a policeman pulled out his revolver and reinforcements were called was the boy's mangled corpse extracted from the wheels.

When the police inexplicably ruled his horrible death an accident, Havemeyer's family's only recourse was to have the stone mason carve their bitter complaint on their boy's headstone.

Christopher Miller's Dragons

Other than with those two obvious expressions of rage, anybody hoping to psychoanalyze people through their cemetery monuments is asking for difficulties. Take, for example, the Roeder sandstone castle in Verdant Slope. At first glance this seems to be sure evidence of a grandiose personality, yet it was built by a modest clergyman, the Reverend Charles W. Roeder, a member of an old Dutch family who was rector of the Flatlands Dutch Reform Church for thirty-three years. Was the good pastor a secret Napoleon?

Stranger still is the Miller monument on Hickory Knoll. If Douglas Keister is correct in saying, "Dead men may tell no tales, but their tombstones do," the tale that Christopher Miller and his wife, Elizabeth, were attempting to tell awaits clarification. A prominent figure in the Eastern District of Brooklyn (meaning Williamsburg or Bushwick), Miller had the means to finance the construction of this monument at a cost reported as $18,000 ($380,000 in 2007). The most prominent features are a large marble plinth said to weigh several tons, the face of a goateed man, and, on high, a statue of a sad-eyed woman holding a wreath. The man must be Miller; the woman a goddess who will coronate him as he rises to Mount Olympus. The monument is more fanciful near ground level. Standing on the base are statues of two charming children, perhaps Miller's own, and at their feet are—amazingly—four dragon heads, the only dragons at the Evergreens.

The Strange Guild Vault

The most confounding monument at the Evergreens is the William H. Guild vault on Hickory Knoll. Round, metal, and gray, it boasts only one decorative feature— an urn at its peak decorated with the head of a cheerful King Neptune. Its only other charm is the dual mystery of its origins and the man who created it and is buried there with his family, including the photographer we met in Chapter 10. Guild came down from Connecticut in around 1840 and co-founded Guild & Garrison, a successful manufacturer of steam pumps for the high-pressure boilers in many steamships that were built in Brooklyn's Wallabout area and repaired at the Brooklyn Navy Yard, adjacent to Guild's factory. Guild remained active into his old age, taking out a patent on a new injection condenser in his seventieth year. When his wife died in 1878, he had his unusual tomb constructed. Around that time he was swept up in a delayed mid-life crisis that brought him even more notoriety than this strange burial vault that has been mystifying visitors to the Evergreens for one hundred thirty years

The inspiration for the vault has long been in dispute. The most intriguing idea is that Guild chose to be entombed in a gun turret like the one on the famous *Monitor*, the ironclad warship built in 1862. Designed by John Ericsson, a Swede, the hull was built by the Continental Iron Works, in Brooklyn, and the turret was constructed by the area's largest and most advanced ironworks, Novelty Iron Works, on the Manhattan side of the East River. Twenty feet in diameter and nine high, the turret was armed with two seven-ton guns and pro-

tected by eight layers of one-inch iron plate riveted together. In the first fight between two ironclads, on March 9, 1862 the *Monitor* and the larger Confederate ironclad *Virginia* (formerly *Merrimac*) fought to a draw in Hampton Roads, at the mouth of the Chesapeake Bay, as Brooklyn's Williamsburg Regiment—the Twentieth Regiment, New York State Volunteer Infantry—looked on from the mainland. Many *Monitor* sisterships and close cousins were later built, several for the Peruvian navy under the supervision of Charles R. Flint, the longtime Evergreens Cemetery trustee.

As tempting as it is to link Flint, the Evergreens, the *Monitor*, and William H. Guild in a way that makes it inevitable that his tomb was modeled after a gun turret, there simply are too many problems to support that conclusion. The vault is sixteen feet in diameter, not a turret's twenty, and it is welded, not riveted. There are no holes for gun ports. A turret was flat-topped, but the vault's lid is similar to the one on a boiler as it curves gracefully up to Neptune's smiling face. And then there is this question: When plenty of boilers were available, why would a man who spent his life in the boiler business haul an armored turret several miles inland to serve as his last resting place?

True, Guild could be a little irrational. A year after he commissioned the vault, on July 28, 1879, a newspaper editor named Amos B. Stillman and his eighteen-year-old daughter, Rosa, spent the morning enjoying themselves at Coney Island. Back home in Williamsburg, they walked down to the ferry wharf, where Stillman boarded a boat for Manhattan as Rosa waved a good-bye before going shopping. Or so her father thought. She did not return home that night. After a frantic search, Stillman and his wife learned that Rosa and seventy-year-old William H. Guild had been married in a local church and were on their way to Ireland by steamship.

The honeymoon proved unsatisfactory. As soon as the couple reached Ireland, they booked return passage, and on arriving back in New York, Guild put his wife into a carriage to Williamsburg, promising to see her

later, and boarded a train across the country to San Francisco. There he initiated divorce proceedings and married another woman. Rosa went to court in New York to have the California divorce declared a fraud, file for a legal divorce, and sue Guild for damages to her reputation. Amid all the court cases, William H. Guild dropped dead and was buried inside his vault.

Captain Woolsey at the Helm

The entertaining story of William H. Guild brings up the subject of maritime history at the Evergreens. Given New York's stature as a seaport, a big local cemetery inevitably has a salt-water connection, though it often is vague because sailors' lives can be undocumented. Lost in time are the stories of the thousands of merchant seamen buried in the Seaman's Grounds. The same can be said about the brothers John H. Foote and James C. Foote. Their headstones report that they sailed as seamen with Commodore Matthew C. Perry on the famous voyage to Japan in 1853 that (to quote one of the epitaphs) "opened the closed doors to that empire." What did these two young men do on the voyage? What did they see in Japan? What memories did they have of Perry and his imposing black sidewheel steam frigate *Mississippi*? None of that is known.

Much more is known about the two Sandy Hook pilots buried at the Evergreens. Ever since New York began appointing pilots in 1694, they have served a number of vital jobs. Most recently, after the attacks of September 11, 2001, the Sandy Hook pilots were charged by the Homeland Security Department to keep track of all boats and ships in New York City's waters. But the primary job of a Sandy Hook pilot has always been to sail out into the Atlantic, board ships, and guide them through the harbor's narrow, shallow, twisting channels. Eighteen pilot schooners were lost off New York before 1858, some run down by other vessels and others wrecked on the shore. This risky trade demanded a special sort of man. The pilots comported themselves with the dignity of naval commodores, and were treated with commensurate respect.

HICKORY KNOLL,
GUILD TOMB

Some symbols are combined, like the cross and a stump stone indicating a life cut short.

James J. Wilkie, a Sandy Hook pilot for thirty-five years before he was laid to rest at the Evergreens, was described as "the personification of the bluff, honest sailor." In 1846 he served as first mate on the first pilot boat to make a trans-Atlantic voyage, the *W. J. Romer*, when she sailed in February to Ireland, reportedly to retrieve an escaped criminal. After a stormy passage, Wilkie was confronted by Irishmen insisting that, out of respect to their hosts, the ship not fly United States colors. Wilkie's defiant and decisive "No!" made him a hero back home.

The character of the other Evergreens pilot is made even clearer on his memorial, which portrays him at work at a sailing ship's wheel. Captain Charles H. Woolsey stands in all his stolid commanding glory, his hands on the spokes. Lower is a spot-on image of a classic New York pilot schooner looking exactly like the great racing yacht that the breed inspired, the New York Yacht Club's yacht *America*, the vessel for which the America's Cup is named. Woolsey was born in 1823 up the Hudson near West Point and got his first taste of the salt water in a whaling ship. After a spell as a crewmember in the lightship anchored out in the ocean off Sandy Hook, New Jersey, near the mouth of New York Bay, he was licensed to join the Sandy Hook pilots and became the longtime captain of the pilot boat *Fannie*.

Woolsey died of heart disease in 1884. Perhaps he chose to be buried at the Evergreens because the tall Seaman's Monument beacon on Howard Point had served him as a navigational aid on stormy days, or maybe he wanted to be buried near his Williamsburg home. Whatever his reasons for being interred at the Evergreens, he commissioned one of the cemetery's most striking structures—a statue of himself so lifelike that it displays his pinkie ring.

The statue was cast in zinc (also called white bronze) by the Monumental Bronze Company of Bridgeport, Connecticut, a famous manufacturer of cemetery monuments and statues. Monumental Bronze's statues of Civil War soldiers stand in town squares across thirty-one states. Monument authority Richard Welch described the Woolsey memorial as one of Monument Bronze's "most exceptional examples of funerary art." Any gravemarker is expected to show the deceased at his or her best, but Captain Woolsey's presents an unusually vibrant drama. The representation is so realistic that visitors could not keep their hands off it. By 1894 it carried a "no trespassing" sign, with limited effect. Toy boats and Mason jars full of sand and

A beacon for sailors for more than a century (see page 14), the Seaman's Monument may have attracted two pilot captains to the Evergreens.

seawater have been found at the good captain's feet. Someone made off with one of his fingers and a steering wheel spoke.

As appealing as it is, Captain Woolsey's tomb is incomplete. There are three sarcophagi alongside the captain at the wheel, but only two are filled. He is there, and also his wife, but not their only child. Elizabeth Woolsey was a performer who called herself Lillie Weston and took on the nickname of "The Musical Wonder" when she went on the vaudeville circuit with her act, which was playing many musical instruments simultaneously. Apparently, she never returned home.

Louis Mathot's Secret

The graves of Civil War veterans range from simple to elaborate. The large sandstone vault structure of the Story family in the Sumachs section is marked with a large badge of the Lafayette Post of the Grand Army of the Republic. Joseph G. Story, a Civil War veteran, was a high officer in the New York National Guard at the time of its greatest prestige, when regimental armories were built in New York and Brooklyn. When he served in the guard's summer camp during the Spanish-American War, the *Eagle* called him "the hardest working man in camp. . . . Everything that comes into camp, from the blankets that cover the servants to the ammunition fired from the guns, goes through his hands." Story retired with the rank of major general. Among others buried in the tomb are Story's father-in-law, Henry P. Freeman, a prominent executive of the Williamsburg Savings Bank, and Seth Crosby, of whom little is known except that he lived in Brooklyn and probably was related to Story.

Less easy to find are two veterans' graves with government standard–issue headstones, on the back side of

MT. GRACE, CAPTAIN
WOOLSEY MONUMENT

CAPTAIN CHARLES H. WOOLSEY.
SANDY HOOK PILOT, DIED APR. 3, 1884.

Hickory Knoll. What is odd is that one of them marks the last resting place of one of the best known men in New York, Louis Mathot. Beside him lies his son, Guy V. Mathot. As close as these two men lie in death, in life they followed very—even tragically—different paths.

In the very many interviews that Louis Mathot gave over his ninety-three-year lifetime, he told a number of fascinating tales. He said he was born in Belgium in a well-to-do military family, traveled around Egypt and Asia Minor until he was mugged in Alexandria, hitched a ride home in a small sailboat, and eventually emigrated in 1863 to New York. There, standing on the wharf and knowing just one word of English (it was "yes"), he promptly joined an independent volunteer battalion that had been raised in New York by French speakers and was called *Les Enfants Perdu* (the lost children). It is much easier to document the fact that he later transferred to a regiment of mounted infantry and saw important service in Florida under General Guy V. Henry, a Medal of Honor winner, doing well enough to be one of the many Union Army officers with honorable records who were awarded an end-of-war honorary promotion, called a brevet—in Mathot's case, to captain. Not so easy to believe and verify is his account that, a few days after the war ended and a few hours before he went to a play at Ford's Theatre, Abraham Lincoln sent for Mathot and called him "Frenchie" (sometimes Mathot's account ended with Lincoln's writing a citation honoring Mathot's courage).

Louis Mathot found his calling when he became a trial lawyer. (In another of the many impossible to confirm claims that he made over his lifetime, he said he was the last French lawyer in the United States.) His specialty was headline-grabbing divorce and personal injury cases. This was a time when the best entertain-

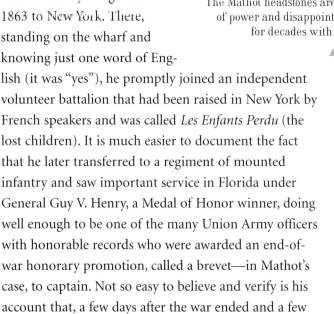

The Mathot headstones are evidence of a curious tale of power and disappointment after being buried for decades with their namesakes.

ment in town took place in courtrooms. Active in the Grand Army of the Republic and a commissioner of education in Queens, he was often seen on reviewing stands at Memorial Day parades. Either a fervent citizen-patriot or a fervent gadfly-busybody, depending on one's perspective, he demanded that an American flag be displayed in every school classroom, that a volunteer cavalry company be organized in Bayside, Queens, that the police prosecute the owners of automobiles with loud engines, and that the city place under arrest the officers of any golf club that did not cease and desist from inducing truancy by hiring boys as caddies.

Louis Mathot had three sons by two wives. The oldest, his father's true son, was William L. Mathot, a Deputy Police Commissioner in the very early 1900s. The *Times* once called William "the legal luminary of the Commissioner's office" for (among other reasons) personally leading raids on gambling parlors. He made more headlines in 1906 when he prosecuted the opera star Enrico Caruso for flirting with a woman in the monkey house at the Central Park Zoo. Caruso was fined $10, and the Metropolitan Opera adjusted its schedule so that his first role after his arrest would not be as the seducer in *La Bohème*. William Mathot proceeded to call Caruso "a Man of Misfit Morals" and announce that many similar prosecutions of famous people—none of whom he named—had been hushed up by bribes to police officers. Such behavior has helped some prosecutors get elected to high office (even mayor), but all William Mathot got was fired.

When William died of tuberculosis at the age of thirty-six, Louis Mathot was left with two much younger and very different sons from his second marriage. Louis Jr. seems to have left no traces, which means he avoided trouble. Not so his brother Guy. Named for his father's Civil War general, he served as a private in a support unit in World War I. After the war, he became a bootlegger, and at one point served time in prison for attempting to bribe a policeman. The misfit son and do-right father are buried side by side on Hickory Knoll under government-issue soldiers' headstones. Louis Mathot died first, in 1929, and had a military funeral, with an honor guard firing blanks over his grave. Six years later Guy was buried beside him with less ceremony, and then, in accordance with his father's instructions, the two headstones were covered over with six inches of Green Hills dirt. Sixty years later, a landscaper's shovel hit one of the headstones. The soil was cleared, the markers were put back upright, and the Mathots were back in the world once again.

The Diehl name is on two sections at the Evergreens, and also on this Civil War coin and advertisement.

John Diehl's Coin

Scattered throughout the Evergreens are many identifiable ethnic sections. The largest and most visible, of course, are the half-dozen areas for Chinese on south-facing down slopes of hills. But there also are sections for Czechs on Mt. Magnolia, Norwegians on Mt. Lebanon, Swedes at Holly Dell, and African Americans at Cedar Vale. Among the group plots are intriguing individual monuments, for example, the large plot and obelisk at Lake View for Joseph Gressak, a Hungarian-born jeweler in Brooklyn who left home after the failed revolutions of the 1840s. Here is the inscription:

> *Exiled thou wert from the fair Magyar home,*
> *From parents, kindred, friends compelled to roam*
> *In death alone was grace vouchsafed to thee*
> *Since freedom's thy burial shroud should be.*

The ethnic groups looked after their own. Some families and groups came to the Evergreens because they had a trusting relationship with an undertaker or a funeral director who, in turn, had a relationship with the cemetery. There were many undertakers to choose from—one hundred thirty-eight in Manhattan and Brooklyn in 1858, and, almost forty years later, five hundred eighty in 1897—yet despite the enormous number of recently arrived Germans, Irish, and Scandinavians, more than three-fourths of these establishments were owned by undertakers with English names. A small number of ethnic funeral homes, therefore, had great influence among immigrants, who naturally looked out for one another individually and also through their institutions. Scandinavians first came to Brooklyn in the 1820s and then arrived in large numbers after the Civil War to settle in or near Bay Ridge, Sunset Park, and the Gowanus area. There were Lutheran churches and benevolent associations, like the Swedish Vasa Clubs, and also Scandinavian undertakers, like the Edward C. Halvorsen Funeral Home, which reserved a lot in the Evergreens' Holly Dell section that came to be called "Halvorsen row" for all the Olsens, Svendsens, and Christensens buried there.

The many thousands of German immigrants who flooded into New York and Brooklyn were no different. After Julius Rensch was clubbed to death during an altercation with a policeman outside a beer garden on New Year's Day 1885, the funeral was held in the lodge of one German fraternal organization, with choral settings sung by members of another lodge. His employer, a German-American contractor named John Rueger, followed the hearse to the Evergreens at the head of a march of two hundred of his employees and three hundred other German-Americans. (Rueger himself would be buried at the Evergreens under a fine monument on the eastern slope of fashionable Hickory Knoll.)

Had Julius Rensch lived in Manhattan the undertaker in charge of his funeral probably would have been John J. Diehl. The funeral home that Diehl established at

133 Essex Street in 1844, soon after arriving from Germany, became so important to the Evergreens under his and his son's management that two sections, Diehl's Mound and Diehl's Slope, were reserved for Diehl clients and another area is dominated by the family's monument.

James Sharkey's Dismay

Of necessity, a cemetery had to stay close with its friends. James Sharkey was a monument builder, the president of his profession's trade association, and a figure in Democratic Party politics. As a Roman Catholic, he was buried at Holy Cross Cemetery after his death in 1897, but in a corner of the Evergreens he left behind an imposing but curiously plain monument carrying only one inscription, his last name. All the other panels are empty. The explanation for this silence was that several members of Sharkey's family had died in a fire, leaving this man whose business it was to be florid and expressive so devastated that the only way to memorialize them was without words.

The Death of Children

Take a step, look down, and your heart is broken. One of the first things that careful visitors to a cemetery notice is the children's graves marked with images of tiny angels, little lambs, sleeping babies, and branchless logs, or with an epitaph such as "How Much of Light, how much of joy, / Is buried with a darling boy." The cemetery's initial interment was of a four-year-old boy, and from then on many stillborns and infants were interred in marked individual graves or unmarked common graves. It was a time when whole sets of siblings were wiped out in a few days by whooping cough or other suddenly arising ailments for which doctors had little or no recourse. According to Edwin G. Burrow and Mike Wallace in *Gotham*, New York City's child mortality rate during the 1850s, the Evergreens' first decade, was 50 percent of all children younger than five years, and 70 percent of those younger than two. (Thanks to this devastation of youngsters, in 1856 the city's overall

death rate exceeded its birth rate.) As late as 1896, almost seven out of every ten deaths in metropolitan New York was of a child under the age of five. That year, there were 16,307 deaths of children under the age of one (in 2005 there were seven hundred thirty-one).

To talk seriously about children's graves is to become enmeshed in one of the most controversial issues in the study of cemeteries and death. A generation ago the French historian Philippe Ariès, in *Centuries of Childhood*, *Western Attitudes Toward Death*, and his other books, propounded the theory that from about 1400 to 1800, parents and families did not deeply mourn the loss of their children. The reason for this parental indifference, he said, was that the high rate of that infant and childhood mortality made parents reluctant to invest deep emotional commitments in their offspring. His evidence for what Ariès called the "restraint of emotional outpouring" was limited. The parental indifference hypothesis was subsequently tested and found weak, most recently by Robert Woods in his sweeping study of mourning for children, *Children Remembered: Responses to Untimely Death in the Past*. The fact is that while some dead children were not deeply mourned, most were. After the English poet John Donne and his wife lost three children in the year 1613, Donne wrote this devastating epigram: "By childrens births, and deaths, I am become / So dry, that I am now mine own sad tomb." It is a feeling that a cemetery visitor has no difficulty understanding.

The Newsboy's Grave

The children's deaths that were mourned most publicly and deeply in New York and Brooklyn were those of inner-city boys and girls called "street Arabs," including runaway children working as newsboys in New York and Brooklyn. The problem of the newsboy attracted the attention of the pioneer New York social reformer, Charles Loring Brace, the founder and leader of the Children's Aid Society who created a dormitory exclusively for newsboys and others in the class of youngsters

that he called "poor and vicious children." One newsboy stood out among the others. He was Johnny Morrow, known far and wide simply as "The Newsboy." The lame, abused nine-year-old son of alcoholic parents was making a small living as a street beggar until a pack of dogs drove him to the refuge of Brace's News Boys' Lodging House. When not peddling in the streets, he learned to read, and began to study theology at Union Theological Seminary. In 1860, helped by a ghostwriter, Morrow wrote an autobiography that was published by A. S. Barnes, founder of the Barnes & Nobles empire. Titled *A Voice from the Newsboys*, and written in the intimate, pathos-rich style of *Great Expectations,* the book was endorsed by Henry Ward Beecher and other well-known clergymen, and made Morrow a celebrity. He was said to have donated much of the book's proceeds to other newsboys.

The saddest children's stories were of Johnny Morrow and other homeless newsboys and "street Arabs" who inspired Horatio Alger.

In May 1861 seventeen-year-old Johnny Morrow's stunted leg was operated on. A few days later, while changing his bandages he accidentally opened an artery and bled to death. His martyr's end was confirmed by reports of his last words: "Please send my love to all the friends that love me. If it is God's will, I am ready to die. Only I wish he would take me as quickly." Here was a child that Victorians instinctively loved and idolized with deep and broad sentimentality, another Tiny Tim in what one mourner called his "witching charm." Brace wrote, "A more heroic life, or a more Christian death, we cannot wish for our own beloved little ones."

When Morrow expressed revulsion at the thought that he might end up in a potter's field, his friends made sure he would receive a proper funeral and burial. By coincidence, they occurred on the same day as the massive funeral for New York's first casualty of the Civil War, Colonel Elmer Ellsworth. The only sorry note was that, as the Newsboy's body was being carried to the Evergreens, a rock-throwing brawl broke out between groups of Brooklyn and Manhattan street Arabs.

Johnny Morrow's example and death put newsboys on America's moral map. They often were the heroes of the rags-to-riches novels of Horatio Alger, with their plucky boys working in solidarity and resilience to rise above a world where, as one of his characters says, "A feller has to look sharp in this city, or he'll lose his eye-teeth before he knows it." (The Horatio Alger Society Newsletter is called *The Newsboy*.) It seemed proper that the rites over the remains of Johnny Morrow and Colonel Ellsworth were conducted at the same time. "A hero's funeral, however humble, allowed newsboys to assert their collective and individual identities," observes Vincent DiGirolamo in a study of the importance of newsboy funerals. Only through ritual could the death of one enhance the status of all." Like Strod Putnam, "the Brooklyn Child" who died in the Civil War and is also buried at the Evergreens, Johnny Morrow put a face on American childhood, and not always its cheerful side.

CHAPTER FOURTEEN

WHAT COULD ANYONE DO? BROOKLYN'S DISASTERS

AT THE SOUTHWEST CORNER of the Ever-greens, near the tracks of the L line subway train, there stand a few acres of low-lying, often damp land sloping down from the hills. Much of that property forms the cemetery of Most Holy Trinity Church, an historically German Roman Catholic church in Williamsburg. This small churchyard is distinctive for its many wooden and metal gravemarkers. According to rumor, the land was donated by a local tinsmith with the stipulation that the markers be made of tin or copper, which of course would have benefited him. Unfortunately for this good story, the facts are different. This was the style of gravemarkers in the old country, the priests wanted to avoid a costly competition for largest monument, in any case the land was too damp to support large monuments, and finally, Most Holy Trinity acquired the property from the Evergreens in 1851.

PAGE 204, DIEHL'S SLOPE, LOOKING TOWARD CHURCH HILL

LEFT, SUMACHS, EASTERN DISTRICT FIRE DEPARTMENT MEMORIAL

Some of the adjacent land in the Evergreens is just as soft, which made it unpopular among families wanting to mark graves with large stones or monuments. This area of the Evergreens, therefore, became dedicated primarily to charity burials without markers. Called Pathside, this section was the destination for unidentified remains from the old Wallabout Burial Ground in Williamsburg, and also for the bodies of infants. An adjacent six-acre plot was acquired by the City of Brooklyn in 1859 for use as a potter's field. After Brooklyn was consolidated into New York in 1898, the city neglected the grounds and in time the Evergreens bought it back and renamed it Memory Gardens.

Near Pathside and Memory Gardens are two of the most strikingly simple monuments at the Evergreens. One is a spruce tree, the other a tall slab on which a woman is shown kneeling in despair. Each marks a plot for victims of a terrible New York disaster.

On March 25, 1911, a fire broke out inside the locked exit doors of the Triangle Shirtwaist clothing factory located high in a ten-story building in Greenwich Village. (A woman's shirt or blouse tailored like a man's shirt, the shirtwaist was popular women's clothing at that time.) Within twenty minutes, one hundred forty-six people—most of them Jewish immigrant women—were dead either from the fire or by throwing themselves out windows onto the sidewalks below. The victims of the fire whose remains were not claimed by friends or family were given a funeral attended by an estimated four hundred thousand mourners in a pouring rain, and then buried in several cemeteries. In the Evergreens' burial ledger for 1911, listed on April 5 under "U" (for Unknown) are eight interments (numbered from 214,654 to 214,661). These were an uncertain number of victims of the Triangle Shirtwaist fire who were burned beyond recognition: an "unknown male," six "unknown females," and (most devastating) "several persons" so badly burned that not even their gender could be identified. One of the victims was subsequently identified and her remains were transferred to her family's plot at Mount Zion Cemetery, a Jewish

This moving monument stands in the cemetery's southwest corner, near unidentified victims of the 1911 Triangle Shirtwaist fire.

cemetery. Originally interred elsewhere in the grounds, today the victims of the Triangle Shirtwaist fire at the Evergreens lie under the kneeling woman, a statement both of mourning and of dedication to the safer workplaces that were mandated by state and federal laws after the Triangle Shirtwaist fire.

Near the Triangle Shirtwaist monument, the boughs of a spruce tree arch over the remains of nineteen victims of another early twentieth-century fire, this one in a New York mental hospital at Ward's Island. Now primarily a site of athletic fields under the Triborough Bridge, Ward's Island for many years was the site of almshouses, mental health facilities, and potter's fields, and facilities for processing immigrants. After Ellis Island became the immigration center in 1892, Ward's became the home of the Manhattan State Hospital, which with 4,400 patients was, reportedly, the world's largest psychiatric hospital (among its patients was William Steinitz, the world chess champion featured in Chapter 9). One of the very few of the twenty-seven victims of the Manhattan State Hospital fire of February 18, 1923, who were positively unidentified was a World War I veteran named Peter Tappas, who was being treated for shell shock, today called post-traumatic stress disorder (PTSD). After the funeral at Ward's Island, the remains of Tappas and seventeen unidentified men were taken to the Evergreens for burial. The procession was an extraordinary one: the coffins containing the remains of Tappas and four other men who were believed to be veterans were placed on gun caissons (Tappas' under an American flag) and, escorted by delegations from American Legion posts in Manhattan and the Bronx, carried across the river by boat and then through the streets of Queens and Brooklyn to the Evergreens.

"The whole mass struggled to the doors."
Horrified actors watch helplessly as a small fire
turns into the worst disaster in Brooklyn history.

The Doom That Was Waiting

When two hundred seventy-eight men, women, and children died in a fire that broke out during a performance in a downtown theatre in 1876, it was the worst disaster in Brooklyn's history, in terms of the number of fatalities, and the second worst theatre fire in American history. Considering Brooklyn's strong conservative religious traditions, to even build a theatre there was risky. It took a decade after the Brooklyn Academy of Music opened in 1861 for another big new theatre to be constructed. Adding to its notoriety, Mrs. F. B. Conway's Brooklyn Theatre (named for its owner's wife) was built on formerly sanctified ground, the old site of St. John's Episcopal Church, which had been built in 1826 by the first rector, the Reverend Evan Malbone Johnson (who was related to a founder of the Evergreens), on family property on Johnson Street in Brooklyn Heights. The congregation later moved out, the remains in its churchyard were transferred to the Evergreens' Church Hill, and in 1871 the controversial theatre opened.

Five years later, on December 5, 1876, a crowded house was settling in for the last act of a play with the unintentionally apt title of *The Two Orphans* when a painted canvas backdrop brushed against a lamp and ignited. As the small blaze rapidly spread in full view of the audience, the orchestra and first mezzanine were cleared quickly through nearby exits, but the balcony gallery was not so well blessed, and the spectators were still crowding the aisles as the fire reached them. "The panic that possessed these poor beings is something too intense to be described," reported one newspaper. "The whole mass struggled to the doors, when a huge block occurred. The young and the weak were knocked down and trampled upon, and at the doors the people were literally wedged together." Within two hours the theatre was in ruins, its outer walls caved in. The next morning, two layers of corpses were found on one stairway, many in such a state that they could not be identified. Of the two hundred seventy-eight bodies recovered, one hundred and two were classified "unknown."

"The Holocaust" (as the *Eagle* called the fire) dominated New York in much the same way as the attacks on September 11, 2001. The first stage was the frantic search for the dead, and then came the tears and eulogies in synagogues and churches of all denominations all across metropolitan New York. The program for one of the mass funerals included a poem with these opening lines:

> *Death! Death! Death!*
> *Stifling, terrible death!*
> *That shriveled the body and parched the breath*
> *Until Hell seemed open, and men could see*
> *The doom that was waiting so fearfully. . . .*

The unidentified dead were buried in a common grave at Green-Wood, and more than two dozen identified victims were interred individually in separate sections at the Evergreens, including an eight-year-old and a seventeen-year-old. The Evergreens burial ledger gave their address simply as "Brooklyn Theatre." Despite some popular feeling that the fire was a divine punishment for building a theatre on sanctified ground, the Brooklyn Theatre was rebuilt. It eventually gave way to the offices of the *Brooklyn Eagle*, and after the newspaper folded in 1955, a courthouse was built on the site.

The Firemen: "Worthy of More Honor"

Until just a few years before the Brooklyn Theatre fire, all Kings County firemen were volunteers. When Caret de Beauvois was appointed Brooklyn's first schoolmaster in 1661, he was instructed to serve also as the village's clerk, its chorister, its grave digger, and its bell-ringer, which meant that he sounded the alarm when fires broke out. Brooklyn's first true fire company was organized in 1785. Williamsburg got its first one five decades

later. After the two cities were merged in 1855, the old Williamsburg and Bushwick volunteer companies were renamed the Eastern District section of the Brooklyn Fire Department. It remained a volunteer operation until 1869, when firemen were at last paid.

The risks these men faced before government fire codes were tremendous. According to a history of New York and Brooklyn firefighters, *The Last Alarm*, two hundred uniformed firefighters in the metropolitan area had lost their lives by 1900. (The total in early 2007 was 1,241, including three hundred forty-three on 9/11.) In the 1850s the Evergreens set aside a plot of high land in the Sumachs area for the Eastern District firemen force. Seventy-seven Brooklyn firefighters have been buried there, a few with their wives. The area was landscaped in the curvilinear style characteristic of the Evergreens, with the headstones arranged in a circle in whose center two striking monuments were raised.

One of those monuments memorializes an individual fireman. On January 14, 1880, a fire broke out in one of the large breweries in Bushwick, the Otto Huber Brewery, which had been founded some twenty years earlier by a German immigrant. Engine Company 16 rushed to the blaze and seemed to have it completely under control when, without warning, a brick wall collapsed on six firemen. All survived except William Baldwin, the company's foreman. The funeral was at the South Third Street Methodist Episcopal Church in Williamsburg, with interment in the Eastern District Fire Department plot at the Evergreens. Attending were the fire chief, hundreds of firefighters, Brooklyn's leading political figures, and a large contingent from the press. The services were as somberly formal as the ones for firefighters today. "Uniform overcoat, fatigue cap, and white gloves will be worn," went the order of the day. "Badge, shrouded in crepe, on the left breast." After Baldwin's funeral, the fire department's chiefs decided to honor all Brooklyn firemen with a monument at the Evergreens, the first in a Brooklyn cemetery. On May 24, 1881, thousands of spectators—including two men from each of the borough's companies, all formally dressed in

The Eastern District Fire Department plot stands out in this panoramic photograph
from the 1920s. Now a wooded glen, the plot is even more dramatic.

white gloves and white shirts—gathered at the front gate of the Evergreens and marched into the cemetery's grounds behind a Fire Department band. At the Eastern District plot they halted and stood silently at attention as Brooklyn Mayor James Howell unveiled a white marble statue of Baldwin in uniform, his right hand resting on a fire hydrant. "Fireman Baldwin is counted among the heroes whose monuments are in human hearts," said the clergyman who presided. "When a man does a noble deed, he is never forgotten, but the man who saves human life is worthy of more honor than the mere claim to be a hero."

The markers for deceased firemen have unique designs, some of them chosen by a former Brooklyn Assistant Fire Chief, John W. Smith. One shows the firefighter looking for the best place to direct the hose. In another, the fireman waits patiently for orders, hand on hydrant. A third motif, the most emotional, is the one on the statue that was put up at the other end of the Eastern District Fire Department plot in 1896, showing a firefighter holding a child in one arm with the other upraised in salute. More simple memorials show a fireman's hat resting on a stone. The cost of monuments was largely covered by the firemen themselves, who contributed one cent daily for a year after a fatality.

Bill Anthony and the Fog of War

Among the veterans buried at the Evergreens since the Civil War is one of the best-known figures of the Spanish-American War, the tragic Bill Anthony, who famously sounded the alarm on the *Maine* in Havana Harbor. Anthony's fame was dramatic and tragically

brief, as we will see, but military glory is never assured.

For example, consider the three men at the Evergreens who won the Medal of Honor between 1900 and 1918. Boatswains Mate Edward G. Allen was awarded the country's highest military honor in 1900 for conspicuous bravery in the China Relief Expedition to relieve the siege on foreign embassies during the Boxer Rebellion. Two years later Coxwain Joseph Quick was cited for saving a shipmate from drowning at Yokohama, Japan. The Evergreens' only World War I Medal of Honor winner actually won two of these prestigious awards. On June 6, 1918, an American known as Charles F. Hoffman fought off a dozen Germans armed with five machine guns, killing two of them with his bayonet. Because he was a U. S. Marine temporarily assigned to an army unit, he was presented with two Medals of Honor—one from the navy, and the other from the army. Making the story even more curious, the navy's award went to Ernest A. Janson, which was Hoffman's real name.

Bill Anthony did not win a Medal of Honor, but for a brief time he was one of the most famous men in America, not for what he did during one of the worst of all American military, but for what he said. A former army enlisted man, in February 1898 William Anthony was a forty-five-year-old private in the Marine Corps assigned as a guard on board the battleship *Maine*. With a crew of more than three hundred, she was anchored off Havana, Cuba, as a show of force following anti-American riots. At 9:40 P.M. on February 15, 1898, a violent explosion rocked the ship and the *Maine* began to go down. According to various accounts, Anthony ran to Captain Charles D. Sigsbee, drew himself up to a stance of attention, and (as legend has it) saluted and offered one of the most famous reports in American military history. "Sir!, I have the honor to report that the ship has been blown up and is sinking." The explosion sank the ship and left two hundred sixty-six enlisted men and officers dead or missing.

Now we know that the cause of the explosion was a fire in the ship's coal bunker, but in 1898, many Americans wanted to believe the *Maine* was blown up by the Spanish. Good-hearted churchgoing Americans felt sympathy for Cuban dissidents, and William Randolph Hearst was itchy to recruit readers for his newspapers. Out of this came a declaration of war on Spain, which then controlled Cuba. As "Remember the *Maine*" was shouted in the streets, Bill Anthony was roped into serving as a spokesman for the prowar lobby. In a letter to a newspaper that he signed, he promised a young woman in Chicago, "dear lady, a day of vengeance is near at hand, when the starry banner of freedom will be unfurled on the battlements of El Moro and Cabannas; when American womanhood will greet the return of husbands, sons, or fathers, who went forth to avenge the foul murder of Yankee seamen." Undoubtedly written by a prowar public relations advisor or journalist, this note and the reports of his stoic heroism made Bill Anthony into something he was not all prepared to be—a celebrity. As a wave of frenetic jingoism swept across the country, the navy cooperated fully by giving him leave so he could appear in a patriotic musical spectacular titled "The Red White, and Blue."

War was declared on Spain in April. Its end less than four months later also ended Bill Anthony's career as a

"The Nation's Hero," Bill Anthony survived the sinking of the *Maine* but not the fame that dogged him. He lies in the Seaman's Grounds (opposite).

national hero as the country moved on to other things. Unemployment and marriage to a much younger pregnant woman (who, it seemed, had not quite broken up with her first husband) left him destitute. On November 24, 1899, the man popularly known as Sigsbee's Marine drank a solution of cocaine and soon after died. Once again a celebrity, though in death, Anthony became a pawn in a cynical tug-of-war over who would have the honor of paying for his funeral. (The winner was the boss of Tammany Hall, Richard Coker, who beat out a Philadelphia newspaper.) After a singing of "Rock of Ages" and a recitation of a poem titled "Bill Anthony, Hero," by an elderly actress named "Aunt" Louisa Eldridge, Anthony's remains were carried from the undertaker's to the Evergreens, where he was interred on the slope of a hill overlooking the Seaman's Grounds.

What Americans admired most in Bill Anthony was his coolness under fire. He was cited as a prime example of the advice in Rudyard Kipling's famous poem, "If" ("If you can keep your head when all about you / Are losing theirs and blaming it on you . . ."). But as war fever cooled and skepticism became tolerated once again, people began to wonder out loud if his stories of the sinking of the *Maine* and his almost inhuman self-control were true.

Captain Sigsbee came forward with an account that was even better than the original. "We bumped into each other in the dark," he told the war correspondent Richard Harding Davis, "and if he had saluted and spoken with that formality, he would have been thinking of himself or of making an effect, and not his duty." Sigsbee went on, "What he really said and did is better without any of the additions which came later." At least

SEAMAN'S GROUNDS,
BILL ANTHONY HEADSTONE

THE NATIONS HERO
SERGEANT MAJOR
WILLIAM ANTHONY
DIED NOV. 24, 1899.
AGED 46 YEARS.

"EXCUSE ME SIR-I HAVE TO
REPORT THAT THE SHIP HAS BEEN
BLOWN UP AND IS SINKING."

BILL ANTHONY'S WARNING TO
CAPTAIN SIGSBEE OF THE BATTLE
SHIP MAINE.

this victim of others' agendas was properly mourned. For several years after his grim death, the Mansfield Post of the Grand Army of the Republic came to his grave on Memorial Day and sang patriotic anthems as two members of the post's Women's Relief Corps scattered flowers on poor Bill Anthony's grave.

The *Slocum* Disaster

On a warm mid-June morning in 1904, approximately 1,500 parishioners of St. Mark's German Lutheran Church (the exact number was never known) from the Lower East Side piled aboard the ferry boat *General Slocum* for an excursion up the East River and into Long Island Sound to their annual church picnic on Eaton's Neck, near Huntington, Long Island. As a band played and children danced, Captain William Van Schaick had the paddlewheeler (named for Henry Warner Slocum, a Civil War hero and leading Brooklyn political figure) steam up the river and into Hell Gate. It was there when a tongue of flame from a stove in the bow started a fire that spread into a nearby locker where drinking glasses were packed in hay, and then to several barrels of oil.

A stiff headwind blew the fire toward the stern, and the passengers crowded aft, with little or no attempt by the crew to bring order. People threw themselves over the side into the path of the paddlewheels, and the captain was dangerously incompetent. Back in 1880, the death toll on the burning *Seawanhaka* (as William R. Grace and his wife calmed the passengers) had been limited by her captain's decisive beaching of the ship at the first opportunity. But Van Schaick delayed and delayed, and when the *Slocum* finally grounded at North Brother's Island, the ship was almost entirely consumed, and hundreds of men, women, or children had been drowned or burned or trampled to death. The final death toll was estimated at more than 1,000. Of the eight hundred forty-eight bodies that were found, one hundred thirty-two could not be identified. Corpses that could be found   many burned beyond recognition— were wrapped in blankets provided by the hospitals of Ward's Island and Blackwell's (now Roosevelt) Island,

and then brought by dories and other small craft— "death boats" they were called—to Manhattan wharves, where they were laid out for identification, a procedure that became more dignified once hundreds of hastily constructed pine coffins were delivered to the water-front. Thousands of people desperately crowded into morgues in search of relatives and friends as newspaper reporters and police conducted house-to-house searches—all these efforts handicapped by repeated inconsistencies in translating and spelling German names.

After days of funerals at thirty churches, the burials took place in many cemeteries around the city. Sixty-one of the unidentified dead were buried at Lutheran All Faiths Cemetery in Middle Village, Queens, where a monument was placed in 1912 with the words "Let Us Not Have Died in Vain." The Evergreens buried fifty-eight of the *Slocum*'s victims, all identified, in nineteen sections of the grounds. Twenty-six of the dead were between five months and fifteen years of age; twenty-six were related to at least one other victim.

Billy Lewis and the Malbone Street Wreck

The *Slocum* disaster was one of the many recent examples of the terrible price that must be paid for careless handling of powerful technology. On shore there were numerous fatal accidents involving trains and street-cars, usually with just one or two deaths (as in the case of Henry Havemeyer). But on one day in Brooklyn the devastation was horrific.

On November, 1, 1918, as New Yorkers were struggling with the last stages of the Great War and an epidemic of influenza, the engineers on the Brooklyn Rapid Transit trolley and subway line were out on strike. Among the dispatchers and other desk workers recruited as motormen was a man known as both Billy Lewis and Anthony Lewis, although his real name was Edward Luciano (a secret kept out of fear of prejudice against Italians). Although Lewis had never run a train except in the storage yard during a brief training period, the B. R. T. assigned him to take charge of one on the challenging Brighton Beach line during the crowded evening rush hour. The route ran from Park Row in Manhattan across the Brooklyn Bridge, up Fulton Street on today's A line tracks to Franklin Street, south on the elevated right of way on which the Franklin Avenue Shuttle now runs, and then—dangerously—onto a steep downgrade into a twisting tunnel under Prospect Park. The train had no automatic brakes, and it had to be actively steered. This was a difficult assignment for even an experienced motorman, and tonight Billy Lewis was barely in control. He over-

shot the Sands Street station near the bridge, sped by another station altogether, and instead of turning south at Franklin Avenue, kept on the Fulton Avenue tracks. Correcting that mistake, he backed out. Behind schedule, he gunned the motor and raced on at a high rate of speed that left passengers exchanging nervous glances.

Hearses lined the city's streets, carrying remains of victims of the *Slocum* horror to cemeteries throughout the city.

Then came the downgrade approaching the Prospect Park station near the Botanic Garden. The posted speed limit was 6 miles per hour. The train reportedly was doing at least 30 as it entered the S-turns under Malbone Street. The second and third cars, both wooden, flew off the tracks, sideswiped a concrete wall, and smashed into a mass of splinters and broken bodies. People said the crash could be heard a mile away. The survivors were slowly extracted from the wreckage and carried to nearby Ebbets Field, the home of the Brooklyn Dodgers. As Lewis-Luciano staggered away toward his home in Flatbush, someone asked him what happened. "I don't know," he replied. "I lost control of the damn thing. That's all." Under police questioning that night, he had an equally simple explanation for why he had taken the job at all, given his minimal experience: "A man has to earn a living."

Ten of the dead in Brooklyn's third worst accident and second worst nonaviation accident—six men and four women—were taken to the Evergreens. The accident was so notorious that the city changed the name of the road under which it occurred from Malbone Street to Empire Boulevard.

Purple Death: The 1918 Flu Pandemic

One of the burdens on the weary shoulders of Billy Lewis on November 1, 1918, was the influenza epidemic. The flu almost killed him; in mid-October it killed his baby daughter, leaving him exhausted and in despair.

The influenza epidemic of 1918–19 may be the only worldwide disaster that people do not talk about. But it flattened America. In June 1918, a twenty-four-year-old Brooklynite named William Hermann Hudaff graduated from a divinity school in Pennsylvania and was ordained a minister in the Lutheran church. A figure fit for an Horatio Alger story, he was an improbable up-and-comer. The only one of four children of German immigrants to survive beyond the age of two, William Hudaff was the family's chosen child. "The family all pulled for him," his great-nephew, Richard Kilbride, said in an interview in 2007. "He was the one for whom they all sacrificed. No one in the family's history had been educated to the extent he was. He was their scholar." Hudaff's father labored in a Williamsburg grocery, his mother took in washing, and William sold bibles to help pay his tuition, first at Wagner College (then in Rochester, N.Y.) and later at Philadelphia Seminary. During the summer of 1918 the newly ordained Reverend William Hudaff became a clergyman at St. Mark's Lutheran Church, at Windsor Terrace, in Brooklyn. On October 18 he presided at a funeral.

Somewhere he caught the flu. On November 16 he was dead. He was buried in the family's lot at the Evergreens. His exact location in the lot was unknown because the cemetery was so overwhelmed by the epidemic that it could not attend to all its records. Said Richard Kilbride, "So many were being buried at that point that the Evergreens did not record which position in the family plot was his."

If young Hudaff was a typical victim of the vast influenza epidemic of 1918–1920, his first symptom was so wrenchingly painful that he would have understood that his life had been catastrophically altered. Another flu victim said it was as though he been run over by a milk truck. A more scientific description was offered by the father of modern medicine, Sir William Osler. First came violent coughing. "For two days I felt very ill & exhausted by the paroxysms." Then came "a stab and then fireworks" in his side, then more coughing "which ripped all pleural attachments to smithereens & with it the pain." By this stage, victims were bleeding internally with such force that the skin was blue (some people called the flu "the purple death"). Usually an optimistic man, Osler was overheard reciting Tennyson's poem "Tithonus": "Of happy men that have the power to die / And grassy barrows of the happier dead. / Release me, and restore me to the ground." Osler very soon got his release.

It was called Spanish flu because Spain suffered badly, but any country's name would have worked in this worldwide pandemic. A type of avian flu, it was spread from its point of origination (which some scientists believe was eastern Asia, others northern France)

Streetcars frightened horses, shoved wagons out of the way, and crashed violently. The Malbone Street wreck killed more than ninety Brooklynites.

by birds, pigs, and the dense crowds of millions of soldiers and sailors who were in constant international motion. Fighting a major war can be "an epidemic-conducive environment," say the epidemiologists. Every continent suffered. India, New Zealand, Latin America, South Africa, North America, Europe—all were brutally battered. In Tahiti, six hundred forty citizens of Papeete—one-seventh of the population—were killed by the flu.

It may have first surfaced in March 1918 in the United States in rural southwestern Kansas, and was unknowingly carried from there by one or more soldiers to a U.S. Army post near Dodge City, where 56,000 men were undergoing training and living in poorly insulated barracks. To quote the pandemic's most thorough historian, John Barry, all the soldiers who finished training in Kansas and moved on to the next posts by train or troopship were "rolling through camps like a bowling ball knocking down pins." Dr. Victor Vaughan, an army medical officer, arrived at one post and was greeted by a horrific sight: "I saw hundreds of young stalwart men in uniform coming into the wards of the hospital. Every bed was full, yet others crowded in." At some posts bodies were stacked like cordwood. Passenger ships were no less vulnerable than troopships. After its initial outbreaks in rural Army camps, the virus was carried by troops to Europe, where it spread in barracks and rebounded back to America on steamships. One well-known passenger on the *Leviathan*, Assistant Secretary of the Navy Franklin Delano Roosevelt, was so ill that he was isolated from his office and advisors for weeks and almost died. President Woodrow Wilson caught the flu—"I am feeling

SUMACHS, EASTERN DISTRICT
FIRE DEPARTMENT MEMORIAL

terribly bad," he cried out—and though he survived, his consequent weakness left him vulnerable. (Five months later he suffered a debilitating stroke.) Barry has estimated the worldwide death toll as more than 50 million—the largest outbreak of disease in human history. More than half a million were killed in less than two years in the United States. New York lost more than 33,000. When public health officials realized how wildly contagious the flu virus was, they isolated sick people and banned crowds by shutting down schools, dance halls, theatres, and even churches. Eleven cities mandated that all funerals be private; only family members could attend.

The pressure on cemeteries was intense. In Brooklyn gravediggers labored seven days a week and were so overworked that they were given a raise from $3.75 a day to $4.00. At a few cemeteries, men struck for higher wages and shorter hours. The supply of gravediggers and caskets in Baltimore was so limited that the city budgeted $25,000 to provide laborers to dig graves and build coffins. In Washington, D.C., the government took over the distribution of coffins to the poor in order to guard against hording.

Interments at the Evergreens increased 20 percent from 4,438 in 1917 to 5,346 in 1918. A sample of names in the cemetery's burial ledgers reveals the cause. One hundred twenty-one individuals with names beginning with the letters B, J, M, and S were buried at the Evergreens in November 1916. One died of influenza and thirteen of pneumonia—11 percent of the total. A survey of the same letters in November 1918 shows one hundred eighty-two burials, with fifty-three deaths due to flu and thirty-seven to pneumonia—49 percent of all deaths. The duty to bury so many thousands, and quickly, was so great that for the first time in many years interments were regularly performed on Sundays. There even were night burials. In the ten months between August 1918 and June 1919, some days had as many as forty burials—so many that the daily schedule did not fit on a single page in the Evergreens Cemetery's gravediggers' diary but ran over onto other pages. After

a large new area called Nazareth Graves was opened in the far northeast corner of the cemetery, people living nearby were awakened at night by trucks or horse-drawn wagons carrying loads of pine coffins down Cypress Avenue to the Evergreens gate.

The epidemic did have a few productive consequences. Medical and demographic records, as well as personal accounts, provide a tremendous base of knowledge for doctors and government officials concerned with preventing or at least alleviating future pandemics. Hundreds of peer-reviewed scientific studies of the flu epidemic have been conducted with the aim of identifying problems that should be addressed should another holocaust-level epidemic appear, whether initiated by terrorists or carried by birds.

A New Relationship with Death

If the most remarkable aspect of the pandemic was its unsurpassed lethality, the second was the calm that appeared to surround it. Perhaps Americans were in denial, or distracted by the war, or feeling the hand of government censors who feared showing weakness to the enemy. Going public also had practical considerations. If one resident of an apartment house had the flu, the building, perhaps even the entire block, would be quickly and publicly quarantined by the authorities, who placed large black-and-white cards in windows. Silence also was a sign of passivity. When everybody considers the common air they breath to be a threat (children skipping rope routinely sang a ditty, "I had a little bird, its name was Enza, / I opened the window and in-flu-enza"), fatalism can set in. "No one really knew what to do," one survivor looked back, "No one knew how to treat it. What could anyone do? You couldn't stop living."

A wall of silence fragmented communities into the sick and the well. Walt Whitman noted this phenomenon in *Leaves of Grass* when he took the Job-like point of view of a victim of the 1849 cholera epidemic: "My face is ash-colored, my sinews gnarl . . . away from me people retreat." Many held off passivity and alienation with one tactic or another. Families and local governments engaged in frenzies of hyperenergetic cleaning of homes and neighborhoods. "Urban sanitation movements and the shock of the influenza experience helped fuel a cleanliness craze in American homes in the 1920s," wrote the historian Harvey Green in his aptly titled *The Uncertainty of Everyday Life, 1915–1945*. And then there were the numerous home remedies. Repeated shots of whiskey or cups of tea were rumored to keep the flu at bay, as was observance of an ancient Jewish tradition that a wedding in a burial ground could beat the plague (a hopeful Brooklyn couple exchanged vows before 2,000 witnesses in Mount Hebron Cemetery). In parts of America, those people would have been breaking the law because, there, public health officials shut down schools, dance halls, theatres, churches, and other gathering places. People stopped meeting face to face. "So many died from the flu they just rang the church bells," recalled one survivor; "they didn't dare take [corpses] into the church." Eleven cities in the United States passed laws requiring that all funerals be private, with no nonfamily member in attendance. (Recent studies have concluded that such measures may not have lessened mortality and may have helped erode sensible customs.)

The flu pandemic remained a secret for decades, rarely (or never) discussed in homes, and almost never mentioned in history classes. The writer H. L. Mencken offered an explanation: "The human mind always tries to expunge the intolerable from memory, just as it tries to conceal it while current." This silence may well have had a profound long-term consequence on the way we grieve. The British anthropologist Geoffrey Gorer speculated that the end of widespread observance of formal funeral rituals can be dated to the years 1914–1918. The cause, Gorer believed, was World War I, when so many young men died so quickly and randomly that the experience wore down survivors and families. If that timeline is accurate, then perhaps the influenza pandemic also made a contribution to the demise of many old mourning rituals. Death by flu in New York seemed no less random than death by machine gun on the Western Front, and when funerals are rigorously circumscribed and almost forbidden, rituals lose their institutional support. "We are unable to maintain our former attitudes toward death," commented Sigmund Freud at that time, "and have not yet found a new one."

Since then, when death and mourning are discussed it is often done skeptically. The most famous book ever written on the subject, Jessica Mitford's assault on the funeral business, *The American Way of Death*, published in 1963, covers many topics, but awareness of and sympathy for the need for organized displays of grief are not among them. The paradox is that Americans are extremely familiar with grief in its public form. "The days that really live in our public memories, aren't birthdays, they're death days," Sandra M. Gilbert wrote in *Death's Door: Modern Dying and the Ways We Grieve*. Depending on our age and nationality, we have heard "the tolling, tolling bells' perpetual clang" (as Walt Whitman wrote soon after the assassination of Lincoln) many times—following the violent deaths of Mahatma Gandhi, John and Robert Kennedy, Martin Luther King Jr., John Lennon, and the people in the buildings and airplanes on 9/11. Yet an acute sensitivity to mass, public, organized grief may not help people in times of private grief.

公墓

WAH PEI

華北同鄉會

北國英靈萬古存

華光彩映五雲中

CHAPTER FIFTEEN

FENG SHUI AT THE EVERGREENS

ON AN AUGUST SUNDAY in 1899, the many strollers on the grounds of the Evergreens Cemetery were fascinated to see a vast number of Chinese men, women, and children— some in traditional dress, others in American garb, their pigtails curled under hats—emerge from under the trees, carrying baskets. "A smile like a summer sea spread over all," noted a *Brooklyn Eagle* reporter who happened to be on hand, "breaking now and then into chuckles that rippled through the crowd as it would through a Sunday School picnic." A picnic was exactly what the Chinese had in mind, though it was not one with which most Americans were familiar. The purpose today was to reach out to the spirits of the dead by serving a good meal on cemetery graves.

Arriving at the Celestial Hill area at the northeast corner of the Evergreens, the crowd of Chinese broke up into family groups. After solemnly bowing to the headstones, they got to work, some cooking chicken, beef, vegetables, and rice in ovens, and others lighting joss sticks, setting off firecrackers, and tossing counterfeit bills—ghost money, they called it—onto the graves and fires. All were honoring the spirits of the dead on this ancestor day, one of two that has been observed at the Evergreens ever since Chinese fall and Ching Ming (which Westerners nicknamed "Chinese Easter") in the spring were major events on the cemetery's calendar.

If Ching Ming impressed native-born Americans, Chinese funerals astounded them. Even men and women who observed the most stringent Western mourning rituals were impressed by Chinese burial rites. Despite the poverty of the typical Chinese family in America in the 1800s, nobody stinted when it came to funerals. In 1888 the remains of Lee Yo Doo, who had fought the French in Vietnam, were carried out to the Green Hills from Chinatown ahead of sixty carriages. Amid the noise of drums, cymbals, and flutes, the mourners in their bright white suits sucked on sugar cubes and candies to eliminate any bitterness, and tossed ghost money and bits of paper out the carriage windows to distract the devils who, they knew, were chasing the dead man's spirit. The long procession crossed the Brooklyn Bridge, made its way along Bushwick Avenue past the breweries, entered the cemetery's main gate, and wound along the Evergreens' roads to the Chinese cemetery within the Evergreens, Celestial Hill. There joss sticks were lit, the casket was buried, the grave was strewn with flowers and covered with an American flag, the deceased's clothing was burned in an incinerator, and food was cooked and laid out on the grave for the feast of the spirit of the dead soldier and his family and friends.

Families attend to graves during Ching Ming in the early 1980s. Even anti-immigrant fanatics were impressed by the faithful attention the Chinese paid their dead.

Notable at the Evergreens, these ceremonies were highlights in the lives of the children in the ethnic enclaves of East New York and Bushwick. An Irishman who attended an elementary school near the Evergreens recalled that whenever the teacher pulled down the window shades, he knew to start listening for "the tom-tom cadence of Chinese funerals." After school he and the other children ran over to Celestial Hill and hid in the bushes to watch until the last mourner departed, when they ventured out and took a little food.

The Celestials

Peeking out school windows at processions of immigrants has long been a normal activity in New York and Brooklyn, but Chinese-Americans attracted more attention than most because they were so different and so few. In 1870 83 percent of the population of Manhattan had at least one foreign-born parent, and none of them was Chinese. Of the approximately 8 million immigrants who arrived between 1855 and 1900, 43 percent were German, 32 percent Irish, and of the remaining 25 percent, the Chinese were one of the very least represented. Fewer than 2,000 Chinese-born legal immigrants were believed to be in New York in 1880, and about 10,000 at the turn of the century. Many more illegal Chinese immigrants were living in New York despite the harsh federal exclusion laws—the same laws that, ironically, helped make a cemetery that had been created to meet the needs of German immigrants into one of the country's largest Chinese burial grounds.

"Celestials," as the Chinese-Americans were often called (their homeland was known as the Celestial Empire), seem to have originally appeared in America as the occasional merchant seamen. The first Chinese individual buried in New York is believed to be the sailor interred at the Evergreens in the Seaman's Grounds in 1853. His recorded name is John Shu, though because Americans often called Chinese men "John," his real first name very likely was different. (This is a good place to note that the same newspapers that would be harshly critical of the Evergreens when it later created Chinese burial plots expressed nothing but pride about the Seaman's Grounds, the Evergreens' first group plot, where indigent merchant sailors of all nationalities and races were buried. The sections reserved for Asians, Africans, and others, boasted the *Eagle*, enhanced the Evergreens' "cosmopolitan character.")

Subsequent Chinese immigrants included coolies who had worked in William R. Grace's ships in Peru and more than 20,000 émigrés from a province near Canton (Guangdong today) who came to the West Coast in the 1850s and afterward to work on the transcontinental railroad and in California's gold fields. Many Chinese called America "the Gold Mountain." A few of them married local women and settled down, but most were temporary workers aiming to make money to send home, where they intended to return. After the transcontinental railroad was completed in 1869, the first Chinese to come East in large numbers were transported by factory owners to be strikebreakers. They moved on to whatever work they were allowed, usually menial labor in the streets and in steam laundries, whose heavy irons gave the job the nickname "the eight-pound livelihood." When chop suey (the words mean something like "leftovers") became popular, some Chinese immigrants opened restaurants. These men were not always received with open arms. Besides the widespread racial prejudice, there were many Americans who lost jobs to low-wage

"Coolie, slave, pauper and rat-eater" reads one of the epithets in this Thomas Nast portrayal of the plight of the Chinese in 1871. The Evergreens was already burying Chinese and later established Celestial Hill.

Chinese immigrants, and others who were annoyed by their unwillingness to put down roots and become citizens. All this tended to confirm white Americans' impressions of Chinese as a contrary, different, and strange people. "Popular opinion, when considering our foreign immigrants, has given the lowest rank among them to the Chinese," observed an American social worker in the 1890s. Their filial devotion was respected, and the detailed reports of funerals in the newspapers did cause sensitive Americans to recognize that even the Chinese suffered their losses. Otherwise, however, they were regarded as aliens in every sense of the word. If their skin color and facial features were not objectionable, it was their language, their religion, their manners (for some reason, the Chinese habit of wearing hats indoors attracted considerable scorn), and their holding themselves separate and seemingly aloof. Adjectives that Americans applied to Chinese told the story, from the relatively tame "inscrutable" and "peculiar," to the patronizing "fascinating" and "exotic," and on to the hard-boiled contempt of "primitive" and "yellow-skinned coolies" who would take any American's job. In 1882 Congress barred immigration by almost all Chinese (exceptions were made for government officials and professionals). The only legislation of its kind in American history before the severe immigration restrictions of the 1920s, the Chinese Exclusion Act did not apply to any other Asian nationality. It was not repealed until World War II, in recognition of China's role as an ally.

Seeking Harmony

With that background, it may seem a surprise that an American cemetery was willing to bury Chinese.

In 1877 a large area on Hickory Knoll at the Evergreens was sold to a Chinese benevolent organization, which buried thirty-two people there (thirty years later, the remains were moved to one of the cemetery's Chinese sections). The Evergreens' policy of providing Chinese with graves at all, much less among white people, stirred an uproar. The *Eagle* expressed shock that Celestials not only were buried at the Evergreens but were interred in the fashionable Hickory Knoll section. In 1885 the *New York Herald* was so outraged that it dispatched a reporter to look into the matter.

His first stop was at a Manhattan funeral home. "Is it true that the Chinese are allowed to bury their dead among the Christians in the Brooklyn Evergreens Cemetery?" the reporter asked. The undertaker said he could not believe that such terrible things actually were occurring.

The reporter went out to the Evergreens, where he found Superintendent Charles Pfeiffer and half-asked, half-demanded, "Have you any Chinamen buried in these grounds?"

"Yes, dozens of them," replied Pfeiffer. "Why should we not receive a Chinaman's body?"

Not hearing what he wanted, the reporter located a foreman, but he looked at it from the point of view of immigrants. "It's all the same to me. I am Irish, thank God. The chief clerk, Mr. Pfeiffer, is German, and we bury any man who comes along." And as far as he was concerned, that was that. When a later Evergreens president, Paul Grassi, was asked in 2007 about this overblown controversy, he shrugged. "That's what we do. We bury people."

The fact is that the Evergreens was the Chinese government's official cemetery in New York. In 1883, the year after the Exclusion Act was legislated, the local Chinese consul, Au Yang Ming, made a point of looking after the burial-related concerns of local Chinese, most of whom knew no English and were exploited by cemeteries. "I found my poor people had been cruelly robbed in the matter of burial," he said in an interview. The solution was to establish a Chinese-American cemetery within an existing cemetery. The consul and the newly established Chinese Consolidated Benevolent Association approached the Evergreens, which was amenable to their proposal. That was the birth of a long relationship. Today, when a visitor to the Museum of Chinese in the Americas, in Chinatown, mentions the Evergreens, a staff member is likely to reply, "Oh, the Chinese cemetery."

The consul, the benevolent association, and the Evergreens staff set about selecting a proper place for Celestial Hill, the group burial site. Their standard was feng shui, the system for finding harmony with the environment. Pronounced "fung shway," it means "wind and water." The feng shui of cemeteries prescribed that a grave site be hilly and sunlit and have a view of water. "A hillside location affords the spirits of the dead a pleasant view of nature and of village life below," says an authority on Chinese cemetery design, Nanette Napoleon Purnell, "while the mountains and the water serve as boundaries for the spirits who dwell in and around the burial grounds in the afterworld of the dead." Because evil spirits tend to become lost, it would also be a very good thing if the roads to and through the Chinese section were winding.

The Green Hills and Andrew Jackson Downing's concepts satisfied feng shui. With its many hills, twisting roads and paths, seven lakes, and grand prospects of the ocean, Jamaica Bay, New York Bay, and the East River, the Evergreens seemed especially well suited for a Chinese cemetery. The consul, the Benevolent Association, and the Evergreens' management agreed on a broad, undeveloped slope on the eastern side of the grounds that fronted on a lake (which has since been filled in). There were approximately two hundred interments at Celestial Hill by 1891, and the area was regularly crowded at funerals and ancestor days. A number of other Chinese areas were later laid out, several with a spirit gate over the entrance. One Chinese area is on the south-facing slope under the Summer House across from the chapel.

The Associations

Like the burials of many non-Chinese, Chinese burials were arranged by benevolent associations. It is not an exaggeration to say that group burial plots made the Evergreens. The authority of these organizations in matters as intimate as burial may surprise many Americans today, when the decision is usually left to the family. But in an earlier time, when there was less security, fraternal and maternal orders provided their members with order, identity, a sense of purpose, and a number of valuable services, including free or low-cost burials in their plots.

Some of these were affinity groups, like the Elks for actors and their friends, the Order of Tents for former slaves, and the Grand Army of the Republic for Union army Civil War veterans. Other groups were defined by work (the Metallic Lathers Union has a plot at the Evergreens), and many more by convictions, which ranged from the religious beliefs of churchgoers to the bonds of mysticism and friendship shared by the Freemasons and the less well-known Knights of Pythias, one of few fraternal organizations to espouse racial equality. Then there were the nationality organizations. Besides the many German groups, on Orient Hill several headstones of émigré Scots surround a marker for the New York Arbroath Association, named for what has been called Scotland's Declaration of Independence. (At Arbroath Abbey on April 6, 1320, the Scots lords put their seals on a successful request to Pope John XXII to not take the English side.)

The Arbroath Association should not be confused with the Amaranth Council, another of the many organizations that, in one way or another, addressed the human need to bond together, provide joy in good times, and offer solace in hard ones. The Amaranth Council, Royal Arcanum, raised a plinth dedicated to the memory of their Brother, Grand Trustee, District Deputy Grand Regent Thomas W. Kelley, a take-charge sort of fellow of whom it was said, "his appearance on the floor of the Grand Council meetings was the signal for a large and attentive audience." After his death his fellow Royal Arcanumites collected $1,300 to build the plinth, which they dedicated before a crowd of 1,000 on Easter Sunday, 1902. Similar leaders and similar stories can be found at many other organizations, which also left their marks in cemeteries. The Chinese are especially prominent in their dependence on associations. "Clan or regionally based benevolent associations were the glue that held the American Chinese together," an historian of Chinatown, Bruce Edward Hall, wrote. Among the grave sites at the Evergreens is the Wing Lok plot, which adjoins a churchyard of one of the very oldest Christian sects, the Syrian Orthodox Church of Antioch.

For Chinese-Americans, a burial society offered one extremely important assurance that other groups did not require. That was the promise that the remains would be sent back to China to be buried in the soil of the motherland. "As every good Chinese son knew," Hall explained, "if you weren't buried in your home soil, your spirit would wander the earth forever." Five or six years after a burial, tents and pots of boiling water were set up under a tent near the grave, the remains were disinterred and professional bone cleaners got to work. The bones were then packed up in zinc boxes and shipped by rail to San Francisco and from there by ship to China.

This process continued for decades until a ship carrying bones was torpedoed in the Pacific during World War II. According to Frank Trupia, the Evergreens' grounds superintendent from 1987 through 2007, "The Japanese would capture the ships and ransack the boxes for the zinc. When that happened, the shipments stopped." After the war further shipment of bones was cut off by the Communist government. Boxes containing the remains of more than two hundred Chinese-Americans were stored in the Evergreens' receiving vault for almost forty years. When the rent checks stopped appearing in 1987, Evergreens President Paul Grassi initiated negotiations with the Chinese Consolidated Benevolent Association that led to an agree- ment to return all remains that could be identified to China, and to inter the others at the Evergreens. "We want to do things the proper way," said the benevolent association's president, George Hui. "They deserve respect."

Ou Loo, War Casualty

Two Chinese-American war heroes are buried at the Evergreens. Benjamin Ralph Kimlau was a World War II pilot whose plane was shot down over New Guinea in March 1944. The son of one of the first Chinese-American undertakers in Chinatown, he was honored in the name of two Chinatown institutions—the Ralph Kimlau Post of the American Legion and the Kimlau Square portion of Chatham Square, where a large memorial commemorates those Chinese-Americans who lost their lives in war.

The other hero was a seaman in the U.S. Navy during World War I whose stone reads simply:

Ou Loo
Fireman M.M.
S.S. Diomed
15th October 1918

The Chinese seaman buried in the Seaman's Grounds was one of the last casualties of the submarine war by the Germans.

As we saw in Chapter 1, the terror weapon of the eighteenth century was the British bayonet. In the early twentieth century it was the submarine. During World War I German U-boats sank some 5,000 war, passenger, or merchant ships with a total tonnage of 12 million and the loss of as many as 15,000 lives. Any ship that went to sea was subject to being stopped, inspected, and—if the cargo was a military one—sunk by a German submarine. Ou Loo's ship, a 4,700-ton British freighter in the Blue Funnel Line, was one of the last U-boat victims.

On August 21, 1918, the *Diomed* was steaming to America under a captain named Baker, three officers, and one hundred Chinese-American seamen, many of them coolies in the engine room, one of whom very likely was Ou Loo. Two hundred miles southeast of Nantucket, the *Diomed* was spotted by a German sub-

marine, U-140, with torpedos and deck guns both forward and aft. Its commander was Korvettenkapitan Waldemar Kophamel. U-140 was making her way home from a lethally successful raiding expedition in U.S. coastal waters, where it and five other U-boats had sunk a total of ninety-one vessels, with almost four hundred fatalities. Though U-140 was leaking fuel after being shaken by a U.S. Navy depth charge, Kophamel was not about to let this target get away. Baker returned fire, but after taking a dozen hits the *Diomed* was slowly settling into the Atlantic with damaged boilers, disabled steering gear, one man killed, and several casualties due to shrapnel or—in the case of many coolies—scalding by steam in the engine room.

The crew lay drifting in the lifeboats when the submarine slowly approached. The men must have held their breath; some U-boat captains treated vanquished enemies as honored guests, and others machine-gunned them. U-140 stopped, Kophamel looked down from the conning tower, and in very good English politely asked, "Do you need a surgeon to attend to your injured men?"

Captain Baker was sorely tempted to ask for help. Despite his need and the friendly tone, he said not a word, fearing that if he spoke the Germans would take him and his officers prisoner. His well-disciplined officers and crew followed his lead. U-140 did not go away. After two hours of this silent cat-and-mouse game, a plume of smoke appeared on the horizon and U-140 raced off, toward Germany. The second ship, a friendly, rescued the men from the lifeboats.

Ou Loo survived the sinking but not his wounds, and a kind soul arranged to have him laid to rest on an autumn day under the red leaves of the maples at the crest of the hill overlooking the Seaman's Grounds.

CHAPTER SIXTEEN

THE TWO ANTHONIES: THE SHOWMAN AND THE SCOLD

T HE CHINESE ARE THE MOST noticeable of the former American pariahs represented in large numbers at the Evergreens, but they are hardly the only social outcasts who have been buried in dignity and even splendor. Many actors and other entertainers, white and black, are there, too. The person mostly responsible for the Evergreens' becoming the last home and resting place for hundreds of performers was also the man widely known as "the father of vaudeville," Tony Pastor. Ironically, just a five minutes' walk from Pastor's grave lies a very different sort of Anthony. Anthony Comstock never met a liberty or pleasure he did not hate, and he made it his life's work not to tolerate pariahs, but to scold them.

PAGE 230,
SHADOWY WAY,
PASTOR LOT

LEFT, ST.MARK'S
CHURCH
GROUNDS

The Father of Vaudeville

Born Antonio Pastore in 1832 in Greenwich Village, when it really was a village, Tony Pastor was the son of a grocer and violinist who, knowing the vagaries of show business, tried to steer his boy into farming. Tony, however, was a natural showman. In his youth he sang in temperance meetings then moved on to the circus, where, as P. T. Barnum's well-hyped "Infant Prodigy," he performed gymnastic tumbles, danced on horses' backs, and sang in an operatic tenor. Performing did not wholly satisfy Pastor's grand ambitions. As the impresario of Tony Pastor's Opera House, he presented cleaned-up versions of the smutty shows that were the norm in the typical smoke-filled, beery, prostitute-friendly Bowery saloon. He even introduced a nightly singing of "The Star-Spangled Banner" during the Civil War. Pastor's theatre was so clean, the saying went, that "a child could take his parents."

He and other showmen created a new form of entertainment that dominated America from the 1870s until the arrival of the movies. What he called "variety" and others called "vaudeville" developed from minstrel shows. White men, their faces blackened by burned corks, sat on long benches and, at the command of their leader, the "end man," stood up and told jokes and sang and danced to songs by Stephen Foster and other composers inspired by the music of slaves. Broadening out beyond these minstrel skits, Pastor nurtured a brilliant and amazingly diverse array of talent. One of his discoveries was a pretty, Iowa-born church choir singer named Helen Louise Leonard, who became the superstar Lillian Russell. With the exception of his unfortunate (but hardly unusual at that time) refusal to hire African American performers, his shows had true variety. Russell and Pastor (who kept on performing) headlined bills that included knife throwers, gymnasts, jugglers, acro-

Juggler, producer, and always the showman, Tony Pastor helped his fellow entertainers when they were among the most scorned Americans.

bats, humorists, tightrope walkers, clog dancers, tap dancers, ballet dancers, zither players, dialect comedians, English women who were male impersonators, French women who were always billed as "the latest Parisian sensation," you-name-it specialists who (for want of a more precise term) were called "funambulists," and an array of actors and singers in hilarious take-offs of Shakespearean plays and Gilbert & Sullivan operettas.

This universe of entertainment played all day, from morning to midnight, in theatres often nicknamed "the great family resort" because they were safe and comfortable enough for women and children. A genius at promotion, Pastor attracted women by offering silk dresses and fancy bonnets as door prizes ("twenty-five policemen had to be present to keep the ladies from breaking ranks," he once claimed). Just because his brand of entertainment was tasteful enough for family audiences did not mean it was without teeth. Robert W. Snyder observed in his history of popular entertainment in New York, *The Voice of the City*, that Pastor did not remove all the Bowery from vaudeville. He particularly enjoyed puncturing the pretensions and advantages of "The Upper Ten Thousand in mansions reside"—the wealthy men of New York, many of whom had legally evaded Abraham Lincoln's Civil War draft by purchasing substitutes for $300:

We are coming Father Abraham
Three hundred dollars more;
We're rich enough to stay at home,
Let them go out that's poor.
But Uncle Abe, we're not afraid
To stay behind in clover;
We'll nobly fight, defend the right,
When this cruel war is over.

Burying Actors

Pastor felt no such bitterness about his fellow performers or the Evergreens. One of his most popular acts was put on by a famous blackface minstrel end man named Eph Horn. A star on a circuit that took him from Brooklyn and New York to San Francisco to London, Eph Horn was a good friend of Pastor's and often lived in his home in New York. On Christmas Day, 1876, a show promoter abandoned Horn on an open train platform in New Jersey. He came down sick, and as he lay dying in Pastor's home, Pastor tried to cheer up him with promises of recovery. A showman to the end, Horn replied, "Oh, I guess I'll get over it. I always was a good man on the end." Pastor paid for the funeral at the Episcopal Church of the Transfiguration in Manhattan, and arranged for Horn to be buried at the Evergreens on Hickory Knoll

phraim Horn, Esq, the Minstrel Boy.

The minstrel star Eph Horn was buried on Hickory Knoll in a grave donated by his friend Pastor.

Most Americans in 1876 (and for many years afterward) would have been surprised to learn that a minstrel player was buried out of a respectable church and in a respectable cemetery. Stage people were widely scorned as unreliable and troublesome, generally one small step above common thieves. In Irving Berlin's song "There's No Business Like Show Business," among the characters who make "show business like no business I know" there is "The sheriff who escorts you out of town."

This reputation reached even into the churches and cemeteries. A few days before Christmas in 1870, an actor named George Holland died in New York and one of his friends, Joseph Jefferson, America's star comic actor famous for playing Rip Van Winkle, approached the rector of a Manhattan church about presiding at Holland's funeral. The clergyman contemptuously replied that he could not possibly do it but, he said, "I believe there's a little church around the corner that

does that sort of thing." Jefferson (who had been subjected to more than his share of prejudice during his long career) replied, "If this be so, then God bless the little church around the corner!" The church was the Episcopal Church of the Transfiguration on 29th Street near Fifth Avenue. Its rector, the Reverend George Hendric Houghton, was an orthodox Anglican churchman with a congregation of Astors, Drexels, Gerrys, and Roosevelts, but he turned away no one. His credo (from the Roman poet Terence) was, "I am a man: nothing human is alien to me." Houghton buried Holland, and continued to bury, marry, and care for performers throughout the forty-nine years of his rectorship. Transfiguration came to be known as both "the Actors' Church" and "the Church Around the Corner" (today its website address is www.little church.org). Houghton was later elected an honorary member of the Actors' Fund, and at his death in 1897, the Actors' National Protective Union of New York issued a statement mourning the passing of "our best and most esteemed friend, who was ever ready to extend the right hand of fellowship."

In keeping with his own traditions and his actor-congregants' affection for spectacle, Houghton made sure that the church's rituals were dramatic. One of the many performers buried out of Transfiguration and interred in the Actors' Fund Plot at the Evergreens was a famous old trooper named Charles W. Couldock. Born in England in 1815, he was apprenticed in the silk business, but rebelled and became an actor. In order to play his first part, as Othello, he paid the producer £10 and, to avoid trouble with his family, temporarily adopted a stage name, "Mr. Forrescue." On the boards in America from the 1840s, he created sensations with his leonine figure and intensely emotional style in Shakespearean roles, in the smash hit *Our American Cousin*, and in the long-running play *Hazel Kirke*, where he sang "Abide with Me"—a gentle hymn with which he was closely identified despite his ungentle, curmudgeonly personality. Once, just moments before the curtain rose on a performance, his sobbing leading lady ran to the director and complained that Couldock had insulted her. "I told her Hades was full of such leading ladies as she is," Couldock admitted, but he assured the director that he was taking it back because "The place isn't quite full. There's still room for her."

Along the circuitous route that took him to stages across North America, Couldock had suffered the loss of his daughter and favorite supporting actress, Eliza, whom he had buried in Salt Lake City. By the time it was his turn, in 1898, eighty-three-year-old Charles Couldock was in Manhattan, broke as usual, and with his all-forgiving friends rallying around. On his funeral bier at the Little Church Around the Corner lay a wreath of white roses tied with a purple ribbon, a memorial gift from Joseph Jefferson. A soprano soloist and the men's choir encircled the bier and sang "Abide with Me." With hardly a dry eye in the house, the service proceeded, and that afternoon Charles Couldock joined his friends at the Evergreens.

"The little church around the corner" was the only well-established church to welcome actors and the last stop for many performers on their final journey to the Evergreens.

Caring for the nomads of the theatre was not limited to one church. Billy Black was a blackface comic of limited talent who drifted around the country on the minstrel circuit from flophouse to flophouse. Actors were used to long disappearances. "You? Why, I thought you were dead long ago," friends would say when Black resurfaced in New York. "Somebody told me you were dead, like the rest of 'em. Good joke, eh? Let's have a drink." When Billy Black failed to appear for a performance, friends found his body at an undertaker's and a chaplain found the money for the funeral. Some three hundred performers came to the church to lay flowers on his casket and say a few prayers, and then his remains were carried out to the Evergreens at the head of a procession of fourteen carriages.

The Poor Player's Sacred Home

The Tony Pastor productions included two burial sections for actors at the Evergreens. In 1867 he helped found the first actors' fraternal organization, the Jolly Corks, and this drinking society morphed into a benevolent and protective order called the Elks (animal names were popular for men's organizations). In 1873 Pastor and his fellow Elks purchased a burial plot at the Evergreens that they called Elks Rest. For years it was guarded by a large stuffed elk that on Memorial Day was joined by a floral reindeer.

Under Pastor's leadership, in the early 1880s actors formed a new benevolent organization, the Actors' Fund of America, that recruited within the entire entertainment business. The fund raised money at benefit performances and a fair attended by J. P. Morgan, former President Grover Cleveland, and various Astors and Vanderbilts. By 1899 the fund had spent $332,000 on benefits to members, and the membership totaled nearly nine hundred, more than half of them playwrights, set designers, stagehands, and others who stood in the theatre wings.

In 1887 the Actors' Fund purchased a large plot at the Evergreens that was landscaped by Samuel Parsons Jr., with a grand monument and, around it, a field of simple headstones (more is said about Parsons and the design in Chapter 11). The plot was dedicated on June 6, 1887, before more than 8,000 spectators—probably the largest single gathering in the Evergreens' history. Father Houghton of the Church of the Transfiguration presided, alongside the silver-tongued Brooklyn preacher Henry Ward Beecher, Joseph Jefferson, whose outrage had been so important to giving actors decent funerals, and Edwin Booth, the great tragedian who came with his niece, Blanche DeBar, who herself would be buried in the Actors' Plot (and of whom much is said in Chapter 6). Music was provided by the famous Seventh Regiment band, led by Carlo Cappa (who would be buried at the Evergreens) and by a chorus that sang a hymn written for the occasion titled "In the Evergreens." There was a moment of tragicomedy when the temporary grandstand gave way under the crush of spectators. Fearful cries gave way to laughter when the people realized there were no injuries.

In the main oration, Edwin Booth acknowledged that actors had long suffered "the brand of vagabondage, which is, in truth, the true condition of our calling—that actors can hardly ever have a permanent abode." Westminster Abbey had dedicated a plot to writers, and now the Evergreens was doing it for actors. "In far humbler form this our modest beacon shall denote the no less sacred home of the poor player to whom, with fervent prayers for God's blessing, we, his brothers and sisters, dedicate it in token of our affectionate veneration." The inscription on the monument captured the mood. It was written by a drama critic, Shakespearean specialist, and biographer of actors, William Winter:

> *Here to your eyes, our earthly labors done,*
> *We who played many parts now play but one.*
> *We knew the stops, could give the viol breath,*
> *Yet even thus our relics may impart*
> *A truth beyond the reach of living art,*
> *Teaching the strong, the beautiful, the brave,*
> *That all life's pathways centre in the grave;*
> *Bidding them live, nor negligent nor fond,*
> *To bless the world, yet ever look beyond.*

Nearly four hundred fifty actors and other stage people were buried in the Actors' Fund Plot before it was filled.

Almost five hundred entertainers found
their last homes in plots owned by the Actors' Fund
(above, at its opening) and the Elks
(with their trademark animal).

Tony Pastor continued to produce and star in vaudeville shows for almost twenty years until he fell ill in 1908. The newspapers ran daily bulletins about his health, and covered his funeral like opening night at his Opera House. The Evergreens was the stage for his last extravaganza, with 2,000 spectators, five carriage loads of floral pieces, a quartet singing "Nearer My God to Thee," a dramatic recitation of William Cullen Bryant's ode to death, "Thanatopsis," and the playing of Chopin's funeral march by Pastor's own band. Pastor was laid to rest in the plot he had arranged for his family, overlooked by angels and placed dramatically at the intersection of two of the Evergreens' roads, directly across from some of Brooklyn's oldest families. He would be remembered for years to come when his band returned to the Evergreens on Sundays to give concerts for people strolling through the grounds.

Another Anthony

Tony Pastor may have pleased families by cleaning up the theatre, but he never could have pleased another Anthony whose whole being ran against not only vaudeville but the spirit of joyful release that was its foundation. When H. L. Mencken defined a Puritan as a person who fears that somebody, somewhere, is having a good time, he could easily have been thinking of scolding Anthony Comstock, whose name for almost one hundred fifty years has been a byword for "American inquisition." Comstock's long reign as New York's most visible (and powerful) censor introduced a new noun to the American vocabulary, "Comstockery," coined by the playwright George Bernard Shaw. Although Comstock had neither seen nor read Shaw's play *Mrs. Warren's Profession*, he publicly warned actors against acting in it. A century later a movie reviewer at the *New York Times*, Manohla Dargis, used the phrases "atomic-age Comstock" and "tireless, cheerless band of Comstocks" to describe modern-day censors.

Born in 1844, the son of a Connecticut sawmill operator and farmer, Comstock devoted most of his seventy-one years to taking his own personal moral buzz

saw to anything he considered evil, salacious, or merely titillating. After service in the Civil War he became a salesman. One day in 1872 he discovered two of his colleagues reading books that he considered indecent and promptly had the bookstore's owner arrested. That set him off on a forty-three-year career of complaining, prodding, entrapping, arresting, and generally harassing anyone he believed was evil—and he found such people everywhere. His behavior eventually won him a roster of nicknames like "the One-Man Traveling Vice Squad," "the Protector of the Public Morals," "the Self-Constituted Censor," and "Sir Anthony." Self-righteous, prudish, arrogant, and given to statements suggesting a Christ complex ("I cannot expect to have better treatment than our blessed Master" he said about one critic's attacks on his behavior), Comstock still deserves to be credited with accomplishing much that was good in a time when pornographers and swindlers seized on the new phenomena of cheap printing and quick national distribution by railroads. In his five-hundred-page book *Frauds Exposed*, he shed light on scams by financial and real estate institutions, lotteries, other get-rich-quick schemers, and medical quacks. He successfully lobbied Congress to pass a law in 1873 regulating the shipment of obscene materials through the mails, and he was appointed a special agent of the United States Post Office (his only government office) with powers to prosecute violators, which he did with chilling enthusiasm.

Such efforts initially earned him considerable respect from well-meaning government and church officials, who praised his concern for the community. But he became corrupted by his power, and his arrogance and rough tactics scared away many of his early friends. Fifty thousand men and women signed a petition calling for the repeal of all national and state "Comstock laws." After he raided an exhibit of French paintings in 1887, the Society of American Artists attacked the interference of "incompetent persons" in artistic matters. Comstock's response was to issue a rousing statement titled "Morals vs. Art" in which he declared morality—or at least his version of it—to be the ultimate arbiter of taste.

MT. GRACE,
THE KNIGHT OF PYTHIAS

The *Times* (probably using figures that he provided) reported that as of the beginning of 1914 (the year before his death), Comstock had helped bring about the arraignment of 3,697 persons in New York or federal courts, 2,740 of whom either pleaded guilty or were convicted. They served a total of five hundred sixty-six years in prison and paid fines totaling $237,134.30 (the equivalent today of more than $4.6 million).

With the help of wealthy patrons Comstock founded the New York Society for the Suppression of Vice to conduct a war on what he called "obscenity," a term that he defined broadly. He took aim at Margaret Sanger and other proponents of contraception and abortion, and reportedly rejoiced when one of them chose to commit suicide rather than go to trial. Sometimes he just looked silly. He confiscated posters of sweaty bodies promoting physical fitness, attempted to halt an exhibition of Paul Chabas' sweetly innocent painting of a dainty nude, "September Morn," and prosecuted a Brooklyn photographer for the pre-PhotoShop

St. Peter rejects Anthony Comstock at the gates of heaven, saying, "We may have things here you would object to."

trick of taking pictures of pretty actresses and replacing their faces with those of prominent socialites. A bull of a man—his friends compared him with Atlas—he could get physical. His muttonchops concealed a scar acquired during one attempted arrest, and in 1903, in his fiftieth year, he was seriously injured while tackling another one of his targets. (He sustained deeper wounds. After his infant daughter died in 1872, he arranged to adopt another girl whose mother was dying, but this child turned out to be mentally impaired. Perhaps Comstock's anger was fueled by personal loss.)

Anthony Comstock died after a short illness in 1915. He is buried at the Evergreens under a large headstone whose epitaph includes a characteristically defiant Comstockian quote from the New Testament's Letter to the Hebrews, "Lay aside every weight . . . looking unto Jesus . . . despising the shame."

CHAPTER SEVENTEEN

SHOW PEOPLE

WITH THE EVERGREENS CEMETERY'S long connections with the Elks, the Actors' Fund, and the vaudeville impresario Tony Pastor—not to mention Brooklyn's history as a home for entertainers—it should come as no surprise that the Evergreens has been a last resting place for performers for well over a century, from the early stage to television.

The first performers interred at the Evergreens were English-born John Barnes, who began touring American theatres in 1816, and his actress-wife, Charlotte, both of whose remains were transferred from St. Mark's in the Bowery Church in 1862. Besides Tony Pastor and Eph Horn, vaudeville was represented by Gus Hill (born Gustave Metz), who, when not swinging and juggling hundred-pound bowling pins, dramatized "the Yellow Kid," the first figure in the color funny papers. Harry Lennie represented the rare breed of Scottish clergymen turned vaudevillians. And of course there were the Irish: James Casey and Maggie Le Claire sang in Pastor's shows, and so did Pat Rooney Sr., who is buried side by side on Mt. Seir with his son, Pat Rooney Jr.—a soft-shoe dancer so adept that the normally curmudgeonly W. C. Fields said he seemed to be floating in air. (Pat Jr. sang the haunting and very Hibernian "More I Cannot Wish You" in the original cast of *Guys and Dolls*.)

Vaudeville had a streak of strangeness. Ella Wesner was the foremost male impersonator of the vaudeville era and was wearing men's clothing when she was buried at the Evergreens. Anyone hearing the woman called "the Phenomenal Baritone," Helene Mora, sing her hit song "Don't Forget, My Boy, You're Leaving Home" could be forgiven for suffering a bout of gender confusion. The twenty-five-inch Australian Little Princess Victoria (sometimes called "Madame Melba") claimed to be the world's smallest female entertainer, but that honor should go to Little Dot Winters, a child star for one-half her brief span of eight years before she, too, was interred in the Green Hills.

Some performers were tiny, others not so. Two expansive stars of the sideshows buried at the Evergreens in the 1880s were Jessie Waldron, "the Fat Woman of Bunnell's Museum," and five-hundred-twenty-five-pound Annie Price, who often appeared alongside her husband, "the white-haired albino." Another hefty entertainer, Maggie Arlington, was so touchy about her bulk that she physically assaulted a performer named Miss Adelaide Cherie, who accused her of having feet a yard long. "Big Mag," as she was called, had such a hard life that her grave in the Actors' Fund Plot was called "Maggie's Rest."

Among the flamboyant show folk at the Evergreens are the male impersonator Ella Wesner (above) and the actor John T. Raymond.

Man of the Gilded Age

One of the stars of the stage, John T. Raymond, owed his success in equal parts to timely plagiarism and his comedic ability. Born in 1836 in Buffalo, Raymond was in show business for twenty years before his big break came along, a lead role in West Coast theatres in a dramatization of the best-selling novel *The Gilded Age* that had not been cleared with the book's authors, Mark Twain (the pen name of Samuel Longhorn Clemens) and Charles Dudley Warner. Twain went to court and blocked the production, then brought Raymond to New York and produced the play himself. Raymond played one of America's favorite scoundrels, Colonel Mulberry Sellers, a shady character who was forever hoping—and failing—to make a fast buck. His best-known line was "There's millions in it!," always expressed with comically desperate optimism. The *New York Times* raved about the part and its performer. "The character of Colonel Sellers, enthusiast, land speculator, humbug—a type of the boastful American new to the stage—became in Raymond's personation a delightful, fascinating, exquisitely humorous creation." Raymond helped launch two American icons.

One was the name "Gilded Age" for the years 1870–1900, when the greed exemplified by the scrambling Colonel Sellers was commonplace. The other icon was Mark Twain. Running for more than 1,000 performances in New York, *The Gilded Age* made enough money to allow Clemens to concentrate on writing fiction, and out of that came the classics *Tom Sawyer* and *Huckleberry Finn*.

When Raymond died suddenly in 1887 while on tour, his body was embalmed and returned to New York, where after the funeral at the Little Church Around the Corner, he was buried at the foot of a sizeable monument overlooking the new Actors' Fund Plot. The *Times* gave him a rare front-page obituary whose headline (of course) was "Colonel Sellers Is Dead."

Raymond was luckier than another actor who ventured west. After a show in Marshall, Texas, in March 1879, Benjamin C. Porter and his co-stars, Maurice Barrymore and Minnie Cummings, were walking into a saloon when they attracted the malicious interest of an inebriated, well-armed railroad detective named Currie. Barrymore called Currie a loafer, Currie insulted Cummings, Barrymore challenged Currie to a fist fight, and Porter was trying to calm everybody down when Currie shot him in the stomach. As he lay dying, Porter moaned, "Oh, my God, why did that man want to kill me? What harm did I do to him?" Barrymore (the father of three famous actors and the great-grandfather of movie star Drew Barrymore) was wounded in the shoulder and later testified at the trial, where Currie was acquitted on two grounds that may have made sense in frontier Texas: he was drunk and Barrymore had called him a loafer. (Ironically, the name of the play was *Diplomacy*.)

The American Nightingale

Among singers in the Gilded Age, none was more elegant than Brooklyn's own Emma Cicilia Thursby, called "the American Nightingale" to distinguish her from the Swedish version of the same bird, Jenny Lind. The daughter of an Eastern District firefighter, she was born in Bushwick in 1845 and first showed vocal talent while singing in a local church choir. When she became the lead soprano at Henry Ward Beecher's Plymouth Con-

"The Nightingale has flown away" mourned a newspaper after the death of Emma Thursby, a Bushwick girl who became a singing superstar.

gregational Church, her career took off. One critic hailed her as the woman "from whose throat such mysteries of sound proceed." In 1876, billed as "Brooklyn's Favorite Vocalist," Thursby shared the lead with Mark Twain at the Brooklyn Academy of Music, she singing Mozart and he reading from his books. Her celebrity was enhanced by her pet multilingual talking mynah bird and her carefully groomed striking appearance, featuring what was described as "hair of a curious silky texture, where the colors seem to change from a dull gold to a deep rich brown." Thursby's ambitious performing schedule, with national and international tours, led to several breakdowns, but her life changed when she met a Hindu monk, Swami Vivekananda, at the Chicago World's Fair in 1893. For years she followed his teachings and passed them on to friends in gatherings called "Thursby Fridays" in her Manhattan apartment. After her death in 1931 at age eighty-six, Emma Thursby was buried in her family's plot at Greenwood Shade. One obituary said simply, "The Nightingale has flown away."

Other Evergreens vocalists were a far sight less refined than the Nightingale. Brooklyn and Queens accents (which is to say blends of about every accent there is) were well represented by the team of Gus Van and Joe Schenck. Both were born and raised near the Evergreens in Ridgewood, Queens. Van (born August Von Glahn) was a baritone who drove trolley cars in Williamsburg and moonlighted as a saloon singer. After he teamed up with Schenck, a piano-playing tenor and member of an old Brooklyn family, they first attracted attention in 1916 with their recordings of "Yaddie Kaddie Kiddie Kaddie Koo," "That's How You Can Tell They're Irish," "For Me and My Gal," and other novelty songs. Later they pioneered on radio and in movies. Schenck, the older of the two, died in 1930 as he was about to go on stage in Detroit. Sixty-five automobiles with 1,500 mourners, plus ten cars of flowers, followed the hearse out to the Evergreens. Gus Van continued performing almost until his death in 1968.

The Lady in the Red Hat

The world of performers is big-hearted and sentimental, as the story of the woman known as "the little old lady in the little red hat" proves. When Ida Robinson died in a Manhattan hospital in 1958, little was known of her except that she was ninety-four, lived in a $10-a-week room, shuffled down the street to daily Mass, and always wore a red hat with a feather. She became less anonymous when a yellowed clipping was found in her room identifying her as retired costume designer for vaudeville comedians, actors, and elephants at Billy Rose's Hippodrome and the 1901 Buffalo World's Fair. In his "Around New York" column in the *New York Times*, the conscience of the city, Meyer Berger, asked that some relative step forward, for otherwise "the little old lady in the little red hat" would end up in a pauper's grave. "She carried her fire too long for that," Berger chided his readers.

No family member came forward, but an official at the Actors' Fund read Berger's plea and decided that, though Ida Robinson had not been an actor, she was very definitely a person of the stage and deserved to be buried in the fund's Actors' Plot. Her funeral Mass was sung by two monks while a third played the organ. "It was a rather unusual mass," Berger reported, "somewhat the same as a priest might have after passing."

The March Princes

In the mid to late 1800s, a handful of émigré European musicians—several of whom are buried in the Actors' Fund Plot—taught Americans to love opera and classical music. One of these maestros was August Bischoff, the director of Brooklyn's Deutscher Liederkranz for twenty-seven years, in its own concert hall. Another was Edward Remenyi, a Hungarian violinist who had accompanied Johannes Brahms and gained a large following in America through his affection for patriotic songs from both his native and adopted countries. (When he expired while conducting "The Star-Spangled Banner," his friends said it was the death he had always wanted.)

Even more famous was an Italian, Carlo Alberto Cappa, who after early musical training in 1856, when he was twenty-one, signed aboard a U.S. Navy frigate at Genoa. Two years later he was playing trombone for New York's Seventh Regiment band. Three years after that, in 1861, he was marching through the streets of New York on the way to war. He led the band for many years, taking classical music to the people in summer concerts in Central Park and at Brighton Beach, and making North American tours. Cappa was knighted by Italy and Venezuela, and after his death in 1893, he was buried under weeping willows and tall oaks in the Shadowy Way section near a monument whose inscription speaks of a gentle soul: "The first time he ever hurt anyone was when he died, and then the pain was deep."

Cappa was a co-creator (with Patrick S. Gilmore and the U.S.–born "March King" John Philip Sousa) of one of the greatest of all American musical crazes, the era of the marching bands. The march could take almost any form—a boom-boom, blare-blare parade tune blasted out by a brass band; a rhythmic dance like the two-step, cake walk, or polka; or a pianist's soft solo variation on a ragtime theme. Distinctively American, the march, according to music historian Nicholas E. Tawa, "captured the confidence, vitality, colorful contrasts, and often the sadness found in turn-of-century America." Fueling the march craze was the new availability of inexpensive upright pianos to place and play in the home parlor. William Clark, who is buried at the Evergreens, built some of the first pianos in New York and kept at it for years until his death in 1898. Between 1857 and 1887 alone, Americans bought more than 800,000 pianos from Clark and other piano makers.

The Prince of March Marketing

Also helping Americans to love music was a new, aggressive way of marketing it. E. T. Paull, who also is at the Evergreens, reportedly was the second most popular

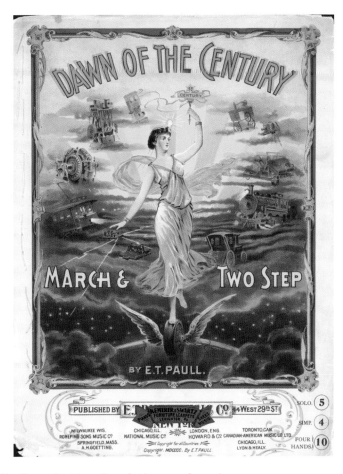

He may not have been the march king, but E.T. Paull was the king of marketing march music, with tunes and fancy packaging for every occasion.

composer and arranger of marches after Sousa. Thirty million copies of sheet music were sold in 1910 at between 10 and 30 cents a copy, and a lot of it was sold by E. T. Paull. While not as gifted a bandmaster as Cappa or Sousa, Edward Taylor Paull was an important figure in the national music business that was loosely identified as "Tin Pan Alley" (the nickname for West 28th Street in Manhattan, where many music companies were located). He chose song subjects and titles that appealed to Americans at a time when they were forging a broader and stronger national identity, and he presented his and other composers' music to the public in an unusually colorful style, like that of rock music album cover art in the 1960s.

Paull learned the business from the bottom up. At age twenty in 1878, he was managing a music store in his hometown of Martinsburg, Virginia, selling pianos,

organs, and the sheet music required to play them. After moving to Richmond in the 1890s Paull composed marches in danceable two-step styles while developing new approaches to titles and packaging. Where Sousa gave his tunes patriotic titles like "Stars and Stripes Forever," Paull linked his songs to well-known contemporary cultural icons in somewhat the same way that today's country singer-composers do. He titled his first published march "The Chariot Race, or *Ben Hur* March," after General Lew Wallace's wildly successful novel (which was later adapted to the screen). Paull's later titles referred to action-packed events in European history ("Burning of Rome," "Napoleon's Last Charge"), the American Revolution ("Paul Revere's Ride"), the Civil War ("Sheridan's Ride," "Battle of Gettysburg"), and the Indian wars ("Custer's Last Charge" was broken into four sections, "Indian Camp Awakens," "Shrill Cry of Indian Pickets," "Bugle Sounding," and "White Chief Long Hair Is Coming"). Oddly, Paull responded to the sinking of the *Maine* in 1898, with atypical bland titles like "We'll Stand by the Flag" and "America Forever."

Choosing an apt title was only one part of E. T. Paull's marketing scheme. He worked with artists and a Richmond printer who could do splendid colorful lithograph covers that are a match for the best Beatles' record jackets and 1940s movie posters. The one for "Custer's Last Charge" shows the general in buckskin calmly holding off several dozen Native American savages. Paull could be simple, too. When Coney Island and bicycles became popular around the turn of the century, he produced "The New York and Coney Island Cycle March Two Step." The chorus goes:

Now for a song as we go wheeling on,
And for the glorious "bike" we'll shout,
It's up to date in all that's new and great,
This wonder that we sing about.

In fact, it was all about wonder. That was the appeal. When H. G. Wells and other early science fiction writers were speculating about space travel, Paull wrote a march called "A Signal from Mars," with a telescope on the cover. Amid the debate over permitting women to vote, he turned out a march titled "Woman Forever." Carefully appealing to both traditionalists and proto-feminists alike, he placed an enthroned queen on the cover and dedicated the song to "womanhood of the universe."

He was far less cautious in 1924 when he wrote a new march titled "The Four Horsemen of the Apocalypse," featuring the Grim Reaper. Perhaps Paull felt an omen; he died later that year.

John Bunny, Movie Clown

When Winsor McCay was making his breakthrough animated cartoon, *Little Nemo*, in 1911, he prefaced it with a live-action sequence in which several human skeptics are gradually converted. Perhaps McCay believed the medium was too novel for viewers to be exposed to it

JOHN BUNNY
OF THE
VITAGRAPH PLAYERS
IN CHARACTER

"The best-known man in the world" at the time of his death. John Bunny was the movies' first star comedian.

suddenly, without a buildup, but whatever the reason, he chose the right man to play the doubter. A heavyset, forceful fellow with a pumpkin-sized head creased by an ear-to-ear grin, he was a former circus performer and vaudevillian who was just then launching his own movie career in a series of one-reel comedies. Over the next four years before his premature death, John Bunny became America's first great comedy movie star, a tremendous international favorite, and a forerunner who helped legitimize the new medium and prepare audiences for Charlie Chaplin, Harold Lloyd, and the other great cinema comedians.

"There was a clown named John Bunny. Now he is

dead," wrote a commentator on popular culture, Joyce Kilmer, not long after Bunny died. "But we still may see and our children's children may see, the gestures and grimaces that made him a welcome visitor in every quarter of the globe. For by the grace of the motion-picture camera, John Bunny's art endures." Kilmer was right about Bunny's popularity (though not, sadly, about its longevity; the self-destructive capabilities of nitrate film stock meant that very few of his one hundred fifty films survive). When Bunny died of Bright's disease at age fifty-two in 1915, the following headline ran in a paper in Dublin, Ireland: "John Bunny Is Dead. The Best-Known Man in the World." A U.S. newspaper speculated that he was more deeply mourned than any president of the United States ever would be.

Born in New York in 1863 and raised in Brooklyn, the son of an Irish mother and English father, Bunny was clerking in a general store when he got the itch to join a minstrel show. Blessed with an agile (if round) body and a rubbery (if ugly) face, he fit into the Falstaff school of acting that Kilmer described as "fat humorously." After twenty-five years on the stage, he saw movies coming along. In 1909 he made a film about Brooklyn's big seaside resort, *Cohen's Dream of Coney Island*, then went over to Vitagraph Company, a film production operation with a studio in Flatbush, and asked for a job in the movies. One of Vitagraph's officers recalled his and a colleague's first encounter with Bunny: "A very fat man was leaning against the wall of the studio, like a buttress supporting the wall of Notre Dame. 'We need a new comedy man,' said Albert, 'maybe this one will be funny.'

"He saw us coming. 'Look,' he said, 'can either of you gentlemen do this?' Springing into the air, he clicked his heels together three times before he hit the ground again. 'I want a chance at the pictures,' he pleaded, 'just a chance.'

"He got his chance."

Many films made by the man known as "Funny Bunny" were of the domestic situation comedy genre, like *Everybody Loves Raymond* and *The Honeymooners*,

where a childlike husband is brought to task by his sensible wife. Bunny was the husband, and the wife was an actress named Flora Flinch, described by the Vitagraph historian, Anthony Slade, as "a tall, thin, spinsterish actress with pinched features." Although occasionally tackling larger, more serious projects, such as productions of Thackery's *Vanity Fair* and Dickens' *The Pickwick Papers*, Bunny generally stuck to the tried-and-true story line. By 1914 the star had become more important than the story, and his name was in most of the films' titles (*Bunny's Swell Affair*, *Bunny's Scheme*, *Bunny Buys a Harem*, *Bunny Backslides*, and so on).

Bunny's weekly salary at first was $40, but as these one-reel films—churned out at a rate of almost one a week—found an audience, his pay advanced dramatically to $1,000. He invested in a chain of movies theatres in New York, each with images of bunny rabbits on its facade. As successful and funny as he was, Bunny had a way of tossing it all away, leaving an estate of just $8,000 and very few friends, thanks to his immense ego. Bunny and Flora Finch reserved a special dislike for each other, and the feelings of his real wife and children may be gauged by the fact that the only person interred in the large Bunny lot at the Evergreens is John Bunny.

If the real John Bunny was not the man people saw on the screen, at least the better John Bunny was. Audiences everywhere adored him. When the news went out in the spring of 1915 that he was seriously ill in his Flatbush home, his decline and death were treated with the seriousness reserved for kings and popes. A newspaper in Georgia said this: "Good old John Bunny! The man who made the whole world laugh on countless gloomy days, has made it weep at last."

"BOJANGLES"
BILL ROBINSON

BORN MAY 25, 1877
DIED NOVEMBER 25, 1949

DANCED HIS WAY
INTO THE HEARTS OF MILLIONS

"WITH MALICE TOWARD NONE,
WITH CHARITY FOR ALL."
A.Lincoln

CHAPTER EIGHTEEN

BLIND TOM, THE QUEEN OF THE TRUMPET, BOJANGLES, AND THE PRES

THE PERFORMERS WHOM we have been talking about shared two traits. First, they were strong characters; there was nothing bland about a one of them. Second, they all were Caucasians. The first can be said about another line of entertainers but not the second, for there is a long, distinguished tradition of African American entertainers at the Evergreens.

I. MINSTREL DAYS

Before the 1920s the range of black parts in the mainstream American theatre was exceedingly narrow, with the typical role an ever-cheerful, ever-compliant slave like the one in the title of Harriet Beecher Stowe's pre-Civil War novel, *Uncle Tom's Cabin.* "In the beginning, there was an Uncle Tom," writes Donald Bogle in his history of African Americans in movies, *Toms, Coons, Mulattoes, Mammies, and Bucks.* Tom and his friends were almost always played by white actors who darkened ("blackfaced") their skin using corks that had been singed in a flame. Blanche DeBar once appeared in blackface when she played Eliza. Another entertainer at the Evergreens who specialized in playing African Americans, John Mulligan, was described in his obituary as "an Ethiopian comedian" whose "appearance on the stage was ever a signal for hearty laughter." In fact, John Mulligan was no Ethiopian or any other kind of African for that matter, but an Irishman. To outward appearances, however, on stage he fit the typical white American's image of the typical black American—in short, a coal-black buffoon. This look was so widely expected that the very few African American performers who were allowed on stage were, like the white men who played them, obliged to apply burnt cork because their skin was deemed to be insufficiently black.

Eph Horn was famous for his mock-dignified air, pompous speeches, and large and flexible mouth that, according to one fan, when "surrounded by burnt cork and opened at intervals, was calculated to set even the Pilgrim Fathers roaring." Had he lived another fifty years, he would have been a magnificent Kingfish, the humbug on the Amos 'n Andy radio and television shows. The best known of the Evergreens' pseudoblack minstrel stars, Thomas K. Heath, teamed up with James McIntyre in 1878 to form the Georgia Minstrels, Heath playing the too-clever-for-his-own-good city slicker taking advantage of McIntyre's Uncle Tom country boob. Half a century later, McIntyre & Heath were still in blackface, dancing the buck-and-wing and singing "There'll Be a Hot Time in the Old Town Tonight." Close friends who lived near each other on Eastern Long Island, they died just months apart—first McIntyre and then Heath, from whom the news of the passing of his dear old colleague had been carefully kept.

It takes nothing away from these gifted character actors to point out that, at the same time they were doing well by parodying African Americans in theatres frequented by white audiences, most real African Americans could not even get a job pushing a broom in those establishments. The typical white American would have considered this an inevitability: "Colored performers cannot vie with white ones, and colored producers cannot play within an apple's throw of Ziegfeld," *Variety* magazine editorialized as late as 1921. "They may be good, but they're different, and in their entertainment they should remain different, distinct, and indigenous." And that remained the rule for many years.

Japanese Tommy and the Dahomeyite

When a black player was permitted on a white theatre's stage, it usually was because the act was bizarre. A black dwarf named Thomas Dilverd made his living in the same way blackface white actors did, by satirizing a pariah people, in his case Asians. Dressed up in vaguely Asian garb, "Japanese Tommy" performed contortionist tricks while cracking jokes in pigeon Japanese-Chinese. He reportedly coined the phrase "hunky dory," meaning "just great." In Brooklyn, Hooley's Opera House ran an advertisement that said, "Japanese Tommy, the Wonder of the World. Don't Fail to See the Little Man." Off stage, Dilverd lived black and died black, passing away at age forty-five in 1887 in the Colored Home and Hospital in Manhattan. He was buried at the Evergreens in the Actors' Fund Plot.

There is a black performer at the Evergreens who never made it onto an American stage. John Ussagah, as his name is recorded in burial records, was an African from the Kingdom of Dahomey (now the Republic of Benin) who with more than seventy other male and female members of a group of Fon people crossed the Atlantic in 1893 to establish a village and perform at the World's Columbian Exposition, better known as the Chicago World's Fair. The first black performers that most Americans ever encountered, the Dahomey Villagers introduced the power of drumming to Western music. Here is a review of one concert: "The drum-major opens the performance with gentle, rhythmic tapping of drums, rapidly increasing in tone. Then another drum is heard, and presently the clashing of a cymbal, the sound gradually gaining in volume until all the musicians are hard at work." They might be the Rolling Stones. The ragtime composer and pianist Scott Joplin heard the Dahomeyites play in Chicago, as did the Czech composer

Antonín Dvořák (some of whose compositions may have been influenced by African and slave music); his student, the African American composer Will Marion Cook; and the black poet James Weldon Johnson. When Cook and Johnson put a ragtime operetta on the stage in 1902, they called it *In Dahomey.* John Coltrane later played a composition he called "Dahomey Dance."

Whatever John Ussagah had contributed to the Dahomey sound, he was unable to perform in Chicago. He died of pneumonia soon after the troupe arrived in New York from West Africa. As the body was prepared for interment at the Evergreens, his friends snipped off fragments of his hair and toenails to send back for burial at his home. That Ussagah and the other Dahomeyites were even allowed in the country outraged many Americans, including the editors of the *Brooklyn Eagle,* who thundered, "From the point of morality and intelligence, they are the lowest class of strange creatures that have yet landed at the Immigration building." But Ussagah was buried in Brooklyn, in an unmarked charity grave in the Mt. Pisgah section of the Evergreens.

Blind Tom

"He is certainly a wonder," exclaimed a Confederate soldier on hearing the thirteen-year-old boy known as "Blind Tom" play the piano in 1862. That was the usual response to Thomas Greene Wiggins who, though a blind, autistic slave on a Georgia plantation, was a musical genius. The *Chicago Defender,* the leading African American newspaper, once headlined a story about him, "Blind Tom, Unsolved Problem in Musical History."

Wiggins very early demonstrated an astounding aptitude for flawlessly repeating any music he heard and

Mark Twain said Blind Tom Wiggins "lorded it over the emotions of his audience like an autocrat."

then adapting it to create new tunes. As a composer, he employed a flowing, naturalistic style that inspired such titles as "Daylight," "Voice of the Waves," "Water in the Moonlight," and (his favorite) "What the Wind and the Waves Told Tom." This gift was thoroughly exploited by Wiggins' owner, James Hill Bethune, who changed the boy's name to Thomas Greene Bethune and leased him out to a concert promoter. Playing command performances (including in the White House) and touring America and Europe, he enthralled his audiences. "If ever there was an inspired idiot this is the individual," Samuel Longhorn Clemons (Mark Twain) wrote, using the then common term for what we call an idiot savant. "He lorded it over the emotions of his audience like an autocrat. He swept them like a storm, with his battle-pieces; he lulled them to rest again with melodies as tender as those we hear in dreams; he gladdened them with others that rippled through the charmed air as happily and cheerily as the riot the linnets make in California woods; and now and then he threw in queer imitations of the tuning of discordant harps and fiddles, and the groaning and wheezing of bag-pipes, that sent the rapt silence into tempests of laughter." As icing on an already rich cake, Tom sang one song while simultaneously playing two more on the piano with his right and left hands.

Ignoring Lincoln's Emancipation Proclamation, Bethune controlled Wiggins for more than twenty years until his daughter-in-law, Eliza Bethune Lerche, went to court, was appointed his guardian, and moved him to Hoboken, New Jersey. Blind Tom performed his last concert in 1904 and died four years later at age fifty-nine. The music played at his funeral included his composition, "Blind Tom's Funeral March." Despite rumors that his remains were sent to Georgia, the Evergreens' records show that he has been in the same grave on Pleasant Hill for one hundred years. The grave, however, was unmarked until a pianist who rediscovered Blind Tom Wiggins' music, John Davis, arranged to have a tombstone placed over it in 2002.

II: WOMEN OF THE HARLEM RENAISSANCE

As jazz developed after 1900, the new music's freewheeling, break-all-rules nature opened opportunities for black performers, three of the most important of whom were women buried at the Evergreens: Lucille Hegamin, Adelaide Hall, and Valaida Snow.

Lucille Hegamin

The oldest of the three was born Lucille Nelson in Macon, Georgia, in 1894, and spent her teen years performing in the South in church choirs and tent shows before joining the northbound African American migration. Blessed with what was called a "vigorous, powerful voice, deep and resonant, youthful and exuberant," she sang in Chicago and West Coast nightclubs and cabarets with groups headed by Jelly Roll Morton and others. She and her then-husband, Bill Hegamin, moved to Harlem in 1919 and took part in the artistic-musical revival known as the Harlem Renaissance. Her specialty was the blues, but with a feminist twist—songs with titles like "I Ain't Givin' Nothin' Away Blues" and "He May Be Your Man, but He Comes to See Me Sometimes." The jazz critic John S. Wilson called this "the other side of the blues—blues sung by independent, outspoken women rather than the more traditional 'victim' types who are always 'dyin' and cryin' because my man left me." She continued to record and perform on radio and in nightclubs into the 1930s. When the Great Depression introduced a new kind of blues that put hers out of fashion, she left show business to become a registered nurse, returning to performing after she retired in the 1960s. Lucille Hegamin Allen died in 1970 and is buried at the Evergreens alongside her mother. Many of her recordings have been collected on compact discs.

Adelaide Hall

In the 1920s the formerly all-white territory of Broadway tentatively began to produce musical reviews with black casts and themes. Out of these successful shows with titles like *Shuffle Along*, *Chocolate Dandies*, *Blackbirds of 1928*, and *Rhapsody in Black* came a generation of African American performers. One of the most gifted was a young woman described in these words: "Flashing eyes, beautiful, witty, vivacious, and she can sing, too." The daughter of a Pennsylvania German father and an African American mother, Adelaide Hall spent her early life in the Clinton section of Brooklyn. Music surrounded her. Her father taught it, held singalongs in the house, and encouraged his daughter, telling her (she lovingly recalled) to "sing to the moon, Addie, and the stars will shine." She did sing, first in the choir at the local Episcopal church and then in school under a demanding music instructor whose former students included Fats Waller. When the girl's best friend, Florence Mills, formed a family group called the Mills Sisters, Adelaide Hall followed suit with her sister Evelyn, who later died in the 1918–19 influenza epidemic.

Hall's first big break was as a member of the chorus of *Shuffle Along*, a landmark 1921 African American musical starring Mills. Within a year there was a popular song about how it was "getting darker on Old Broadway." Though Florence Ziegfeld still declined to use black performers, he at least hired black dancers to teach his showgirls the sexy steps coming down from Harlem's cabarets. "The music had an intensive, pervasive rhythm—sometimes loud and brassy, often weird and wild," Lena Horne would recall. "The dances were elegantly provocative; and if they were occasionally stately, that stateliness served only to heighten their abandon." In 1927 Adelaide Hall, backed by Duke Ellington's orchestra, recorded a sinuous half-chant, half-moan, "Creole Love Call." After Florence Mills died young, Hall was selected to star in *Blackbirds of 1928*, where she sang "I Can't Give You Anything But Love, Baby" and danced with Bill "Bojangles" Robinson. When Harlem's bright lights were dimmed by the Depression and the downtown cabarets shut the door on black performers, she moved to Europe, where she performed for many years, married an Englishman, and became a British citizen. A nightclub she founded in London was bombed and destroyed in the Blitz, and she toured the front, entertaining soldiers. After the war Hall returned to the theatre in London and New York. In 1992, in her nineties, she brought her one-woman show to New York and was hailed for her "undefeatable cheer" and "gregarious optimism." Adelaide Hall Hicks died a year later in England, and was carried back to her old home of Brooklyn to be buried at the Evergreens.

Valaida Snow

While there are many certainties about one of the most exciting and flamboyant women of the Jazz Age, there also are more than a few mysteries. Valaida Snow (her first name was pronounced "Val-i-da") was born in Chattanooga, Tennessee, on June 2—that much is agreed on—but whether that June 2 was in 1903, 1905, 1907, 1914, or any of the other birth years she claimed is unknown. It has also been rumored that she was the child of a white father and black mother who were entertainers and music teachers, and that by her late teens she was professionally singing, dancing, and playing eight instruments, including the harp and cello. What is known for sure is that she played the trumpet so well that she was promoted as "the Queen of the Trumpet" and sometimes other performers called her "Little Louis," in honor of the great Louis Armstrong.

Developing a performance style described as "effervescent with pep and vitality," Valaida Snow went to Harlem in the 1920s. Between shows at the Apollo Theatre and on Broadway, she toured internationally (according to another impossible-to-prove Snow story,

A woman of "undefeatable cheer" throughout her many years, Brooklyn's Adelaide Hall was a star of the Harlem Renaissance.

she taught Shanghai cooks how to prepare soul food). The regal singer-actress Ethel Waters believed that she was the star of a production called *Rhapsody in Black.* That was before Snow made her grand entrance on an immense bass drum, playing high Cs on the trumpet, and then proceeded to lead a sixty-piece orchestra and chorus, wielding the baton (according to one member of the audience) "with a frenzy that would abash a roomful of Toscaninis." After a few weeks of stealing Waters' spotlight, Snow found herself without a job.

Valaida Snow was not inclined to live according to other people's rules. Taking a shine to an eighteen-year-old dancer in one of her shows, Snow (then in her thirties) eloped with him. His angry father discovered that she had not got around to divorcing her last husband, and she spent some time in jail. The cabaret singer Bobby Short remembered seeing her "in an orchid-colored Mercedes-Benz, dressed in an orchid suit, her pet monkey rigged out in an orchid jacket and cap, with the chauffeur in orchid as well." As Earl Hines, a jazz pianist who knew her well, said, "She just loved a good time and she had to have the best of everything." He added, "She was just a beautiful and exceptionally talented woman." When the Depression and racism ended the party she went to Europe, where she played clubs, made records and movies, and performed before royalty; the Queen of the Netherlands was said to be so pleased that she presented Snow a golden trumpet.

Snow's life as she knew it ended suddenly in 1941. Exactly what happened is not clear, but it seems that while she was performing in an all-girl band in Nazi-occupied Scandinavia, she was arrested and sent to the Wester-Faengle internment camp in Copenhagen, which specialized in the confinement of black people. When a prisoner exchange allowed her to return to America, she weighed sixty-eight pounds and spoke of near-starvation rations and regular beatings and rapes. After a long recuperation, she returned to show business, taking her act to mid-level nightclubs and cabarets, but also to burlesque houses and other low-grade venues. She was changed physically and also emotionally. "She was so talented, so beautiful, and so sweet," remembered a friend, Melba Liston. "But she was so unhappy. She was like hurt all the time." Perhaps it was this vulnerability that caused the boxer Joe Louis to announce before she performed at his nightclub, "Tell the bartenders not to serve anything, and ask the waiters to stand still while Miss Snow sings. She's an artist if there ever was one."

Her career as a flashy star well behind her, she gave a recital of sacred, classical, and popular songs at New York's Town Hall. Blaming others for her fall, she told thenewspaper columnist Walter Winchell, "On Broadway, there are always some jealous people when you Stop the Show." When a cerebral hemorrhage finally stopped Valaida Snow's show, fittingly she was backstage at the Palace Theatre on Times Square.

She was buried at the Evergreens on her birthday, June 2 (cemetery records give her age as forty-two, at least a decade less than her real one). The life force that was Valaida Snow went to her reward in a $165 grave that was left unmarked by her husband at the time, a promoter named Edwards.

She is often seen, even in her periods of self-indulgence, as a paradigmatic figure of struggle and rebellion against oppression. "Despite her confinement," writes Clarence Lusane in an account of her wartime captivity, "Snow prevailed and remains a symbol of the tenacity and unyielding spirit of jazz women who refuse

Her vitality and resilience carried Valaida Snow into show business and through Nazi imprisonment, but she was buried in an unmarked grave.

to submit and who live their choices uncompromisingly." She has inspired two works of fiction by African American writers (a short story by John Edgar Wideman in his collection *Fever* and a novel, *Valaida*, by Candace Allen), and there has been talk of a biographical movie. But except for the many stones and ribbons left by her admirers, plot 11134 in the Redemption section at the Evergreens remained without a marker in 2007.

III: Bojangles

Valaida Snow's grave is about halfway between the last resting places of two of the most important black male performers in popular music history. The older man was nicknamed "Bojangles," the younger "the Pres." The dancer Bill Robinson and the jazz saxophonist Lester Young dominated their fields for almost forty years. Although they were buried at the Evergreens only eight years apart, when it came to taste in music and attitudes about race, they were separated by generations

On a late November day in 1949, the man known universally by his childhood nickname, Bojangles, was carried through Manhattan and Brooklyn—from his funeral in Harlem to a brief stop in Times Square, and then on to the Evergreens—along miles of streets lined by a throng of mourners that the police estimated at more than 500,000. Once the flag-draped hearse passed, the men put their hats back on and began to talk about the Bill Robinson they knew. "Some would say how they remembered him showing a child how to dance down the steps of a tenement," a hovering journalist would report. "Others marveled at his slight regard for money, recalling how with indifference he would lose $10,000 on a roll of dice. In church, when the pastor remarked that Mr. Robinson had two vices, 'ice cream and gambling,' the audience laughed over the recollection of his carefree manner." They all assumed one more thing about Bojangles Robinson. As unlucky as he had been at the dice table, with cards, and betting that Joe DiMaggio would hit a home run—so unlucky, in fact, that he blew several fortunes and died flat broke—Bojangles Robinson was a genius at entertaining. Four years after his death, in the classic MGM musical *The Band Wagon* the character played by Jack Buchanan declared, "There is no difference between the magic rhythms of Bill Shakespeare's immortal verse and the magic rhythms of Bill Robinson's immortal feet."

A slave's grandson, he was born Luther Robinson in Richmond, Virginia, in 1878, and quickly earned a common prankster's nickname, Bojangles. He dropped out of school at age seven, first performed at eight, and at fourteen ran away from home, appropriating his younger brother William's first name to become Bill. That larceny reflected a lifelong sense of entitlement of the sort that often accompanies exceptional talent. After he developed his signature "stair dance" routine—a soft-shoe glide up a flight of steps and down again, with no show of effort other then a slight waving of his hands, his fingers light as feathers—Robinson took out a graceless newspaper ad advising that anyone who dared to borrow the routine would end up in court. "This is fair warning. It goes for both sides of the ocean and I go everywhere sooner or later, You be nice and I'll be nice . . . or else!" Throughout his long life, his quick temper regularly got the better of him. With debt collectors often hovering nearby, he was known to carry a knife and even a pistol.

As a young man Robinson played the minstrel and vaudeville circuit with a partner. After several years of knocking around and being knocked around, he took the big chance of going solo, polishing his image from street-corner scruffy to drawing-room classy with the aim of appealing to white audiences. He adopted the word *copacetic* (meaning "first rate" or "excellent") as his personal slogan, always verbalized enthusiastically as "copacetic!" The gamble paid off. In the 1930s Robinson

became the first African American stage and film star to succeed equally well with both black and white audiences. Only a couple of years after making an all-black film titled *Harlem Is Heaven* and being named the unofficial "Mayor of Harlem," Robinson appeared with the white child star Shirley Temple in three extremely popular films. Their stair dance duet in *The Little Colonel* continues to enchant curly-topped little girls (and their parents and grandparents, too). Although his characters were always subservient to whites, Robinson was given remarkable liberties. Film historian Donald Bogle has remarked that "certainly the first time in the history of motion pictures that a black servant was made responsible for a white life" was when Robinson's plantation slave, Uncle Billy, saved the Temple character from a band of threatening soldiers in *The Littlest Rebel.*

The curmudgeonly "colored" hoofer and gambler became a beloved national symbol of avuncular authority and graceful living. The superstar white dancer, Fred Astaire, honored him with the "Bojangles of Harlem" tribute in the movie *Swing Time*, and producers cast him in racially integrated Broadway shows. "Every one knows Bojangles Bill and is devoted to him," wrote the theatre critic Brooks Atkinson. "But this department never ceases admiring the genius of this magnetic master of the taps who treats his feet kindly and preserved all these years the springy step, the impeccable taste of the instinctive artist and honest showman. The rhythm has become so much a part of him that even when he is standing still you feel that he is dancing."

More accurately, *most* people loved Bill Robinson. What Bogle called his "spontaneous effervescence" seemed to some African Americans the sign of a racial sellout. "The biggest Uncle Tom in Show Biz" was how he was characterized by Lena Horne, his co-star in the film *Stormy Weather*. Fiercely protective personally, when it came to racial issues he was a cautious accommodationist. After the black baseball pitcher Don Newcombe was criticized for rejecting a white opponent's challenge to a fight, Robinson assured Newcombe that he had acted correctly; he might have started a race riot. "He told me he was very proud of the way I conducted himself," Newcombe said. Perhaps Robinson had been around too long to fight a system that piled on humiliations. On location, Shirley Temple and other white actors were put up in four-star hotels, but Bojangles of Harlem had to rent a room in the "colored" part of town. Directors filmed his and other black actors' songs or dances in ways that allowed them to be easily dropped from the movie so it would be permitted to play in Southern theatres.

Death did not end the Bill Robinson spectacular. The funeral in Harlem was arranged by two men who knew how to put on a good show, the black clergyman-Congressman Adam Clayton Powell Jr. and the white entertainment columnist and future television impresario Ed Sullivan. The viewing was held in an armory because the churches were too small, and more than 30,000 people filed past his coffin. The honorary pallbearers were sports and Hollywood stars, including Newcombe, Cole Porter, Jackie Robinson, Bob Hope, Joe Louis, Duke Ellington, and Joe DiMaggio. In his eulogy, Powell portrayed Robinson as above the world's problems: "He was a legend because he was ageless and raceless. Bill was a credit not just to the Negro race but to the human race. He was Mister Show Business. He was Broadway. And who is to say that making people happy isn't the finest thing in the world?" Powell put together a fund to pay the bills.

Robinson was buried in the eastern part of the Evergreens Cemetery, in a prominent corner of the Redemption section. Six months later, a choir, a color guard, a rabbi, a priest, and Ed Sullivan were on hand to dedicate his monument, with its bas relief of Robinson's

The marvelous dancer and personalty Bojangles Robinson was a magnet for words like "spontaneous effervescence." He preferred "copacetic."

face, the statement, "Danced his way into the hearts of millions," and Abraham Lincoln's advisory to express malice toward none and charity for all. When the stone was vandalized, a replacement was provided by one of Bojangles Robinson's best black dancer successors, Sammy Davis Jr. Standing high behind a thick field of flowers, it has the appearance of a small but cherished lighthouse marking the channel into a harbor.

IV: The Pres

Effervescent Bill Robinson and Valaida Snow surely were, but effervescence was not a trait of another black star who is buried very near them. Lester Young's authority over his instrument inspired Billie Holiday to refer to him as the President of the Tenor Saxophone, or "the Pres" (he in turn called her "Lady Day"). Though he is widely acknowledged to be one of the giants of jazz, his headstone (unlike Robinson's) says nothing of his accomplishments. There is, however, testimony that here lies a good man who was much loved. "Till we shall meet and never part," reads the epitaph. That is the last line of a poem by an English poet, Henry King, in memory of his wife, whom he called his "matchless never to be forgotten friend." Half a century after Lester Young's death in 1959, the crown of his stone is usually crowded with rocks of remembrance and sheets of music left by his fans.

He usually performed in an ugly flat-topped, wide-brimmed "porkpie" hat, and he cocked his saxophone at an awkward angle across his body so as not to poke the back of the player in front of him. Yet he is widely regarded as one of the transformative figures in the history of popular music. He was a shy, often melancholy, loner with a boyish face and what seemed to some people to be the saddest eyes they had ever seen. Sadness

"I melt with all of it." Lester Young said of jazz.
His distinctive saxophone style and his mystical
pronouncements have had vast influence
among performers like his friend Billie Holiday.

there surely was during his fifty years, what with divorces, violence, alcoholism, drug abuse, and a miserable army stint that included a court martial and a stint in the detention barracks.

Born in southern Mississippi in 1909, he was raised by his musician parents amid the clamor of the New Orleans jazz scene. When he turned ten his father took him off on the minstrel show and carnival circuit with the Young Family Band. He eventually ran off and for years played in jazz bands, becoming close with Holiday, the remarkable young singer with whom he developed similar soft styles. Just as William Steinitz reinvented the rules for winning chess matches, Young turned jazz inside out and upside down—"like nothing we'd ever heard" was the judgment of one of his bandleaders, Count Basie. The jazz critic and historian Gary Giddins

used more technical language, referring to Young's "contrary melodic fragments, each complete in itself and rhythmically invincible, that makes perfect sense." All this shocked the establishment. "Oh, they were terrified of Lester," the jazz composer Gil Evans said of the critics. "They used to be so scared of him because of his rhythmic freedom, for one thing. They were used to having somebody play that would take their hand and hold it all the way through, you know what I mean? But with Pres, it was different." Young, said someone who often played with him, was "the only person I know who could play a song that called for fire and not put fire into it."

His reputation was not founded solely on his musical gifts. People loved the man. A thick collection of affectionate reminiscences, *The Lester Young Reader* was published more than thirty years after his death. Friends and acquaintances shared a sense that they were in the presence of a rare someone—"Gandhi-like" and "a visitor from a small plane" according to the pianist and composer Bobby Scott—who had special knowledge and wisdom, and a special way of expressing it in his sometimes opaque jive talk. "He plays those licks, I play my licks, you play your licks," was how Young explained why he declined to borrow techniques from another musician. Asked why all his performances were unique, he said, "I try not to be a repeater pencil." When Young spoke about music, he sounded like a mystic. "I melt with all of it." Had Blind Tom Wiggins been able to talk, he might have said the same thing.

Young and Billy Holiday did not see each other for years until December 1957, when they played together in a television performance of a blues song of hers, "Fine and Mellow." (It is archived on the Internet.) Dying from their two addictions—alcohol in Young's case, drugs in Holiday's—they put together a piece of magic, Young wrapping the tune in an understated bliss that transfixed Holiday. Within two years they were dead.

CHAPTER NINETEEN

A RURAL CEMETERY
IN THE
TWENTY-FIRST CENTURY

At the time sad-eyed Lester Young was buried in the Redemption section in March 1959, the Evergreens was a very different place from the struggling Cemetery of the Evergreens of a century earlier. For instance, the grounds were rapidly filling up. On the cemetery's ledger, Young was recorded as burial number 402,741. From the original knob-and-bowl central sections laid out in the mid-1800s, to the broad, gently rolling meadows on the Queens side of the county line that were opened in the 1900s, monuments over family lots and headstones over single graves were visible almost everywhere. The cemetery's management was beginning to think about what to do when little or no open land would be left in the early 2000s.

The new areas were named differently from the old ones. When the idea of the rural cemetery was new, its pastoral features were highlighted by naturalistic names—Evergreens, Rustic Fence, Sylvan Dell, Lake View, Ocean View, Beech Side, Hickory

Knoll, Tulip Grove, Mt. Magnolia, and so on. By the turn into the next century, rural cemeteries were so common that the once-innovative picturesque style lost its novelty. The next round of section-naming emphasized the "cemetery" part of "rural cemetery," stressing the land's holy uses with biblical or spiritual names. Many new sections were called after Old Testament landmarks—Mt. Tabor, Mt. Herman, Siloam—or places associated with Jesus' journey to the cross—Nazareth, Bethany, and Mount of Olives. Two new sections, Redemption and Ascension, referred to Christian doctrines. While the cemetery imposed no religious test—gravestones showing the cross and the star of David can be found side by side—neither was its mission wholly secular.

Paradoxically, just as religious names were appearing on the Evergreens map in the early twentieth century, the days of angels looking down benevolently from towering plinths were coming to an end. One reason was a new sense of modesty and proportion. As is well known, death is the great equalizer in every way except in how it is commemorated. Social status is projected sometimes by understatement, sometimes by overstatement, and in the Gilded Age by over-the-top statement. This point was made humorously in 1896 by John Flavel Mines, in his book *Walks in Our Church Yards*: "The shaft in modern times has become merely the marble finger that points down to a grave in which the erstwhile possessor of riches is buried, and is no longer the indication of love and trust that looks up to Heaven." This (temporary) decline in conspicuous memorializing had economic causes. Costs were rising, and since single graves in all but soft soil could accommodate two or three caskets, one atop the other, many families turned away from the traditional family lot and acquired singles. In the 1950s twelve new single graves were being sold for every new family lot. In the new, exclusively single sections, small headstones march like well-drilled troops across the fields, their rows and columns presenting a far more tame and orderly look than that of the old heterogeneous rural cemetery, with its random styles.

There were continuities. One was (and remains) the famous diversity of Brooklynites. Ship captains and farmers, reformers and crooks, former slaves and white vaudevillians who pretended to be black, Bohemian painters and Puritanical scolds, German-Americans, Chinese-Americans, Hispanic-Americans—all and more continued to be received into the sandy soil of the Green Hills. There were the usual ironies. In 1925 a man who was celebrated as Chinatown's peacemaker for ending a violent tong (or gang) war, Lee Kue-Ying, died of natural causes, and after a procession of one hundred cars to the Evergreens, was interred in Celestial Hill. Eleven months later almost to the day, a twenty-car procession to Celestial Hill followed the remains of a tong gunman named Sam Wing, who a week after the peacemaker's funeral had murdered a laundryman and was subsequently electrocuted at Sing Sing. In 1997 the character actor William Hickey, nominated for an Academy Award for his role as the wizened, bizarre, and lethal Don Corrado Prizzi in *Prizzi's Honor*, was buried in Gibron under a headstone with the pictures of two dogs and the epitaph, "Actor, Teacher, Child of God."

Surviving the Depression

In the sunny 1920s the Brooklyn Rapid Transit Company built a subway out from Fourteenth Street in Manhattan to Canarsie. Now called the L line, it ran past the Evergreens on a right of way that it bought from the cemetery, a splinter of land so narrow that the tracks are stacked one atop the other, allowing the outbound passengers a quick view of the cemetery grounds. An even broader panorama of the Green Hills opened as the train climbed up onto the spectacular, roller-coaster-like Broadway Junction elevated station.

The optimism represented by the new B.R.T. line was echoed by the cemetery. The year 1929 was the busiest in Evergreens history, with almost 4,700 interments and sales of new lots and graves totaling an acre and a half of land. The management confidently raised rates and fees by as much as 33 percent—just in time for the Depression and the collapse of the market in family lots. As many more single graves were purchased, the trustees, worried about future maintenance, made a second mistake in 1932 when they added a mandatory $75 charge for perpetual care (called permanent maintenance today) atop the $100 for the grave. The $175 price was more than double the charges at neighboring cemeteries. Sales of single graves declined precipitously. All told, between 1929 and 1935 interments at the Evergreens dropped by one-third and land sales by three-fourths, the investment portfolio lost more than half its value, and profits almost disappeared. Alarmed by the collapse of old, previously safe investments like railroads, the Board of Trustees tore up the old investment policy and bought hundreds of mortgages on Brooklyn and Queens real estate, making long-term loans at 3 or 4 percent interest rates to homeowners and businesses that included Trommer's Brewery and a boat marina in Queens. (A request for a loan by a Brooklyn undertaker was turned down on the sensible grounds that there might be a conflict of interest.)

Even the few bits of sweet news during the Depression were likely to sour. In 1934 New York Parks Commissioner Robert Moses instructed the Evergreens to sell the city a seven and one-half acre strip of land along the eastern border to accommodate a new parkway from Queens into Brooklyn. The trustees initially hoped to realize $278,000 in cash. They ended up with $215,000, much of it in New York City bonds for which there was almost no market. The $29,000 per acre price was one-half what Chinese burial societies were then paying. One piece of good news was that Moses' Interborough Parkway (today's Jackie Robinson Parkway) did not slice through Evergreens' burial grounds. Thirty

The fields in the Evergreens' northern section were developed in the 1900s. Many of the familiar symbols and decorative features were retained.

years later, in 1963, Moses announced plans to build a second parkway, this time through the Evergreens to a new tunnel under the East River that would feed an expressway across lower Manhattan. But Moses' supreme power over the city's roads was in decline, and when the expressway was defeated, the second parkway scheme vanished.

Throughout the Depression and the 1940s the Evergreens trustees and management concentrated on finances. It helped that maintenance became simpler when most of the rail lots were finally removed during the World War II metal drives (as described in Chapter 11). In the late 1930s the Evergreens launched an extensive upgrading project with the publicized aim of leaving the cemetery "looking more like a beautiful park." Birdhouses were erected on tall poles, for example. But the primary goals were financial. The handsome old Alexander Jackson Davis gatehouse was torn down, as were watchmen's cottages and stables. Potential income was increased by opening up land for burials. The last of the seven lakes was filled in, and roads and paths were dug up and replaced with soil.

After all that, in 1947 the trustees seemed to reverse their expansion policy by selling off a twenty-acre notch of the northern part of the grounds to a new Jewish cemetery association, Knollwood Park. The price was $52,000 an acre (half that for land under roads), to be paid in five installments as Knollwood expanded over the next decade. Later generations of Evergreens officials would regret the sale of almost 20 percent of its open grounds, but at the time it seemed to be a prudent business decision to address a whole new problem laid on the cemetery's doorstep by state regulators. After disclosures of abuses in the management of some cemeteries, in 1949, after a long debate, the state legislature established a regulatory agency, the Division of Cemeteries, headed by the Cemetery Board. The first time the Evergreens requested that it be allowed to charge higher prices, the board said no. As long as there was enough of a surplus to pay stockholders dividends even during the Depression, the board believed that the Evergreens could survive with its current rates. Seeing the writing on the wall, the Board of Trustees transformed the Evergreens from a for-profit stockholder-owned business to a nonprofit corporation owned mutually by the owners of graves and lots. To buy out the sixty-eight stockholders, instead of borrowing money they used the proceeds from the Knollwood sale.

The management was already adapting to another dramatic change in its business. In 1942 the cemetery's workers voted overwhelmingly in favor of joining a union. Contract negotiations sometimes were contentious, and there were several strikes (one in 1970 ran eight weeks and delayed 115,000 burials in the metropolitan area). When the union won a five-day work week in 1961, the Evergreens and other cemeteries petitioned the Cemetery Board for higher rates on Saturdays to cover the cost of overtime. "We end up with nine burials on Friday and thirty on Saturday," Vice President Robert Goodwin of the Evergreens told the *Times*. Saturday overtime was costing the cemetery $52,000 a year.

Though new sections were no longer named for natural features, the cemetery's landscapers and gardeners remained sensitive to its environment, including putting up birdhouses.

When the Cemetery Board rejected the request, the Evergreens, Green-Wood, and Lutheran Cemetery announced that henceforth they would not do any burials on Saturday. After a six-month legal and public relations battle, the Cemetery Board permitted a special fee for Saturday interments.

The Twin Dynasty

The cemetery business was nothing like what it once was. The Evergreens no longer was a lightly regulated for-profit company with a low overhead and a nonunion workforce. But one thing remained true: the Evergreens had been run by two families for over a century. One was the blood family of Goodwins and Bennetts, the other the official "family" of Graces and officers of W. R. Grace & Co. and its subsidiary, the Grace National Bank. When one of the cemetery's trustees, Charles Erhart Jr., a Grace official, described the Evergreens' board as "very tight-knit," he was referring to this twin dynasty, which provided all but two presidents and most trustees from the 1870s into the 1980s.

The Bennett-Goodwin family so dominated the management of the Evergreens that there was a myth that they actually had founded the cemetery on their Bushwick homestead. That, of course, was not true; the Evergreens was two decades old when the Bennetts came in as investors. Newspaper publisher George C. Bennett and Congressman Charles Goodwin Bennett served as presidents, and after them came Charles' nephew

Expansion was interrupted by the Great Depression but resumed after World War II.
A new state regulatory regime encouraged the Goodwins and Grace interests
to sell off land and change the Evergreens' structure.

George Bennett Goodwin (1914–24) and his son and grandson, Charles Goodwin (1934–49) and Robert Goodwin (1965–86). Charles Goodwin Jr., a lawyer, was chairman of the board in the 1970s, and his son William, another lawyer, served as secretary of the board. The Goodwins took summer jobs at the cemetery, discussed its operations over the dinner table, apprenticed for their elders, served on the board of trustees, and eventually were buried in the family lot.

As for the Graces, their dedication and that of their employees to the Evergreens cannot be explained easily. The Graces were Roman Catholics, and since there was no Catholic consecrated ground at the Evergreens, they were buried elsewhere. But one thing did unify them and their employees and that was a century of loyalty to William R. Grace. As his biographer, Marquis James, remarked in 1948, W. R. Grace & Co. was one of very few businesses shaped for so long by its founder's "personality and life experience"; decades after his death, the company and its subsidiaries continued to be "still really a part of him." Though not officially a subsidiary, the Evergreens might as well have been one because Grace and his family owned much of its stock. The Evergreens board of trustees, which often met at the Grace offices on Hanover Square in Manhattan, at one time or another included the founder's sons (who, among other things, developed the Grace passenger steamship line and formed an airline to South America in partnership with Pan American Airways) and his grandson J. Peter Grace (who transformed the company into a billion-dollar specialty chemical operation). Until the 1990s,

long after the cemetery ceased being a stockholder-owned company, the family's historic interest in the Evergreens was represented by top officers of the Grace company and the Grace National Bank (which merged with the Marine Midland Bank).

The loyalty of Grace employees was exemplary. J. Louis Schaefer was a fourteen-year-old office boy when he went to work for Grace in 1882. He became the treasurer of the parent company, the president of Grace National Bank, and the vice president of the Grace Steamship line. At his death in 1927 he left an estate of nearly $3 million. Along the way he was as an usher at William R. Grace's funeral, the father of a daughter named "Grace," and a trustee of the Evergreens Cemetery. Schaefer, who was extremely active in Lutheran charities, followed his patron's philanthropic example and sometimes exceeded it. Grace had once helped arrange for a ship to carry food to Ireland during a famine; Schaefer personally chartered a steamship to bring stranded Americans home from Italy after the outbreak of World War I. He was succeeded on the Evergreens board by his son J. Louis Schaefer Jr., who stepped down thirty-seven years later. The Schaefers helped run the Evergreens for fifty-two years.

One of the officials of the Grace banking interests who served on the Evergreens board, Crocker Luther, chaired the grounds committee for years. It was more than a duty to him. Luther's affection for the place is obvious in the words he chose to open a report in 1993: "As would be expected after the severe winter and now a very wet spring, the overall condition of the Cemetery was a little glum." On his retirement from the board, the staff presented Luther with a green groundskeeper's shirt.

The long era of the twin dynasty ended in the 1980s when W. R. Grace & Co. moved to Florida, Marine Midland was bought by a global bank, and the last Goodwin president, Robert, retired. Several years later the last Goodwin at the Evergreens, William, a lawyer who was being groomed to be the next chairman of the board, died of an undiagnosed heart condition.

Shaping the Balance

All the trustees shared an affection for the place. When John Titman, a Time–Warner real estate executive who chaired the board for many years, was asked to describe the appeal of a cemetery trusteeship, he immediately burst out, "It really was the most marvelous experience. On many boards the trustees either do nothing or spend most of their time being briefed by lawyers. But this is a small board, and we needed to contribute, each of us. The six of us, with Paul Grassi, really ran the cemetery. We were involved in investment decisions, and we also addressed personnel problems, made decisions about charitable donations of graves, and stayed in *close* touch with the grounds. I now know a lot about what chemicals work best at killing weeds around monuments, and about how to restore big trees—and I am a tree lover. And we did a *lot* of planning. We retained an architectural firm to design plots, and we spent a great deal of time thinking about the future."

Beginning in the 1980s, there were two worries. One was the cemetery's declining appearance, and the other concerned the shrinking availability of land for burials. For years the two missions in the "rural cemetery" formula had been in balance, with concern for the beauty of the grounds about equal with that for business and financial issues. But from the Depression onward, the second role was emphasized. Even the charming wooded hillside around the rustic Summer House, next to the administration building, was developed. The new generation of trustees, however, reversed the trend. Like

Titman, they were tree-loving Brooklyn residents; most, in fact, were active volunteers at the Brooklyn Botanic Garden.

The prior generation had a different style. "Mr. Goodwin was exactly my idea of a New York businessman," comptroller Roland Cadicamo, a longtime Evergreens employee, said about Robert Goodwin, the last of the Bennett-Goodwin family of Evergreens presidents. "You'd come into the office in the morning, and he'd be sitting there reading the *Wall Street Journal* with his feet up on the desk." Goodwin's successor as president, Paul Grassi, would be more likely to be running out the door shouting over his shoulder, "I'll be on the grounds."

"It's a business like any other, but with some differences," Grassi said in the summer of 2007, his twenty-first as the Evergreens' president. "Like all businesses we have a balance sheet, but the departments are unusual and they're all interrelated. When I first came to work for the Evergreens, I expected that the business office would be in Manhattan, which is where I thought all businesses were, but it's more complicated than that because a cemetery has so many goals and problems. The key is to *know this business.*"

Having been around or at the Evergreens nearly all his life, Grassi knew the business. Born in 1949 and raised in the nearby Bushwick-Ridgewood neighborhood, he played football on an undeveloped part of the grounds ("it was Bethany Lawn before it had any graves, and somebody chased us out"). After graduating from Christ the King High School, he majored in accounting at Long Island University while working part-time at the Evergreens as an assistant bookkeeper. He joined the cemetery's business staff full time in 1972 and was mentored by the vice president, Robert Ilasi, a career cemetery man (a "cemeterian," to use today's term). "He taught me everything I know, and he knew the business very well," Grassi looked back. Unhappy that he was not named to succeed Goodwin, Ilasi tried to gain control through a proxy fight, which failed, and in 1986 the Board of Trustees selected Grassi. To the job he brought

CHAPEL MAUSOLEUM

his intensity, a deep personal commitment to a cemetery's traditional purposes ("*cemeteries are forever*," he would burst out), and an openness to trying new things. Unlike older cemetery officials, he and his contemporary cemeterians made a point of maintaining collegial relations and meeting frequently to discuss common issues. Well-respected by his peers, in 1999 Grassi was elected president of both the New York Metropolitan Cemetery Association and the New York State Association of Cemeteries.

Grassi was not one to either finesse a cemetery's problems or minimize the seriousness of its mission. "My worst winter here was in 1994. Bitter cold, deep snow, frost, ice everywhere. We never saw the pavement of the roads, never. We couldn't even get the machines up the hill onto the high parts of Beacon Hill. For two months we kept guys here late at night working under floodlights with compressors and jack hammers, just to try to break the frost. That was the toughest winter I ever worked. The ground was so frozen, the rain wouldn't penetrate and water was halfway up the monuments and flooding the open graves." He paused. "We had to put remains in the receiving vault. *You're not going to bury someone in a pool of water!*"

In the meantime he was clearing up old misunderstandings. Some concerned land that had long been owned by the government. The Brooklyn City Grounds was a small charity burial site that the old city of Brooklyn had acquired within Evergreens boundaries back in the 1860s. Badly neglected, it was put up for auction by the City of New York. Fearing that a commercial developer would take it over and build on it, the trustees bid $160,000, won the property, cleaned it up, and opened it for new interments. The cemetery also sorted out the

Evergreens President Paul Grassi (right) and Assistant Superintendent Anthony Salamone flank the cemetery's on-site historian, Donato Daddario, on Hickory Knoll.

question of the title to its oldest section, the Seaman's Grounds, which contained the handsome base of the old monument. When Beacon Hill was cleared in 1956 to accommodate new burials and a road, the monument was moved down the slope. Unfortunately, the tall, graceful shaft was so badly deteriorated that it had to be removed (breaking into pieces during the process). The base and the globe survived the move and now sit on the greensward near the main gate. There remained the question of who actually owned the Grounds. Although the U.S. government was known to have held the title at the time it was founded, the paperwork went astray and the Evergreens carried the cost of maintenance for over a century. A new arrangement was made, giving the Evergreens more land high up the slope.

There were problems concerning Ching Ming and other Chinese-American events. The Evergreens' neighbors were complaining about firecrackers and open fires, and buses bringing people out were veering off the cemetery's narrow roads and tearing up the grass. "Frank Trupia, our grounds superintendent, and I and another person in the office sat down and wrote a new set of rules and regulations," Grassi recalled. "We went to Chinatown and had a combination discussion and fact-finding mission with the Chinese funeral directors. We told them the Evergreens couldn't have big buses just coming in whenever they liked. They would have to make appointments for guides to direct them. The fireworks and fires had to stop. There are state laws about open fires. And we told them that the leftovers from Ching Ming had to be properly put away in big metal garbage cans so we wouldn't have a rodent problem. Ching Ming is so big that we still assign a man for the weekend whose only job is to pick up."

Those negotiations went well. Grassi scheduled another meeting with representatives of the Chinese community associations and burial societies. "I wanted it to be publicized to the community. I asked them if they would publish a report of our meeting in the newspaper, and they chose to put it on television so everybody would know about our concerns. We wanted them to know that the Evergreens is not a Chinese cemetery. It's a *nonsectarian* cemetery for many other people who use it, too." The point got across.

"I've learned over the years that I have to treat every instance differently, and I'm very happy to be doing just that," Grassi went on. "When I come in every morning, I just don't know what the daily agenda will be. Once, the union struck a day before Mother's Day, the busiest day of the year for visitors! One thing we're finding is that the people who come here are expecting more guidance from us than they used to." Families may need an introduction to cemetery law and customs. People whose great-grandparents put a few hundred dollars into a perpetual-care fund to provide extra maintenance for a family lot may be displeased to be told that the endowment is insufficient. "We explain to them that we're allowed only to use the *income* from the endowment, not the principal. Sometimes they don't want to hear that." (State law now requires that 25 percent of the price of a lot or grave goes into maintenance funds.)

Upkeep was an ongoing problem. "When I started, we needed to upgrade our maintenance. The old board was less active than it is today. There had been some cutbacks and the grounds just didn't look very pretty." He recruited an experienced cemetery groundskeeper, Frank Trupia. While improving the quality of mainte-

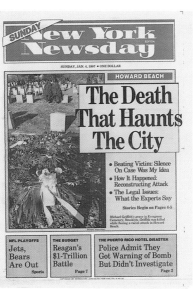

The brutal 1986 racial incident at Howard Beach touched the Evergreens when the victim, Michael Griffith, was buried at the cemetery.

nance, Trupia took advantage of technological improvements to trim the grounds staff from forty-seven all-year regular workers and sixty-four seasonal workers, to twenty-four regulars and twenty-six seasonals. The trustees were concerned about the state and appearance of the grounds, and especially its foliage. "Frank is passionate about trees, and we want to preserve what is there and keep the leafy aspect," said trustee Francesca Anderson, a botanic artist and Crocker Luther's successor as chair of the grounds committee. They established a policy to replace dying trees, many of which were planted around 1900. "The average lifetime of a tree is one hundred years and we're reaching that in many places," she explained. "We can't simply replace a tree when it comes down. Unless the old stump has gone, we have to find a new open place where we can start growing again. We've done this in several areas. Mt. Magnolia is named that for a reason, and there we've been able to shoehorn in some new magnolias. We'd like to do more of that—for instance, putting in new evergreens because many of the old ones have been lost, and we planted some camellias near the receiving vault." Anderson arranged for an arborist to inventory the cemetery's trees and recommend new acquisitions. She worked with the Audubon Society to trace birds' migratory routes over the cemetery.

The Right Thing

Toward the end of the twentieth century, therefore, the Evergreens was being reconceived by its trustees along the lines of the traditional mixed-used rural cemetery that was characterized by cemetery historians Blanche Linden-Ward and David C. Sloane as "a museum, arboretum, bird sanctuary, park, historical archive, and landmark."

NEXT PAGE, TULIP GROVE

This panoramic photograph of 2007 was taken from the same spot in Hickory Knoll as the one at the top of page 166, taken eighty years earlier (note the Linz monument at the left of each). The face of the Evergreens was dramatically changed by a policy of managed natural preservation that would have pleased Andrew Jackson Downing.

All this time, of course, it continued to be a burial ground serving the needs of people in distress at times of acute private and public need. Among the many hundreds of children's graves, few are more heart-wrenching than the three for the youngsters of a Nigerian immigrant family who were killed on October 1, 1998, when the car they were in was hit by an ambulance that had needlessly run a red light. Noble Akintunde Morak (age two), Humble Olusegun Morak (five), and Radiant Damilola Morak (seven) were buried side by side in the Nazareth Lots section under simple, expressive stones, each with a kneeling angel and a special inscription for the child.

In the late 1900s, New York and Brooklyn were undergoing their own long-term disaster. "When I walked down Bushwick Avenue as a child in the fifties," Grassi said, "I saw brownstones filled with doctors, lawyers, and other professionals. Later it became a *very tough* neighborhood." Waves of arson, vandalism, gang fights, thefts, and muggings swept across the city, even onto the Evergreens grounds. In 1982 an Evergreens foremen, Stanley Stoehrer, was killed by an employee, a drug addict. Four years later, during a racial attack by a pack of white teenagers on three black men in Howard Beach,

a twenty-three-year-old West Indian, Michael Griffith, was hit and killed by an automobile. Amid one of the most tense racial standoffs in New York history, the Evergreens donated the grave. "It was the right thing to do," said the board chairman at the time, John Titman. Two and a half years later a sixteen-year-old black boy named Yusef Hawkins was buried at the Evergreens after he was shot by a white man in Bensonhurst. The Reverend Al Sharpton led five hundred people on a march from the church through the Evergreens gates to the grave in the Ascension section, near Michael Griffith's.

Griffith's and Hawkins' graves were both dug by Otis Chance, an African American who lived in Williamsburg. The experience touched him deeply. "You don't always know who they're for," Chance told the *New York Daily News* just before Hawkins' burial, "but the foreman told us yesterday this one was for Yusef Hawkins." One measure of these difficult times was the headstone over Hawkins' grave. His mother asked a monument builder in East New York, Robert Pugh, to create a message that would help her move beyond her anger. Pugh drew a clenched fist from which dangles a hanging man. Under that accusatory image there is an epitaph with a slightly garbled but more kindly message:

New York's disruption and violence subsided in the 1990s, yet random acts continued. In August 2003, in New York's City Hall Councilman James E. Davis was murdered by a political rival in plain view of onlookers. The assassin was shot and killed by a policeman. Both men were interred at another cemetery, and as soon as Davis' family discovered that his remains were lying in the same burial ground as his murderer's ashes, they had them transferred to the Evergreens. Grassi told his staff, "*I'm not here to make a burial a media circus!*" and had the crowd of newspaper reporters and photographers held at the front gate. At the family's request Davis has two markers, one on his grave (whose location remains private), and one a memorial stone near the main road.

Banking the Land

Once the grounds were improved, the main worry was one of the concerns that had led to the cemetery's founding in 1849—the crowding of urban burial grounds. This time, the urban burial ground that was filling up was the Evergreens itself. According to the state Division of Cemeteries, of the three hundred twenty-five cemeteries that have existed at one time or another in the City of New York, only seventy-five were still accepting new burials in 2006, and at many of those the flow was slowing dramatically due to lack of space. At one time the Evergreens was regularly conducting more than 4,000 burials annually. In one of the early years of the new millennium, that was about the total number of burials at the Evergreens, Woodlawn, and Green-Wood cemeteries combined. With 60,000 deaths annually in the city, the old cemeteries were filling up while new ones upstate and in New Jersey were thriving, with decades of open access in the future.

As early as the 1930s, the Evergreens' management was regularly projecting when the grounds would be (in the words of John Flavel Mines) "thickly sown with the dead"—in other words, filled. The usual answer was that there would be open space until the early 2000s. That timeline was shortened by the sale of twenty acres to Knollwood in the 1950s, but it was lengthened in the 1970s by increasing longevity, which meant, among other things, that many New Yorkers were living so long that when they died, they were in retirement homes in Florida. The construction of an above-ground mausoleum and columbarium, Chapel Mausoleum, eased some land concerns, and a new state law allowed a cemetery to reclaim vacant portions of family lots where there had not been a burial in seventy-five years. (Grassi, the traditionalist, was unenthusiastic: "I just don't think it's *the right thing to do*.")

When John Titman became the board chairman in

1980, he decided that a well-thought-out plan for the future was required. "The place needed a board that would look to the next generation. Until then planning had taken the form of incremental, ad hoc decisions that resulted in filling open land. From what we were hearing, the cemetery was either single graves or large Chinese lots, and not much else." The Board of Trustees began to make a strategy for the future, planning for a time when so little land would be available for burials that the Evergreens would cease to be an operating cemetery.

Left with two and one-half acres of open land, the trustees approved a proposal made by Fred Bland, a partner at the architecture firm Beyer Bender Bell, and Titman's successor as board chairman, Jonathan Weld, a lawyer. The plan called for limiting the number of interments. Thanks to an investment strategy that had shifted away from low-interest mortgages, there was sufficient endowment to cover the annual budget of approximately $5 million. Because the possibility of further burials was allowed for in case more income was required in the future, the plan was summarized in the phrase "banking the open land."

"In banking the open land, we have this commitment with the state that we will maintain these grounds forever," Titman explained. "We're not making any changes on purpose," Francesca Anderson emphasized. "It's not really a decision. It's *inevitable*. It's a cemetery and it's never going to be a park. But the place has finite acreage. At some point there's simply not enough room." The trustees regretted that the Summer House slope and other attractive areas had already been used. "If we could, the board would take back some of the land that we think has been overdeveloped recently," Weld said. "The board wants to end most burials. We have an obligation to the people already buried here to maintain the cemetery's serenity, and not overcrowd it or put tombstones in every bit of space. We have the funds to do that. Members of the board are inclined to emphasize the role of the grounds as a park, a bird sanctuary, and an historic site."

Weld paused.

"But Paul Grassi, our president, is opposed. He's a cemetery man."

The Cemetery Man

Once again there surfaced the tension between the two words in the formula "rural cemetery." The board's plan rubbed against Grassi's conviction that a cemetery's mission is to use all its available assets to bury people. "We may be in a park-like setting but our first obligation is not to be a park. *It's to bury and care for the remains of human beings.* The biggest change in my years here is in the number of burials. What makes the Evergreens distinctive is our numbers. We have 526,000 people buried here in our two hundred twenty-five acres. Green-Wood has had 600,000 burials, but it's almost five hundred acres, and Woodlawn, in the Bronx, has four hundred acres but just over 300,000 interments. Here, there used to be 2,500 interments a year, even more. Now there are 1,000. One consequence is that we have fewer visitors because the most recent burials get the most visitors, and we've had fewer burials. All around, we just aren't as busy as we once were."

Grassi went along with the decision, developing options for the use of each parcel of reserved land, taking the lead role in the cemetery's successful application for a listing on the National Register of Historic Places, and encouraging tours of the grounds led by employees Anthony Salamone and Donato Daddario and Joe Fodor, a Brooklyn journalist. They sometimes took along a boom box to play jazz at Bill Robinson's and Lester Young's graves. When a headstone was dedicated over the grave of Blind Tom, the former slave musical genius, in 2002, a grand piano was set up. In 2007 there was a small gathering of tap dancers at Bojangle Robinson's grave, and chess players often came out to pay homage to William Steinitz. Grassi hoped that headstones would be placed on the unmarked graves of Valaida Snow and the baseball player Bill Dahlen.

"You know, this is a beautiful cemetery," he said, stretching out his arms. "Some cemeteries are very cold, with few trees. *We make an effort.* We pride ourselves on the quality of our gardens throughout the cemetery. There's the one at Bojangles Robinson's grave, and another big one around our above-ground crypt. Our gardens are one of our selling points."

Asked to name his favorite spot at the Evergreens, Grassi chose the point overlooking East New York that so impressed the first visitors on the fine, fair day in October 1849 when the future home of the Cemetery of the Evergreens was introduced to the world. "The best view in the Evergreens is the one from Beacon Hill. You can see the ocean all the way around to Manhattan." But Grassi preferred not to talk much about the typical prospect from Beacon Hill. His concern lay with a particular day.

"The World Trade Center used to be visible from Beacon Hill, too, and also from other parts of the cemetery, like the Sands Street Church grounds and near the main gate. Every morning I would drive onto the grounds through the main gate and look to the left, and if the day was clear I would be looking right at the twin towers. On 9/11 I was at a New York State Association of Cemeteries conference. Of course, when I heard the news I wanted to get back as soon as I could, but the planes were grounded. We drove the rental car all the way down, and the next day I was back at the Evergreens."

A look of distress came over his face. Grassi took a moment to collect himself.

"Driving in the gate, it was devastating to look off to the left. Where the familiar World Trade Center used to be, it was all smoke." Grassi was certain this was another of the disasters in which the Evergreens would play a large role, but because so many 9/11 victims could not be identified, only one was buried there. Dennis Mojica was a cheerful fifty-year-old New York City Fire Department lieutenant who had served as a rescue specialist and a departmental spokesman and who, in 1997, had saved a man from a collapsed building in the Flatlands section of Brooklyn. Before the interment, Grassi asked the family's permission to allow the cemetery's employees to attend the ceremony. The family agreed, and so all were there.

Another victim of that terrible Tuesday was closer to home. Christine Donovan Flannery was a buoyant twenty-six-year-old whose father, Bill Donovan, was a gravedigger at the Evergreens for almost four decades. Donovan, Grassi, and the others stood in pained shock at the Evergreens that day and watched the towers fall. After Christine Flannery's remains were buried in St. John's Roman Catholic cemetery, the Evergreens created a memorial to her near the main gate at Bushwick Avenue. Behind the marker stands a perfect evergreen, a spruce. "Bill said it was her favorite tree," Grassi said.

He paused again. "It was a memorial for her and for our connection to her, our love for one of our own. You know, we're a cemetery and a *community*."

ACKNOWLEDGMENTS

T O TELL THIS STORY required regular access to the Evergreens—its grounds, its monuments, its archives, and its people. For that and for their support and assistance, I offer my sincere thanks to Jonathan Weld and other members of the Board of Trustees, past and present; to President Paul Grassi, Superintendent Frank Trupia, Comptroller Roland Cadicamo, and my regular tour guides and advisors, Assistant Superintendent Anthony Salamone and his right-hand man, Donato "Danny" Daddario; and to the ladies of the office staff, who regularly went out of their way to provide information and assistance.

My thanks go also to Richard Welch and Ken Druse for their helpful observations during tours of the grounds; to Anthony DellaRocca for sharing his extensive knowledge of the Fourteenth Regiment, New York State Militia Infantry; to Richard Kilbride and Muriel Heilshorn Kilbride for their accounts of their relative William Hermann Hudaff's death during the 1918–19 influenza pandemic; to June Beason, of Rapid City, South Dakota, for providing J. J. Diehl's Civil War record; to David Thaxton and David Shepherd for their assistance concerning John Bunny; to Spencer Smith and Jean Kerr, my publishers, for their keen interest; and to my wife, Leah, for the hours she devoted to discussing topics of deep mutual concern, and for all else. My thanks go to Claire MacMaster for her elegant design and fondness for dramatic illustrations, and to Kara Steere for her copyedit.

The conference "Death and Loss in America: Colonial Era to the Present," presented by the Museum of Funeral Customs, in Springfield, Illinois, in October 2006, provided valuable information and encouragement.

ST MARK'S CHURCH GROUNDS,
LOOKING TOWARD LAKE SIDE

BIBLIOGRAPHICAL NOTE

T HE BEST ONE-VOLUME histories of New York are Edwin G. Burrows and Mike Wallace, *Gotham: A History of New York City to 1898* (N.Y.: Oxford, 1998) and *The Encyclopedia of New York City*, ed. Kenneth T. Jackson (New Haven: Yale, 1995). They are the sources for much of the demographic and other data. For Brooklyn, see Henry R. Stiles, *A History of the City of Brooklyn* (Brooklyn: 1867), Eugene Armbruster, *The Eastern District of Brooklyn* (N.Y.: 1912), Ralph Foster Weld, *Brooklyn Village, 1816–1834* (N.Y.: Columbia, 1938), and Weld, *Brooklyn Is America* (N.Y.: Columbia, 1950).

As for the history of cemeteries, the following have been especially helpful: David Charles Sloane, *The Last Great Necessity: Cemeteries in American History* (Baltimore: Johns Hopkins, 1991), James J. Farrell, *Inventing the American Way of Death, 1830–1920* (Philadelphia: Temple, 1980), Kenneth T. Jackson and Camilo José Vergara, *Silent Cities: The Evolution of the American Cemetery* (Princeton: Princeton Architectural Press, 1989), and Douglas Keister, *Stories in Stone: A Field Guide to Cemetery Symbolism and Iconography* (Salt Lake City: Gibbs Smith, 2004).

Drew Gilpin Faust's *This Republic of Suffering: Death and the American Civil War* (N.Y.: Knopf, 2008) appeared when this book was in final production. It strengthens my conviction that the history of American cemeteries is interwoven with the Civil War and with the longing for a good end and a decent burial in a beautiful place. When Dr. Faust observes that "honoring the dead became inseparable from respecting the living" (page 135), she speaks not only for the mourners of the Civil War era.

I have been aided by three short, unpublished studies of the Evergreens that were supported by the Board of Trustees: Richard F. Welch, "The Funerary Monuments, Memorials, and Gravestones of the Evergreens Cemetery, Brooklyn, New York" (2006); Wayne Morris, "Arboricultural Report for the Evergreens Cemetery"

(2005); and Joe Fodor, "Documentary History of the Evergreens, 1849–2000" (2000). Welch's and Morris' essays, with a summary of the cemetery's history that I wrote, were included in the Evergreens' successful application for listing on the National Register of Historic Places. Let me also acknowledge the work of another Evergreens historian, Victor A. Katinas

All honor to librarians and archivists! Writers owe an immense personal debt to the people who maintain the physical places and cyberspaces. Here I want to acknowledge those that aided me in this wide-ranging project. One, of course, was the Evergreens Cemetery's collection of records, scrapbooks, other documents, and artifacts, not to mention thousands of monuments and headstones and the grounds, for which I have developed considerable affection. Columbia University's enlightened policy of granting research and reading privileges to its graduates made its entire world class library system into my local library, just a short walk from my home. Among the eight branches that I used, Avery, Butler, Rare Books and Manuscripts, and Union Theological Seminary were especially helpful. I spent many fruitful days in the New York Public Library's midtown research library on Fifth Avenue, with its justly famous Room 315 and the Irma and Paul Milstein Division of United States History, Local History, and Genealogy. Other collections and libraries that helped were the New-York Historical Society, the New York Genealogical and Biographical Society, the Brooklyn Public Library and its Brooklyn Collection, the Brooklyn Historical Society, the Long Island Room of the Queens Public Library at Jamaica, the Museum of Chinese in the Americas, and the New York Public Library's Performing Arts Library at Lincoln Center. Of the many websites and databases I relied on, let me highlight those of the *New York Times*, the *Brooklyn Daily Eagle*, Proquest Historical Newspapers, Early American Newspapers, Making of America, the New York State Civil War Data Base, and YouTube, that immense digital vaudeville show where works and performances of Winsor McCay, Bill "Bojangles" Robinson, Adelaide Hall, Lester Young, and many other performers are saved and presented

REFERENCES

CITATIONS ARE BY the initial two words of a quote or brief reference to the subject. Many cite the *Brooklyn Daily Eagle* or the *New York Times*

REFERENCES FOR PAGES 13–22

Chapter 1. A Proper Place in the American Revolution
Grounds in 1849. "In the," Johnson to *Eagle*, Sep. 18, 1858. 1849 visit, "A New Cemetery," *Journal of Commerce*, Oct. 22, 1849. "Dreary aspect," "Cemetery of the Evergreens," *Eagle*, May 1, 1858. **Brick Church.** Shepherd Knapp, *A History of the Brick Presbyterian Church …* (N.Y.: Brick Church, 1909). James McCullough Farr, *Short History of the Brick Presbyterian Church …* (N.Y.: Brick Church, 1943). Theodore Fiske Savage, *Presbyterian Church in New York City* (N.Y.: Presbytery of N.Y., 1949). *Times*, May 15, 1856. Lila James Roney, "Gravestone Inscriptions from the Burial Grounds of the Brick Presbyterian Church," *New York Genealogical and Biographical Record*, vol. 60, no. ii (Jan. 1929), 8–14. **Berrien.** Shipping, *New-York Gazette and Weekly Mercury*, Feb. 16, 1768. Liberty Boys, *Connecticut Courant*, Mar. 30, 1767. "Do you," *Boston Gazette and Country Journal*, Sep. 1, 1766. *Boston Post Boy*, Sep. 8, 1766. "The terror," David Hackett Fischer, *Washington's Crossing* (N.Y.: Oxford, 2004), 97. Jesse Lemisch, *Jack Tar vs. John Bull: The Role of New York's Seamen in Precipitating the Revolution* (N.Y.: Garland, 1997). Isaac Q. Leake, *Memoir of the Life and Times of General John Lamb* (Albany: Munsell, 1850). Roger James Champagne, "Sons of Liberty and the Aristocracy in New York Politics, 1865–1790," Ph.D. diss., Univ. of Wisconsin, 1960. Lincoln Diamant, *Bernard Romans: Forgotten Patriot of the American Revolution* (N.Y.: Harbor Hill, 1985). *The Burghers of New Amsterdam and the Freemen of New York, 1675–1866* (N.Y.: N.-Y. Hist. Soc., 1885). "Women, children," *New-York Gazette and Weekly Mercury*, Aug. 19, 1776. **Battle of Brooklyn.** Barnet Schecter, *Battle for New York* (N.Y.: Walker, 2002). "You are" and Howard account, T. W. Field, *Historic and Antiquarian Scenes in Brooklyn and Its*

Vicinity. (Brooklyn: n.p., 1868), 63–6. "By daybreak," John J. Gallagher, *Battle of Brooklyn* (N.Y.: Castle, 2003), 107. "Good God," Fischer, *Washington's Crossing*, 95. **Berrien later.** Frederic G. Mather et al., *New York in the Revolution …* (Albany: Quayle, 1901). Lincoln Diamant, *Chaining the Hudson* (N.Y.: Stuart, 1989). *Abstracts of Wills, Collections of the New-York Historical Society for the Year 1904*, 85–86.

**Chapter 2. A Pretty Natural Situation:
Founding a Rural Cemetery**
Place names. "Strolls Upon Old Lanes," *Eagle*, Dec. 9, 1888. Wells, "Thirty-Five Years a Pastor," *Eagle*, Jan. 5, 1885, "Fifty Years at One Church," *Times*, Apr. 22, 1894. *Burial.* "Death in," "The Cost of Dying," *Independent*, Apr. 30, 1874, 16. "Urban sanitation, "So many," Harvey Green, *Uncertainty of Everyday Life, 1915–1945* (N.Y.: HarperCollins, 1992), 182. "The human," Robert Pogue Harrison, *Dominion of the Dead* (Chicago: Chicago, 2003), 154. "Show me," Edward Streeter, *Story of the Woodlawn Cemetery* (N.Y.: Woodlawn, n.d.). "For medieval," Eamon Duffy, *Stripping of the Altars*, 2nd ed. (New Haven: Yale, 2005), 328. "Without that," Erik Eckholm, "Burial Insurance Provides Peace of Mind for $2 a Week," *Times*, Dec. 3, 2006. *Founders.* Copland and Hall, Jacob Judd, "Administrative Organization of the City of Brooklyn, 1834–1855," part 1, *Journal of Long Island History*, vol. 5, no. 2 (Spring 1965), 4–16. Crosby, *National Cyclopedia of American Biography*, vol. 10, 61. **Walt Whitman.** *Leaves of Grass* (1st ed., 1855). *I Sit and Look Out*, ed. Emory Halloway and Vernolian Schwarz (N.Y.: AMS, 1966). *Specimen Days*, in *Prose Works 1892*, ed. Floyd Stovall (N.Y.: NYU, 1963). *Journalism*, ed. Herbert Bergman (N.Y.: Lang, 1998). "What a," *Walt Whitman's New York*, ed. Henry M. Christman (N.Y.: Macmillan, 1963), 77. "The settlement," "East Long-Island Correspondence," *Eagle*, Sep. 16, 1847. See David S. Reynolds, *Walt Whitman's America* (N.Y.: Vintage, 1995), Justin Kaplan, *Walt Whitman: A Life* (N.Y.: Simon & Schuster, 1980), Joel Myerson, *Whitman in His Own Time* (Iowa City: Iowa, 2000), Whitman obituary, *Times*, Mar. 27,

1892. **Seaman's Grounds.** "There is," Weld, *Brooklyn Is America*, 233. "The captain," Leah Robinson Rousmaniere, *Anchored Within the Vail* (N.Y.: Seamen's Church Institute, 1995), 4. "Cemetery for," *Eagle*, Jul. 25, 1857. "When a," "Why He Should Not Be Buried in Potter's Field," *Evening Telegram*, May 9, 1883. "When Jack Tar Dies in Port: A Final Resting Place in the Evergreens Cemetery," *Times*, May 28, 1893.

Chapter 3. New York's Burial Crisis
"Brooklyn Stands," "Our Cities of the Dead," *Eagle*, Apr. 28, 1895. "Eternal slumber," Donald E. Simon, "The Public Park Movement in Brooklyn, 1824–1873," Ph.D. diss., NYU, 1973, 72. **Cremation.** Anthony Fleege, "The Origins of Cremation in the United States from Dr. LeMoyne to the 1960s," paper presented at conference on "Death and Loss in America: Colonial Era to the Present," Museum of Funeral Customs, Springfield, Il., Oct. 19, 2006. **Epidemics.** "Death and," Burrows and Wallace, *Gotham*, 358. "The face," John Pintard, *Letters from John Pintard to His Daughter, Eliza Noel Pintard Davidson, 1816–1833* (N.Y.: N.-Y. Hist. Soc., 1940–41), vol. 4, 91. Louisiana, "Antebellum Louisiana: Disease, Death, and Mourning," *Cabildo*, http://lsm.crt.state.la.us/cabildo/cab8a.htm. "A long," Farr, *Short History*, 4. Ships, James C. Brandow, "A Visit to New York and Long Island in 1837," *New York History*, vol. 67, no. 1 (Jan. 1986), 23–39. "The streets," Andrew Delbanco, *Melville* (N.Y.: Knopf, 2005), 99. "Human carcasses," James Hardie Mitchell, *Account of the Malignant Fever …* (N.Y.: Hurtin, 1799), 17. Springs, James Ruel Smith, *Springs and Wells of Manhattan and the Bronx* (N.Y.: N.-Y. Hist. Soc., 1938). "Very sink," Burrows and Wallace, *Gotham*, 359. **Transfer controversy.** "Menace to," Louis Windmuller, "Graveyards as a Menace to the Commonweal," *North American Review*, Aug. 1898, 211–12. "Gray and," Walt Whitman, *Specimen Days*, 6. Philip Roth, *Everyman* (N.Y.: Farrar, Straus, & Giroux, 2006), 171. "Overturn, overturn," *Diary of Philip Hone, 1828–1851*, ed. Allan Nevins (N.Y.: Dodd, Mead, 1927), 730. "The very," "Thoughts Connected with Rural Cemeteries," *Christian*

Review, 1848, 12. "Unholy speculators," "St. Ann's Church Graveyard," *Eagle*, Jun. 11, 1860. "It was," *Letters from John Pintard*, vol. 2, 234–35. "Scandalous," "New-York City-The Burial Ground Excitement," *Times*, Jan. 26, 1854. "Our Fathers, Where Are They?" *Times*, Feb. 17, 1863. Frank A. Biebel, "Church and Cemetery," *New York Researcher*, Fall 2006, 63–64. "The place," "The Dead: Brooklyn Graves That Have Been Opened," *Eagle*, Oct. 2, 1875. **Sectarianism.** "The lines," Robert T. Handy, *A History of Union Theological Seminary in New York* (N.Y.: Columbia, 1987), 2. "In the old," Henry Chadwick, "Reminiscences of School Boy Fun," *Brooklyn Daily Standard Union*, Feb. 19, 1905. "The Funeral of Henry Oltmans," *Eagle*, Feb. 11, 1884. "Mrs. Chovey," *Eagle*, Aug. 2, 1879; *Times*, Nov. 15, 1879 and May 16, 1880. Bangs, Edwin Warriner, *Old Sands Street Methodist Episcopal Church of Brooklyn* (N.Y.: Phillips, 1885), 211. "The border," "Borough Tourist's Guide to the Border Crossing," *Times*, Oct. 9, 1993.

Chapter 4. Designing a Cemetery with Andrew Jackson Downing
Location. "A museum," Blanche Linden-Ward and David C. Sloane, "Spring Grove: The Founding of Cincinnati's Rural Cemetery, 1845–1855," *Queen City Heritage*, vol. 43, no. 1 (Spring 1983), 17. "High rustic," "The Cemetery of the Evergreens," *Eagle*, Sep. 25, 1850. "Knob and," Elizabeth Barlow, *Forests and Wetlands of New York City* (Boston: Little, Brown, 1971), 9. "One thing," Sarah Comstock, *Old Roads from the Heart* (N.Y.: Putnam, 1917), 23. "Scenes that," Burrows and Wallace, *Gotham*, 26–27. Farming, Marc Linder and Lawrence S. Zacharias, *Of Cabbages and Kings County: Agriculture and the Formation of Modern Brooklyn* (Iowa City: Iowa, 1999). "Long Island: The Background of Brooklyn as a Great Farm Garden," *Eagle*, Aug. 7, 1881. "A cluster," *N.Y. Herald*, Apr. 29, 1884. "The improvements," "Cemetery of the Evergreens," *Eagle*, Sep. 25, 1850. **Design background.** "Sepulchers," James Stevens Curl, *A Celebration of Death* (London: Batsford, 1993), 247. "The idea," "Cypress Hills: History of the Origins of the Cemetery,"

Eagle, Jul. 28, 1874. "Sterile acre," Walt Whitman, *Specimen Days*, 6. "A preoccupation," Keister, *Stories in Stone*, 8. "But why," Washington Irving, "Westminster Abbey," *Sketchbook of Geoffrey Crayon*. "It seems," *Letters of Emily Dickinson*, ed. Mabel Loomis Todd (Boston: Roberts, 1894), vol. 1, 21. "Weep and," "Our citizens," Linden-Ward and Sloane, "Spring Grove," 21, 17. "Open air," Timothy Dwight, *Travels in New England and New York*, ed. Barbara Miller Salomon, (Cambridge: Belknap/Harvard, 1969), vol. 1, 490. "A fit," "The Cemetery of the Evergreens," *N.Y. Observer & Chronicle*, Jul. 24, 1851. **Design.** "A green," Downing, *Rural Essays* (N.Y.: Leavitt, 1856), 147. Elizabeth Barlow Rogers, *Landscape Design* (N.Y.: Abrams, 2001). David Schuyler, *Apostle of Taste: Andrew Jackson Downing, 1815–1852* (Baltimore: Johns Hopkins, 1986), "The Evolution of the Anglo-American Rural Cemetery," *Journal of Garden History*, vol. 4, no. 3 (Jul.–Sep. 1984), 291–304, and "Public Landscapes and American Culture, 1800–1870: Rural Cemeteries, City Parks, and Suburbs," Ph.D. diss., Columbia Univ., 1979. Elizabeth Feld and Stuart P. Feld, ed., *In Pointed Style: The Gothic Revival in America, 1800–1860* (Hirschl & Adler, 2006). Jane B. Davies, "Davis and Downing: Collaborators in the Picturesque," *Prophet with Honor: The Career of Andrew Jackson Downing, 1815–1852* (Washington, D.C.: Athenaeum, 1989), 81–123. George B. Tatum, "Nature's Gardener," *Prophet with Honor*, 43–80. Davis' diary for 1849 is in the Manuscripts Division, New York Public Library. "A contemplative," Rogers, *Landscape Design*, 336. "Every laborer," Blanche Linden-Ward, "Strange but Genteel Pleasure Grounds: Tourist and Leisure Uses of Nineteenth-Century Rural Cemeteries," *Cemeteries & Gravemarkers*, ed. Richard E. Meyer (Logan: Utah State, 1992), 312. "The great," "Mr. Downing and *The Horticulturist*," *Horticulturist*, Sep. 1, 1852. "The fundamental," Rogers, *Landscape Design*, 326. "Our rural," *Horticulturist*, Jul. 1849. "Transitional," Schuyler interview, *All Things Considered*, National Public Radio, Jul. 30, 2006. "Scenes abounding," Rogers, *Landscape Design*, 328. "There are," "A New Cemetery," *Journal of Commerce*, Oct. 22, 1849.

"Various beauties," Rogers, *Landscape Design*, 336. "It has," Fredrika Bremer, *America of the Fifties: Letters of Fredrika Bremer*, ed. Adolph B. Benson (N.Y.: American-Scandinavian Foundation, 1924), 17. "We think," "Inexpressibly," "Cemetery of the Evergreens," *Eagle*, May 17, 1856. "Bare thought," "Thoughts Connected with Rural Cemeteries," *Christian Review*, 1848, 11.

Chapter 5. Order Out of Chaos and the Rise of William R. Grace

Problems. "Hills have," Judd, "Administrative Organization," 13. "Embellish, adorn" *Eagle*, May 9, 1872. Green-Wood founding, Jeffrey I. Richman, *Brooklyn's Green-Wood Cemetery* (Brooklyn: Green-Wood Cemetery, 1998), 11–13. "The trustees," "The Evergreen Cemetery-Meeting of the Plot Owners," *Eagle*, Sep. 6, 1859. "Every action," "The Trustees of the Evergreens to the Lotowners and the Public," *Eagle*, Sep. 18, 1858. "In the years," Charles C. Parlin to Nathaniel L. Goldstein, Jan. 16, 1952, copy bound into minutes of Evergreens Board of Trustees, 1952. "That unlucky," "Pending Brooklyn Bills," *Eagle*, Mar. 30, 1870. ***William C. Kneeland.*** "Matrimonial Difficulties," *Eagle*, Nov. 28, 1866. "Evergreen Cemetery Troubles," *Eagle*, Jul. 29, 1871. "Kneeland: Why He Committed Suicide," *Eagle*, Nov. 4, 1877. "Kneeland," *Eagle*, Nov. 24, 1877. ***Recovery and neighborhood.*** "Cemeteries: The Silent Cities of Brooklyn's Dead," *Eagle*, May 19, 1876. "The Evergreens: A Visit to One of the E. D. Cemeteries," *Eagle*, Aug. 30, 1878. "Two or three," Gertrude Lefferts Vanderbilt, *Social History of Flatbush* ... (N.Y.: Appleton, 1887), 299. "Thick forests," "Long Island: The Background of Brooklyn as a Great Farm Garden," *Eagle*, Aug. 7, 1881. "Order out of," "The Evergreens," *Eagle*, Oct. 1, 1873. "A good," "the winter," "We need," President's Annual Report, Evergreens Board of Trustees minutes, Mar. 10, 1873. "Great natural," "Our Cities of the Dead," *Eagle*, Apr. 28, 1895. "Go back," Evergreens Board of Trustees minutes, Jul. 27, 1883. ***Grace and Flint.*** Marquis James, *Merchant Adventurer: the Story of W. R. Grace* (Wilmington: SR Books, 1993). J. Peter Grace Jr., *W. R. Grace and the Enterprises He Cre-*

ated (N.Y.: Newcomen, 1953). "Even in," "Wm. R. Grace's Career," *Times*, Mar. 22, 1904. "Perhaps America's," Burrows and Wallace, *Gotham*, 1104. Charles R. Flint, *Memories of an Active Life* (N.Y.: Putnam, 1923). Harriman and other anecdotes, "Bye-the-Bye in Wall Street," *Wall Street Journal*, Feb. 27, Jun. 8, 1934.

Chapter 6. Soldiers and Conspirators: The Evergreens and the Civil War

Hall. Sarah N. Roth, "The Mind of a Child: Images of African Americans in Early Juvenile Fiction," *Journal of the Early Republic*, vol. 25, no.1 (2005), 79–109. ***Williamsburg and 14th regiments.*** *A Report on the 14th Regiment N.Y.S.M. During the Civil War.* . . . Fourteenth Regiment N.Y.S.M. Co. E. Living History Association, http://14thbrooklyn.info/. "Brooklyn in the Civil War," http://www.brooklynpubliclibrary.org/ civilwar/cwdoc 042.html. "More expressive," "Dutchtown," *Eagle*, Jan. 16, 1881. "Max Weber," *Eagle*, Jun. 17, 1901. "There was," *Eagle*, May 23, 1861. "We were," "At a Camp Fire," *Eagle*, May 19, 1891. "You have," "History of the 14th Brooklyn," www.rootsweb.com/~ny civilw/regiments/ RealHistory.html. See also "The Fourteenth," *Eagle*, Feb. 6, 1898, "Splendid," 84th Regiment, N.Y. Volunteer Infantry, Civil War Newspaper Clippings, www.dmna.state.ny.us/ historic/civil/infantry/84thInf/84thInfCWN.htm. "Welcome home," *Eagle*, May 24, 1864. "Tell my," "Another Young Soldier," *Eagle*, Dec. 21, 1884. ***Medal of Honor.*** Charles W. Hanna, Medal of Honor Historical Society, "Medal of Honor Recipients Buried in the Evergreen Cemetery," Feb. 22, 2005, report in Evergreens Archives. ***Lincoln connection.*** Michael W. Kauffman, *American Brutus: John Wilkes Booth and the Lincoln Conspirators* (N.Y.: Random House, 2004). Notes from Secret Service interviews with Chester are available at www.Footnote.com. See also *Assassination of President Lincoln and the Trial of the Conspirators*, comp. Benn Pitman (N.Y.: Funk & Wagnalls, 1954), Edward Steers Jr., *Blood on the Moon* (Lexington: Kentucky, 2001), and James L. Swanson, *Manhunt* (N.Y.: Harper, 2007). ***Blanche DeBar Booth.*** "This tall," Stanley Kimmel Blanche, *Mad Booths of*

Maryland (N.Y.: Bobbs-Merrill, 1940), 142. "Blanche DeBar," "Sock & Buskin," *Church's Musical Visitor*, Feb. 1874. See also John Wilkes Booth, *"Right or Wrong, God Judge Me": Writings of John Wilkes Booth*, ed. John H. Rhodehamel and Louise Taper (Urbana: Illinois, 1997), Clinton Densmore Odell, *Annals of the New York Stage* (N.Y.: Columbia, 1927–49), Allston Brown Thomas, *A History of the New York Stage* (N.Y.: Dodd, Mead, 1903). **Booth rumors.** "Niece Details Story of Alleged Meeting," *Oakland Tribune*, Feb. 23, 1925. "Services Set for Wife of Lincoln's Guard," *Long Island Press*, Feb. 11, 1958.

Chapter 7. Cover Them Over: Decoration Day at the Cemetery

Memorial Day origins. "There are," "Another Young Soldier," *Eagle,* Dec. 21, 1884. "Culture of," "old soldiers," David W. Blight, *Beyond the Battlefield: Race, Memory, and the American Civil War* (Amherst: Massachusetts, 2002), 178, 185. Kurdistan graves, Ralph Solecki, "In the Beginning," *Looting of the Iraq Museum, Baghdad*, ed. Milbury Polle and Amanda M. H. Schuster (N.Y.: Abrams, 2005), 45. "The dead," "Id al-Fitr: Time to Eat, to Honor, to Shop," *Times*, Oct. 13, 2007. "Not by," "Memorial Day," *Times*, May 31, 1870. "The boy," *Eagle*, May 24, 1881. "Decoration Day," *Eagle*, May 31, 1877. "Cover them," Robert Haven Schauffler, *Memorial Day* (N.Y.: Moffat, 1911). "The festival," "A sacred," Stuart McConnell, *Glorious Contentment: The Grand Army of the Republic, 1865–1900* (Chapel Hill: North Carolina, 1992), 184, 185. "A leaf," "The Grave of Harry Lee," *Eagle*, May 30, 1889. See also George J. Lankevich, "The Grand Army of the Republic in New York State, 1865–1898," Ph.D. diss., Columbia Univ., 1968, and www.usmemorialday.org. **Warren statue.** *Eagle*, Oct. 11, 1890. "The General Warren Statue," *Eagle*, Jun. 17, 1896. "Women Claim the Credit," *Eagle*, Jun. 23, 1896. "Gen. Warren's Statue," *Times*, Jul. 5, 1896. **Eggleston.** "Our ideas," "I saw," George Cary Eggleston, *A Rebel's Recollections* (N.Y.: Hurd, 1875), 31–32, 146. "Just and," "George Cary Eggleston," *Times*, Apr. 23, 1911. "Obnoxious emblems," "Wants No Gray," *Eagle*, Jun. 2, 1891. Brown,

"From the Harry Lee Post," *Eagle*, Mar. 24, 1890. "Memorial Day," "For one day," W. Lloyd Warner, *The Living and the Dead: A Study of the Symbolic Life of Americans* (New Haven: Yale, 1959), 256, 266.

Chapter 8. African Americans in Peace and War

20th Regiment U.S.C.T. Gail Buckley, *American Patriots: The Story of Blacks in the Military from the Revolution to Desert Storm* (N.Y.: Random House, 2001). George Washington Williams, *A History of the Negro Troops in the War of the Rebellion, 1861–65* (N.Y.: Bergman, 1968). John David Smith, "Let Us All Be Grateful That We Have Colored Troops That Will Fight," in John David Smith, ed., *Black Soldiers in Blue* (Chapel Hill: North Carolina, 2002), 1–77. "Give me," "When you," Benjamin Quarles, *The Negro in the Civil War* (N.Y.: Russell, 1953), 190, 191. "A vast," Joseph T. Glatthaar, *Forged in Battle* (N.Y.: Free Press, 1990), 141–42. "It is," *Diary of George Templeton Strong*, ed. Allan Nevins and Milton Halsey Thomas (N.Y.: Macmillan, 1952), vol. 1, 411–12. "We are," "My dear," *Freedom: A Documentary History of Emancipation, 1861–1867. Series II: The Black Military Experience*, ed. Ira Berlin (Cambridge: Cambridge, 1982), 681, 501–502. "We have," Edwin S. Redkey, ed., *A Grand Army of Black Men: Letters from African-American Soldiers in the Union Army, 1861–1865* (N.Y.: Cambridge, 1992), 195. **Cook.** "The Hull Mystery Solved," *National Police Gazette*, Jul. 5, 1879. "Chastine Cox," *Phrenological Journal and Science of Health*, Oct. 1879, 69–71. "The Hull Tragedy," *National Police Reporter*, Jul. 14, 1880. Reports in *Times*, Jun. 24, 1879, and subsequent issues. "Balbo and Cox to Be Hanged," *Times*, Apr. 7, 1880. "Murder as a Means to Grace," *Times*, Jul. 30, 1879. "Our New York Letter," *Philadelphia Inquirer*, Jul. 19, 1880. "The Burial of Chastine Cox," *Times*, Jul. 18, 1880. "Bishop James H. Cook," *Times*, Aug. 12, 1899. **Integrating cemeteries.** "Brooklyn was," Burrows and Wallace, *Gotham*, 972. "One would," "Where the Color Line Exists," *Eagle*, Dec. 7, 1890. Warriner, *Old Sands Street Methodist Episcopal Church*. "Buried Slaves," *Eagle*, May 19, 1888. **The Hornes.** Gail Buckley, *The Hornes: An*

American Family (N.Y.: Knopf, 1986) and *American Patriots*. "Frank S. Horne," www.answers.com/topic/frank-s-horne. "Frank Smith Horne 1899–1974," *Black Renaissance in Washington, D.C., 1920–1930s,* http://dclibrary.org/blkren/bios /hornefs.html.

Chapter 9. Crooks, Competitors, Writers, and Congressmen
Tammany Hall. "He was," "He Says He Paid Byrnes," *Times,* Nov. 12, 1895. "A smooth," "There was," Kenneth D. Ackerman, *Boss Tweed* (N.Y.: Carroll, 2005), 115, 116. Leo Hershkowitz, *Tweed's New York* (Garden City: Anchor, 1977). Denis Tilden Lynch, *"Boss" Tweed* (N.Y.: Boni, 1927). Leo Herskowitz, ed., *Boss Tweed in Court* (Bethesda: Univ. Publications of America, n.d.) "At one," "Obituary: Oliver Cotter," *Eagle,* May 6, 1900. "Oliver Cotter's," *Brooklyn Standard Union,* Sep. 11, 1876.
Dahlen. Harold C. Burr, "Bad Bill Dahlen," *Sporting News,* Jan. 14, 1943. "As good," "Old Time Baseball," *Chicago Daily Tribune,* Apr. 1, 1894. "Has a," "Undervalued, Overlooked, but Far from Forgotten," *Times,* Dec. 2, 2007. **Hall.** William A. Cook, *Louisville Grays Scandal of 1877* (Jefferson, N.C.: McFarland, 2005). Mike Robbins, *Ninety Feet from Fame* (N.Y.: Carroll, 2004). Harold Seymour, *Baseball: The Early Years* (N.Y.: Oxford, 1960). Geoffrey C. Ward and Ken Burns, *Baseball* (N.Y.: Knopf, 1994). "A certain," "Quaint and Odd Things from Baseball Guides of the 60s," *Washington Post,* Jun. 30, 1907. Hall statements, *Chicago Tribune,* Nov. 11, 1877. "Once noted," "Sports and Pastimes,'" *Eagle,* Feb. 14, 1886. "Gambling is," "Unfettered Rose Inquiry a Contrast to N.B.A.'s Case," *Times,* Jul. 25, 2007.
Steinitz. Kurt Landsberger, *William Steinitz, Chess Champion* (Jefferson, N.C.: McFarland, 1993). "Chess Player Steinitz Dead," *Eagle,* Aug. 14, 1900. **Writers.** "I hate," "Etiquette's Arbiter," *Times,* Dec. 24, 1974. Edmund Pearson, *Dime Novels* (Boston: Little, Brown, 1929). "Undoubtedly the," "'Old Sleuth' Passes Away," *Times,* Dec. 18, 1898. "Enemy aliens," "Dr. Alice Salomon Is Honored at 70," *Times,* Apr. 20, 1942. "Dr. Alice Salomon Dies in Exile at Age 76," *Times,* Sep. 1, 1948.

"Everything I," Alice Salomon, *Character Is Destiny: The Autobiography of Alice Salomon* (Ann Arbor: Michigan, 2004), 201. **Congressmen.** *Biographical Directory of the United States Congress.* "No namby-pamby," *Eagle,* May 26, 1914. "Charles G. Bennett Dead," *Times,* May 26, 1914. "This gentleman," *Pittsfield Sun,* Feb. 28, 1833.

Chapter 10. The Poetry of Their Existence: Artists at the Evergreens
Heade. "One of," "Martin Johnson Heade," www.tfaoi.com/newsm1/n1m630.htm. "One of," "The poetry," "I am not," "The fact," Theodore E. Stebbins Jr., *Life and Work of Martin Johnson Heade* (New Haven: Yale, 2000), 76, 166, 165, 166. "Sense of," www.butlerart.com/pc_book/pages/matin_johnson_heade_1819.htm. J. Gray Sweeney, "A 'Very Peculiar' Picture: Martin J. Heade's Thunderstorm over Narragansett Bay," *Archives of American Art Journal,* vol. 28, no. 4 (1988), 2. **Fenn.** "He could," Paul Giambara, *100 Years of Illustration and Design,* giam.typepad.com/100years_of_illustration /2005/03/harry_fenn_pen_.html. "Force and beauty," Sue Rainey, "Harry Fenn," *American Book and Magazine Illustrators to 1920,* ed. Steven E. Smith et al. (Detroit: Gale, 1998), 100. **McCay.** Mark Langer, *Moving Image,* Spring 2005, 149–53. "The two," Dave Kehr, "New DVDs," *Times,* Jun. 1, 2004. Andrew Melomet, "Winsor McCay and the Sinking of the *Lusitania,*" *St. Mihiel Trip-Wire,* Sep. 2006. "Animation should," "Elfin charm," "He and," John Canemaker, *Winsor McCay* (N.Y.: Abrams, 2005), 191, 244, 7.

Chapter 11. The Cemetery-Park and Its Management
"A Lone Fisherman," *Eagle,* Jul. 10, 1881. "A lonely," Isaac Asimov, *In Memory Yet Green* (Garden City: Doubleday, 1979), 131. "Beautiful resorts," "The Cemetery of the Evergreens," *Eagle,* Sep. 25, 1850. "A Beautiful Ride," *Eagle,* May 25, 1852. "In our," "Flowers in Churchyards," *Eagle,* Jul. 23, 1842. "Among the," "Our Cities," "Sunday Recreation," *Eagle,* Aug. 21, 1865. "Our Cities of the Dead," *Eagle,* Apr. 28, 1895. "The great," Simon, "Public Park Movement," 188. "The immediate," "Dead   China-

men," *N.Y. Herald*, 1885. **Reed.** "Makes His Home in a Tomb," *Eagle*, Sep. 2, 1895. "Home Made in Wife's Tomb at Evergreens Cemetery," *Times*, Sep. 2, 1895. *N.Y. Herald*, Oct. 5, 1896. *N.Y. Sun*, Aug. 6, 1897. "Home of the Mysterious Roof Dwellers," *Eagle*, Jul. 29, 1900. "Found, Near Death, in His Wife's Tomb," *Times*, Mar. 24, 1905. "The Whole Town Talked," *N.Y. World Telegram*, May 9, 1939. **Trommer and Lundy.** "Turning through," "Lee Wan's Funeral," *Times*, Sep. 6, 1880. Will Anderson, *Breweries of Brooklyn* (Croton Falls: n.p., 1976). Ben Jankowski, "The Bushwick Pilsners: A Look at Hoppier Days," *Brewing Techniques*, Jan./Feb. 1994. "Frederick W. I. Lundy," *Times*, Sep. 10, 1977. **Landscaping.** "Today the," Charles A. Birnbaum, *Samuel Parsons Jr. …* (Bronx: Wave Hill, 1995), 14. "Let the," "Mrs. Seifert Has Planted Soup Greens," *N.Y. World*, Feb. 27, 1896. "From Me," *New Yorker*, Sep. 12, 1964. Francis R. Kowsky, *Country, Park & City: The Architecture and Life of Calvert Vaux* (N.Y.: Oxford, 1998). Samuel Parsons Jr., "Color Bedding," *Century*, Jun. 1885, "Railway, Church-Yard, and Cemetery Lawn Planting," *Scribners Monthly*, Jul. 1881, and *Memories of Samuel Parsons*, ed. Mabel Parsons (N.Y.: Putnam's, 1926). Wyrick in John Matturri, "Windows in the Garden: Italian-American Memorialization and the American Cemetery," *Ethnicity and the American Cemetery*, ed. Richard E. Meyer (Bowling Green: Bowling Green, 1993), 15. Strauch and Lawn Plan, Sloane, *Last Great Necessity*, chapter 5. **Rail lots and maintenance.** Ellen Marie Snyder, "Victory over Nature: Victorian Cast-Iron Seating Furniture," *Winterthur Portfolio*, vol. 20, no. 4 (Winter 1985), 221. Rules, Evergreens archives. "A sort of," "Cypress Hills: History of the Origins of the Cemetery," *Eagle*, Jul. 28, 1874. Tools, Fodor, "Documentary History of the Evergreens." "Strayed," *Eagle*, Oct. 7, 1868. "The section," "When taking," Hasbrouck H. Wright memoranda to staff, Evergreens archives, May 29, 1943, Jun. 2, 1947.

Chapter 12. Buried from the Home

Funeral customs. "Dying was," David S. Heidler and Jeanne T. Heidler, *Daily Life in the Early American Republic, 1790–1820* (Westport, Conn.: Greenwood, 2004), 77. "The noxious," Vanderbilt, *Social History of Flatbush*, 157. "It seems," Penny Colman, *Corpses, Coffins, and Crypts: A History of Burial* (N.Y.: Holt, 1997), 149. See also Knapp, *History of the Brick Presbyterian Church.* "Trees for Rural Cemeteries," *Horticulturist*, Apr. 1, 1854. "Laud the," Garry Wills, *Lincoln at Gettysburg* (N.Y.: Simon & Schuster, 1992), 59. "Come forward," Harrison, *Dominion of the Dead*, 158–59. Hall, *Eagle*, Apr. 17, 20, 1868, Aug. 16, 1873. Keziah Blackburn, "In Good Style," "With But a Single Aim," *Eagle*, Dec. 28, 1883, and Feb. 17, 1884. "Setting Aside a Will," *Times*, Feb. 18, 1884. **Professionalizing the funeral.** "With scant, "1845–1856," *York Daily Record*, Jan. 25, 2005. www.ydr.com/ntbf/ci_4336797. "Time was," "Oppose Services at Graves." *Eagle*, Feb. 24, 1896. **Suicides.** "Kemlo's Ghastly Crime," *Times*, Sep. 19, 1883. "In One Grave," *Eagle*, Sep. 21, 1883. "Such mistaken," Sloane, *Last Great Necessity*, 17. "An Epidemic of Suicide," *Eagle*, May 24, 1897. Hoffman data, "The Suicide Rate," *Times*, Nov. 9, 1909, and "Suicide," *Times*, Feb. 5, 1905. "Suicides in Cemeteries," *Eagle*, May 18, 1893. "Health News," New York State Department of Health, www.health.state.ny.us/. Cowper, Kay Redfield Jamison, *Night Falls Fast: Understanding Suicide* (N.Y.: Knopf, 1999), 10. Cummings incident, "Poisoned," *Eagle*, Jul. 16, 1874. "Sentimental suicides," *Eagle*, Jul. 18, 1874. "A nice," "The Evergreens Cemetery Suicide," *Eagle*, Jul. 8, 1890.

Chapter 13. Angels Beside the Tomb: Monuments Grand and Humble

Monument symbols. "First-class buyers," Evergreens President's Annual Report, Mar. 10, 1873. "Featuring design," Richard F. Welch, "The Funerary Monuments, Memorials, and Gravestones of the Evergreens Cemetery, Brooklyn, New York," Dec. 2006, unpublished report in Evergreens Archives. "The nineteenth," Robert Woods, *Children Remembered: Responses to Untimely Death in the Past* (Liverpool: Liverpool, 2006), 11. "What sign," Henry Ward Beecher, *Overture of Angels* (N.Y.:

Ford, 1870). "At the," Rowan Williams, *Tokens of Trust: An Introduction to Christian Belief* (Louisville: Westminster John Knox, 2007), 52. Charles Taylor, "The Sting of Death: Why We Yearn for Eternity," *Commonweal*, Oct. 12, 2007, 13–15. Elisabeth L. Roark, "Embodying Immortality: Angels in America's Rural Garden Cemeteries, 1850–1900," *Markers XXIV* (2007), 57–111. On ideas of immortality, see Milton McC. Gatch, *Death: Meaning and Mortality in Christian Thought and Contemporary Culture* (N.Y.: Seabury, 1969). **Accusations.** Havemeyer, "His Wagon Run Down by a Car," *Eagle*, Feb. 8, 1895, "Now the Total Is 104," *Times*, Mar. 14, 1895. **Lots and tombs.** Miller, "The Cemetery of the Evergreens," *Eagle*, May 30, 1880. Guild, "Elopement of a Man of Seventy and a Girl of Eighteen," *Brooklyn Daily Union-Argus*, Jul. 29, 1879. "Cupid's Dart," *Eagle*, Jul. 30, 1879. "Mr. W. H. Guild's Fraudulent Divorce in San Francisco," *Eagle*, Jan. 7, 1882. "The Guild Divorce Suit," *Eagle*, Jun. 13, 1882. Guild Vault plan and records, Evergreens Archives. Woolsey, Welch, "Funerary Monuments … ." Barbara Rotundo, "Monumental Bronze: A Representative American Company," *Cemeteries & Gravemarkers*, ed. Meyer, 263–92. Wilkie, "Death of a Sandy Hook Pilot," *Times*, Feb. 3, 1878. Woolsey death, "Death of an Old Pilot," *Times*, Apr. 4, 1884. Story, "Obituary," *Eagle*, Nov. 19, 1879. "William L. Mathot Dies," *Times*, Nov. 24, 2007. "Another Cavalry Troop," *Eagle*, Mar. 1, 1898. "Druggist Files Suit to Test Liquor Law," *Times*, Jul. 11, 1923. "Captain Louis Mathot, Veteran of '61, Dies," *Times*, Oct. 15, 1929. "The Death of Julius Rensch," *Eagle*, Jan. 5, 1885. **Children.** Burrows and Wallace, *Gotham*, 790. Other data, New York City Department of Health and Mental Hygiene, Sep. 14, 2006. www.nyc.gov/html/doh /html/pr2006/pr088-06.shtml, http://eh.net/encyclo pedia/article/haines.demography. Ariès thesis, Woods, *Children Remembered*, 7–13. Newsboys, John Morrow, *A Voice from the Newsboys* (N.Y.: 1860). "Please send," "Johnny Morrow, the Newsboy," *Farmers' Cabinet*, Jun. 21, 1861. Morrow profile in Charles Loring Brace, *Short Sermons to Newsboys* (N.Y.: Scribner, 1866), 257. "Johnny Morrow, the Newsboy,"

New York Evangelist, Jun. 6, 1861. Vincent Digirolamo, "Newsboy Funerals: Tales of Sorrow and Solidarity in Urban America," *Journal of Social History*, vol. 36, no.1 (Fall, 2002), 5–30.

**Chapter 14. What Could Anyone Do?
Brooklyn's Disasters**
Michael L. Boucher et al., *Last Alarm: The History and Tradition of Supreme Sacrifice in the Fire Departments of New York City* (Evansville, Ill.: M.T. Publishing, 2006). **Holy Trinity Cemetery.** "Our Neighborhood: The Way It Was," *Ridgewood Times*, Apr. 11, Oct. 24, 2002. "The History of Most Holy Trinity Cemetery," www.mht brooklyn.org/en_cemetery.htm. "Holy Trinity Cemetery," *Eagle*, Nov. 26, 1899. **Triangle Shirtwaist.** "Triangle Fire Stirs Outrage and Reform," *NFPA Journal*, May–Jun. 1993, 73–82. **Ward's Island.** "Frantic Battles in the Dark," *Times*, Feb. 19, 1923. "Services for Fire Victims," *Times*, Mar. 1, 3, 1923. "Funeral for 20 Killed in Ward's Island Fire," *Times*, Mar. 12, 1923. **Brooklyn Theatre.** Samuel L. Leiter, "Brooklyn as an American Theatre City, 1861–1898," *Journal of Long Island History*, vol. 7, no. 1 (Winter-Spring 1968), 1–11. "The Holocaust," *Eagle*, Dec. 8, 1776. **Firemen's Monument.** "Monument Unveiled," *Eagle*, May 25, 1881. *Our Firemen: The Official History of the Brooklyn Fire Department* (Brooklyn: 1892). www.bklyn-genealogy-info.com/Fire /Bklyn/3.html. **Anthony.** Navy Historical Center, www.history.navy.mil/photos/pers-us/uspers-a/w-anthony.htm. "Dear lady," "Letter from 'Bill' Anthony," *Los Angeles Times*, Mar. 24, 1898. "Sigsbee's Marine Is Dead," *Times*, Nov. 25, 1899. "To Bury William Anthony," *Times*, Nov. 27, 1899. "Bill Anthony Laid to Rest," *Washington Post*, Nov. 30, 1899. "Bill Anthony's Coolness," *Times*, Feb. 3, 1901. Charles Dwight Sigsbee, "Personal Narrative of the *Maine*," *Century*, Dec. 1898, 241–63. "Flowers for the Graves of Their Honored Dead," *Eagle*, May 31, 1902. **Malbone Street wreck.** Brian J. Cudahy, *Malbone Street Wreck* (N.Y.: Fordham, 1999). Brian J. Cudahy, *How We Got to Coney Island: The Development of Mass Transportation in Brooklyn …*

(N.Y.: Fordham, 2002). "Malbone Street Wreck,"
http://nycsubway. org/lines/brighton.html. "Scores
Killed, Many Hurt on B.R.T.," *Times*, Nov. 2, 1918.
Influenza. Osler, "Before the," "The dead," "Rolling
through," "I saw," John M. Barry, *Great Influenza* (N.Y.:
Penguin, 2004), 242, 4, 190, 148, 189. "You haven't,"
Alfred W. Crosby, *America's Forgotten Pandemic* (N.Y.:
Cambridge, 2003), 29. "No one," "Memories of 1918 Flu
Pandemic Haunt 21st Century," Reuters, May 27, 2006.
"Wed in Graveyard to Stop Influenza," *Brooklyn Stan-
dard Union*, Nov. 4, 1918. Martin C. J. Bootsma and Neil
M. Ferguson, "The Effect of Public Health Measures on
the 1918 Influenza Pandemic in U.S. Cities," and
Richard J. Hatchett, Carter E. Mecher, and Marc Lip-
sitch, "Public Health Interventions and Epidemic Inten-
sity During the 1918 Influenza Pandemic," *Proceedings of
the National Academies of Sciences of the United States*,
May 1, 2007, www.pnas.org. "The human," Richard
Collier, *Plague of the Spanish Lady* (N.Y.: Athenaeum,
1974), 76. "I am," Arthur S. Link, ed., *Papers of Woodrow
Wilson* (Princeton: Princeton, 1987), vol. 56, 556. "Gives
Caskets to City's Poor," *Washington Post*, Oct. 19, 1918.
"Funeral Invitations Barred in Epidemic," *Boston Globe*,
Dec. 29, 1918. "Grave Diggers Strike," *Times*, Jul. 31,
1919. "We are," "The days," Sandra M. Gilbert, *Death's
Door* (N.Y.: Norton, 2006), xvii, 283.

Chapter 15. Feng Shui at the Evergreens
"A smile," *Eagle*, Aug. 21, 1899. "The tom-tom," Roy
Gibbond Doyle, "Red Mike and the Caterpillar," *N.Y.
World-Telegram*, Sep. 2, 1948. Population, *Encyclopedia
of New York City*. "Cosmopolitan character," "Sunday
Recreation," *Eagle*, August 21, 1865. "Popular opinion,"
Helen F. Clark, "The Chinese of New York," *Century*,
Nov. 1896, 104. ***Feng-shui and Celestial Hill.*** Nanette
Napoleon Purnell, "Oriental and Polynesian Cemetery
Traditions," *Ethnicity and the American Cemetery*, ed.
Meyer, 193–221. "Feast of Chinese Dead," *Eagle*, Aug. 20,
1899. "And Thereby Hangs a Tail," *N.Y. World*, Apr. 21,
1891. "Is it," "Dead Chinamen," *N.Y. Herald*, ca. 1885
clipping, Evergreens scrapbook. "I found," "Fatherly Au

Yang Ming," ca. 1883 clipping, Evergreens scrapbook.
"Celestials at the Grave," *Eagle*, Apr. 25, 1881. ***Associa-
tions.*** Amaranth Council, "Monument to T. W. Kelley,"
Eagle, Mar. 16, 1902, "Unveiled a Monument to Thomas
W. Kelley," *Eagle*, Mar. 31, 1902. "Clan or," Bruce Edward
Hall, "Chinatown," *American Heritage*, Apr. 1999. Ship
sinkings, "R.I.P. 50 Years Later," *Sunday News*, May 29,
1994. "We want," Luis J. Beck, *New York's Chinatown*
(N.Y.: Bohemia, 1898). ***Diomed.*** Submarine war, Leah
Rousmaniere, *Anchored Within the Vail*. "In it," "Sunday
Recreation," *Eagle*, Aug. 21, 1865. "*Diomed* Sent Down
off Atlantic Coast," *Atlanta Constitution*, Aug. 24, 1918.
"British Boat Sunk After Long Fight," *Boston Globe*, Aug.
24, 1918. "Submarine Offered Doctor to Victim," *Times*,
Aug. 25, 1918. www.historycentral.com/Navy/ Subma-
rine/u-140.html.

Chapter 16. The Two Anthonies: The Showman and the Scold
Pastor. *American National Biography*. "Vaudeville," *Ency-
clopedia of New York City*. "'Tony' Pastor Dead in His
77th Year," *Times*, Aug. 27, 1908. Arnoud Fields, *Lillian
Russell* (Jefferson, N.C.: McFarland, 1999). "We are,"
Robert W. Snyder, *Voice of the City: Vaudeville and Popu-
lar Culture in New York* (Chicago: Doe, 2000), 15.
Charles Edward Ellis, *An Authentic History of the … Elks*
(Chicago: 1910). Eph Horn, "A Good Man on the End,"
Boston Globe, Jan. 5, 1877. ***Church of Transfiguration.***
www.littlechurch.org. "Little Church Around the Corner
Anniversary," *Times*, Oct. 5, 1902. "Funeral of Dr.
Houghton," *Times*, Nov. 19, 1897. "Tributes to Dr.
Houghton," *Times*, Nov. 20, 1897. "Curtain Falls on the
Life of Charles Couldock," *Times*, Nov. 28, 1898. "An
Ambiguous Apology," *Times*, Mar. 19, 1899. "Funeral of
C. W. Couldock," *Times*, Dec. 1, 1898. Wayne S. Turney,
A Glimpse of Theater History, www.wayneturney.20m.
com/couldock.htm. "Last of Billy, the Minstrel," *Times*,
Dec. 8, 1905. ***Actors' Fund Plot.*** "In far," *Brooklyn Star*,
Jun. 7, 1887. ***Comstock.*** *American National Biography*.
"Comstockery," Manohla Dargis, "The Notorious Bettie
Page," *Times*, Apr. 14, 2006, Weekend Arts, 14, and "A

Cad and a Femme Fatale Simmer," *Times*, Sep. 26, 2007. "He May Not Be Dead After All," *Times*, Dec. 1, 1889. "Anthony Comstock Dies in His Crusade," *Times*, Sep. 22, 1915.

Chapter 17. Show People
Mark Twain, *Mark Twain's Autobiography* (N.Y.: Harper, 1924), vol. 1, 89–92. "Colonel Sellers Is Dead," *Times*, Apr. 11, 1887. "The Murdered Actor," *Eagle*, Mar. 22, 1879. "Buried," *Eagle*, Mar. 26, 1879. "The Sunny South," *Eagle*, Apr. 20, 1879. "A Shady Spot," *Eagle*, May 30, 1880. "Miss Thursby and Mynah," *Eagle*, Oct. 2, 1887. Arthur S. Maynard, review of Richard McCandless Gipson, *Life of Emma Thursby, 1845–1931, New York Genealogical and Biographical Record*, vol. 72, no. 3 (Jul. 1941), 2534. "Guide to the Emma Thursby Papers," N.-Y. Hist. Soc. Tim Gracyk, "Van and Schenck," www.gracyk.com/schenck.shtml. "Joe Schenck is Buried," *Times*, Jul. 4, 1930. Ida Robinson, Meyer Berger, "Around New York," *Times*, Mar. 5, 7, 14, 1958. **March princes.** "Captured the," Nicholas E. Tawa, *Way to Tin Pan Alley: American Popular Song, 1866–1910* (N.Y.: Schirmer, 1990), 139. Clark obituary, *Times*, May 30, 1898. Russell Sanjek, *American Popular Music and Its Business* (N.Y.: Oxford, 1988), vol. 3, 350. Wayland Bunnell, "E. T. Paull," *Sheet Music Exchange*, vol. 7, no. 2 (Apr. 1989), http://parlorsongs.com. **Bunny.** "There was," Joyce Kilmer, "In Memoriam, John Bunny," *Circus and Other Essays* (N.Y.: Gomme, 1916), 63. "John Bunny," Anthony Slide, *Big V* (Metuchen, N.J.: Scarecrow, 1987), 45. "A very," Slide, *Big V*, 46. Bunny films, www.goldensilents.com/comedy/johnbunny.html. "Good old," *Macon Daily Telegraph*, Apr. 28, 1915.

Chapter 18. Blind Tom, the Queen of the Trumpet, Bojangles, and the Pres
"In the," Donald Bogle, *Toms, Coons, Mulattoes, Mammies, and Bucks: An Interpretive History of Blacks in American Films*, 4th ed. (N.Y.: Continuum, 2001), 3. Col. T. Allston Brown, *Early History of Negro Minstrelsy* (1912–14), www.circushistory.org/Cork/Burnt

Cork4.htm. Horn, "A Good Man on the End," *Boston Globe*, Jan. 5, 1877. "Colored performers," Mario A. Charles, "The Age of a Jazzwoman: Valaida Snow, 1900–1956," *Journal of Negro History*, vol. 80, no. 4 (Autumn 1995), 183–91. ***Japanese Tommy and Blind Tom.*** "Japanese Tommy," *Eagle*, May 23, 1873. "'Japanese Tommy's' Funeral," *Times*, Jul. 13, 1887. Hubert Howe Bancroft, *Book of the Fair* (Chicago: Bancroft, 1893). Elizabeth Kolbert, "About Time Dept., Blind Tom's Tombstone," *New Yorker*, Jul. 15, 2002. "Blind Tom, Unsolved Problem in Musical History," *Chicago Defender*, Aug. 19, 1922. "If ever," "Letter from Mark Twain," San Francisco *Alta California*, Aug. 1, 1869. http://twainquotes.com/18690801.html. Barbara Schmidt, "Archangels Unaware: The Story of Thomas Bethune . . .," www.twainquotes.com/archangels.html. ***Harlem Renaissance.*** Bruce Kellner, ed., *Harlem Renaissance* (Westport, Conn.: Greenwood, 1984). Cary D. Wintz and Paul Finkelman, ed., *Encyclopedia of the Harlem Renaissance*, two vols. (N.Y.: Routledge, 2005). Jervis Anderson, *This Was Harlem: A Cultural Portrait, 1900–1950* (N.Y.: Farrar, 1982). ***Hegamin.*** "'Blues Is a Woman' Tonight Explores Other Side of the Blues," *Times*, Jul. 2, 1990. See www.redhotjazz.com/hegamin.html. ***Hall.*** Darlene Clark Hine, ed., *Black Women in America* (N.Y.: Carlson, 1993), vol. 1, 514. "Sing to," Iain Cameron Williams, *Harlem to Paris Years of Adelaide Hall* (N.Y.: Continuum, 2002), 20. "Getting Darker," Ann Douglas, *Terrible Honesty: Mongrel Manhattan in the 1920s* (N.Y.: Farrar, 1995), 385. "The music," Lena Horne, *Lena Horne in Person* (N.Y.: Greenberg, 1950), 41. "Undefeatable cheer," Stephen Holden, "Adelaide Hall," *Times*, Mar. 12, 1992. ***Snow.*** "With a," *Times*, May 5, 1933. Rosetta Reitz, "Hot Snow: Valaida Snow (Queen of the Trumpet Sings & Swings)," *Black American Literature Forum*, vol. 16, no. 4 (Winter 1982), 158–60. "In an," Bobby Short, *Black and White Baby* (N.Y.: Dodd, Mead, 1971). "She used," Reitz, "Hot Snow," 159. "Tell the," *Chicago Defender*, Jun. 23, 1956. Walter Winchell, "On Broadway," *Washington Post*, Sep. 20, 1953. "Despite her," Clarence Lusane, *Hitler's Black Victims* (N.Y.: Routledge, 2002), 172. *Women in History,* www.lkwdpl.org/ wihohio/snow-val.htm. **Robinson.** Donald Bogle, *Bright Boulevards, Bold Dreams: The Story of Black Hollywood* (N.Y.: One World/Ballantine, 2005). Jim Haskins and N. R. Mitgang, *Mr. Bojangles* (N.Y.: Morrow, 1988). "Celebrities and 8 Miles of Crowds Pay Last Tribute to Bill Robinson," *Times,* Nov. 29, 1949. "This is," Williams, *Harlem to Paris Years,* 147. "Certainly the," Bogle, *Toms, Coons,* 47. "But this," "The Play: All in Fun," *Times,* Dec. 28, 1940. "Spontaneous effervescence," "The biggest," Bogle, *Toms, Coons,* 52. "He told," "Sports of the *Times,*" *Times,* Jul. 19, 2007. "He was," Robinson obituary, *Times,* Nov. 29, 1949. **Young.** "Like nothing," Douglas Henry Daniels, "Lester Young: Master of Jive," *American Music,* vol. 3, no. 3 (Autumn, 1985), 313. "Contrary melodic," Gary Giddins, *Visions of Jazz: The First Century* (N.Y.: Oxford, 1998), 178. "Oh, they," Ben Sidran, *Talking Jazz: An Oral History,* expanded edition (N.Y.: Da Capo, 1995), 21. "The only," Douglas Henry Daniels, *Lester Leaps In* (Boston: Beacon, 2002), 323. "Gandhi-like," Bobby Scott, "The House in the Heart," *Reading Jazz,* ed. Robert Gottlieb (N.Y.: Pantheon, 1996), 453. "I try," Lewis Porter, *Lester Young* (Boston: Twayne, 1985). "I Melt," Daniels, "Lester Young," 317.

Chapter 19. A Rural Cemetery in the Twenty-First Century

"The shaft," Felix Oldboy (John Flavel Mines), *Walks in Our Churchyards* (N.Y.: Peck, 1896), 61. "Chinatown to Honor Tong War Peacemaker," *Times,* Aug. 24, 1925. "Chinatown Lays Sam Wing to Rest," *Times,* Jul. 20, 1926. "Lauds W. L. Butcher as Friend of Boys," *Times,* Jan. 18, 1931. "Ancient Tribal Rites to Commend Chief Two Bears to Great Spirit," *N.Y. Daily News,* Jan. 31, 1958. "Neighborhood Report: Harlem, a Closet Full of Genius," *Times,* Feb. 13, 2005. **Depression.** Board of Trustees minutes, 1929–1935. Evergreens sales summary, Jun. 9, 1941. "Looking more," "Evergreens Cemetery Offers New Landscaped Plot Section," *Brooklyn Citizen,* Jun. 30, 1944. "We end," "Week-End Burial Curtailed Here," *Times,* Jan. 3, 1962. "As would," Evergreens Grounds Committee report, Apr. 6, 1993. **Morak children.** "Mourning Three 'Cherubs' Killed by Ambulance," *Times,* Oct. 18, 1998. "You don't," "He'll Bid Yusef His Last Farewell," *N.Y. Daily News,* Aug. 31, 1989. **Hawkins headstone.** Michael Yeh, "The Final Word … ," *NYC24 Ethnic Cemeteries,* issue 3 (2000). www.nyc24.org /2000/ issue03/story03/memorial1.html. "Thickly sown," Oldboy (Mines), *Walks in Our Churchyards,* 74.

ILLUSTRATION CREDITS AND SOURCES

All four-color photographs are by Ken Druse, © Ken Druse, 2008, with the following exceptions:

John Rousmaniere, 15, 122 (bottom), 190 (both), 192 (both), 198, 199, 228, 274

Anthony Salamone, 122 (top)

Historical Illustrations, Sources

Evergreens Cemetery Archives, 35, 49, 63, 64, 66, 67, 68 (both), 70, 79, 124, 140 (top), 159, 160 (all), 162 (top), 166 (both), 169 (both), 170 (both), 196, 211, 237 (bottom), 269, 270 (both), 271 (top)

Brooklyn Museum, 31, 146, 147 (bottom)

Brooklyn Public Library, Brooklyn Collection, 110 (both), 161

Courtesy of Anthony DellaRocca, 111 (Nelson Harding drawing, *Brooklyn Eagle*)

Courtesy of Kurt Landsberger, 135 (bottom)

Fenn editions, *Gray's Elegy in a Country Churchyard* (1883), 46 (both) and 59, and William Cullen Bryant, *The Story of the Fountain* (1871), 150 (top row)

History-Buff.org, 92 (both)

Leo Baeck Institute, 139

Metropolitan Museum of Art, 147 (top), Gift of Erving Wolf Foundation and Mr. and Mrs. Erving Wolf, 1975, photograph © 1992 The Metropolitan Museum of Art, and 150 (bottom), Maria DeWitt Jesup Fund and Morris K. Jesup Fund, 1980, photograph © 1989 The Metropolitan Museum of Art

Museum of Chinese in America (photograph by Paul Calhoun), 224

Museum of Funeral Customs, Springfield, Illinois, 176, 177

New Jersey Historical Society, 135 (top)

New York City Department of Parks and Recreation, 149 (both)

New York Public Library, Astor, Lenox, and Tilden Foundations: Billy Rose Theatre Division, 234, 235, 240, 246 (top), 247, 250; Emmet Collection, Miriam and Ira D. Wallach Division of Arts, Prints, and Photographs, 121; Gustav Scholer Papers, Manuscripts and Archives Division, 215; I. N. Phelps Stokes Collection, Miriam and Ira D. Wallach Division of Arts, Prints, and Photographs, 14; Milstein Division of United States History, Local History, and Genealogy, 44; Music Division, 249 (both); Photography Collection, Miriam and Ira D. Wallach Division of Arts, Prints, and Photographs, 134, 202, 246 (bottom); Picture Collection, The Branch Libraries, 16, 22, 43, 91, 180, 182, 202, 209, 212, 216, 225; Print Division, Miriam and Ira D. Wallach Division of Arts, Prints, and Photographs, 32, 81; Rare Books Division, 34; Schomburg Center for Research in Black Culture, Photographs and Prints Division, 262

Ohio State University Cartoon Research Library, 152 (bottom right), bequest of Henriette Adam Brotherton; 152 (all others), Woody Gelman Collection.

Picture History, 96, 100

U.S. Senate Historical Office, 140 (bottom)

Other images were acquired from collections through eBay.

INDEX